Detail in Contemporary Bathroom Design

Published in 2009 by
Laurence King Publishing Ltd
4th Floor
361–373 City Road
London
EC1V 1LR
United Kingdom
e-mail: enquiries@laurenceking.co.uk
www.laurenceking.co.uk

A catalogue record for this book is available from the British Library.

ISBN: 978 1 85669 590 9

Designed by Hamish Muir
Illustrations by Advanced Illustrations Limited
Picture Research by Sophia Gibb

Cover image:
VDD Residence, Belgium
© Karel Moortgat

Printed in China

Virginia McLeod

Detail in Contemporary Bathroom Design

Laurence King Publishing

Contents

Introduction

Over the past few decades, bathrooms have lost their utilitarian nature and become an integral part of the home. Once relegated to the back of the house, sometimes even outdoors for sanitary reasons, and equipped with the most utilitarian equipment, bathrooms today are about rest, relaxation and recuperation, rather than simply a space for a quick wash.

Bathrooms are often the only place in busy households that provide the opportunity for solitary contemplation time. As a result bathrooms are becoming increasingly generous in proportion, and architects and designers spend more time thinking about specialist lighting, heating and luxury finishes. Many houses, even small ones, feature multiple bathrooms, sometimes one per bedroom – a luxury unheard of until recently. Often master bedrooms will have a dedicated bathing space of the same proportions as the bedroom, equipped in the manner of a luxury spa-like retreat. In addition, luxury bathrooms often have their own dedicated outdoor space, allowing users to indulge in an indoor / outdoor bathing experience.

Second only to the kitchen, bathrooms are the place where a considerable proportion of a budget will be spent when renovating a house and when building from scratch. It is here that people are more likely to want to specify luxury materials such as granite and stone, and, increasingly, hi-tech materials such as Corian and composite stone. Obviously such materials have a practical aspect, being appropriate for a room that must cope with a great deal of water and condensation. But these materials are also chosen purely for their sense of luxury and delight to heighten the sense of indulgence.

Similarly, fittings and fixtures have become more sophisticated. Baths, basins and WCs are no longer straightforward sanitary items. The choice available in design, materials and budget is now virtually limitless. In fact, sanitary fittings have become the focus of attention for world-renowned architects and designers, with Philippe Starck, Norman Foster, Antonio Citterio, Ross Lovegrove and Jasper Morrison, among others, devoting their attention to designing bathroom suites for major manufacturers such as Ideal Standard, Duravit, Hansgrohe and Vitra. Designer items such as these provide specifiers and home owners with the opportunity to make their bathroom as sophisticated and design-orientated as the rest of the home.

In *Detail in Contemporary Bathroom Design*, 35 bathrooms illustrate the diversity of bathroom design in recent years. In addition, three case studies show how architects, clients and builders approach the creative process and the practicalities of creating a new bathroom.

The bathrooms illustrated here range from compact but stylish renovations such as Ullmayer Sylvester Architects' reworking of a mansion block apartment in London, where space is limited but a simple palette of white fittings and dark stone create a contemporary bathroom, to many examples of the most luxurious and spacious bathrooms where no expense has been spared. These include Seth Stein's bathroom for a luxurious house on North Caicos islands, where visual and spatial connections to the beachfront landscape inform the design, to Vincent Van Duysen's VDD Residence, where the simplification of the minimalist design allows the Belgian Bluestone interior to take centre stage.

Detail in Contemporary Bathroom Design, while not intended as a practical manual, provides an invaluable insight into some of the most beautiful and functional bathrooms created by architects and designers in recent years. All of the projects and case studies are presented with photographs, plans, elevations and sections to clearly illustrate how great bathrooms are designed and built.

Notes

US and Metric Measurements
Dimensions have been provided by the architects in metric and converted to US measurements, except in the case of projects from the USA where dimensions have been converted to metric.

Terminology
An attempt has been made to standardize terminology to aid understanding across readerships, for example 'wood' is generally referred to as 'timber' and 'aluminum' as 'aluminium'. However materials or processes that are peculiar to a country, region or architectural practice that have no direct correspondence are presented in the original.

Floor Plans
Throughout the book, the following convention of hierarchy has been used – ground floor, first floor, second floor, and so on. In certain contexts, terms such as basement level or upper level have been used for clarity.

Scale
All floor plans, sections, elevations and construction details are presented at conventional architectural metric scales, typically 1:50, 1:20 or 1:10 as appropriate.

Case Studies

Case Study 1

Old Greenwich Residence Connecticut, USA

Kaehler Architects has been specializing in private residential architecture for 14 years. The focus of the practice is to provide clients with highly personal and effective design solutions that merge everyday practical needs with beautiful spaces.

Kaehler Architects was commissioned in February 2005 to develop a design proposal for a new house on a waterfront site in Old Greenwich. Two existing houses on the site had fallen into disrepair and were demolished to make way for a custom designed and built new home.

Laura Kaehler
Principal Architect
Kaehler Architects

We were commissioned to build a waterfront home on a site that the clients had purchased a year earlier. They had been living on the site for some time and so had many insights on aspects they liked about it and, more importantly, the things they didn't.

The long and narrow lot included a house set close to a busy street that afforded little privacy. A small guest house adjacent to the water and set very low on the sloping site often flooded and was in a precarious state. It was decided to remove both of these structures, salvaging quality elements from both for reuse.

After extensive site analysis we placed the new house to take advantage of the narrow constraints of the site. The house is set further back from the street than many of its neighbours, to allow privacy and to create an appropriately scaled forecourt and a rear yard. The forecourt provides a transition to the house via the stone pathway through the landscape that frames the home's entry porch.

The clients stressed that they wanted to maximize the height to provide a third-floor lookout with water views. Therefore, in order to keep the house in scale with its surroundings, oversized architectural detailing was used. Large doors, windows, mouldings, corner boards and columns all combine to give a sense of scale appropriate to the older homes in the area. When viewed from the street, the effect belies the large size of the house and makes it appear equal in scale to adjacent homes.

We wanted to create an open, simple and elegant interior and the owners stressed their desire for an uncomplicated and relaxed home. They wanted to convey a sense of formality upon entry, but to have an informal family space adjacent to the water on the first floor. We accomplished this by bisecting the floor plan so that the front of the house contains all of the formal spaces including the entry tower, stair hall and formal living room as well as a mud room.

A wide hallway acts as an axis connecting front to rear. Its long timber slat ceiling and floorboards draw the eye towards the magnificent water views through large glass doors and windows. The rear of the first floor is a large open space perforated with a multitude of large windows that bring views and light into the relaxed living spaces including the kitchen, dining room, family room and billiards room. These spaces are all interconnected without dividing walls and are separated only through different ceiling details and architectural lighting. A large timber deck extends the living areas and contains a screened porch whose roof doubles as a second-floor balcony off the master suite.

The second floor contains two bedrooms, an office and the master suite with bedroom, dressing area, balcony and the master bathroom. The suite is designed to capitalize on panoramic water vistas and has large windows overlooking the balcony and water below.

The room is a glimmering study in white. Painted timber-panelled walls on three sides complement a 'wet' wall of white Carrara marble that contains the large shower, the bathtub, toilet and cupboard. All of the doors in the marble wall are made from frosted glass with the shower doors receiving a frosted band only at their centre, leaving the top and bottom clear to visually expand the space whilst affording privacy.

Dark stained mahogany vanities flank the freestanding bathtub and provide a contrast to the pure simplicity of the marble and white-painted walls. The large two-person bathtub sits in front of two lowered windows that allow panoramic views while bathing.

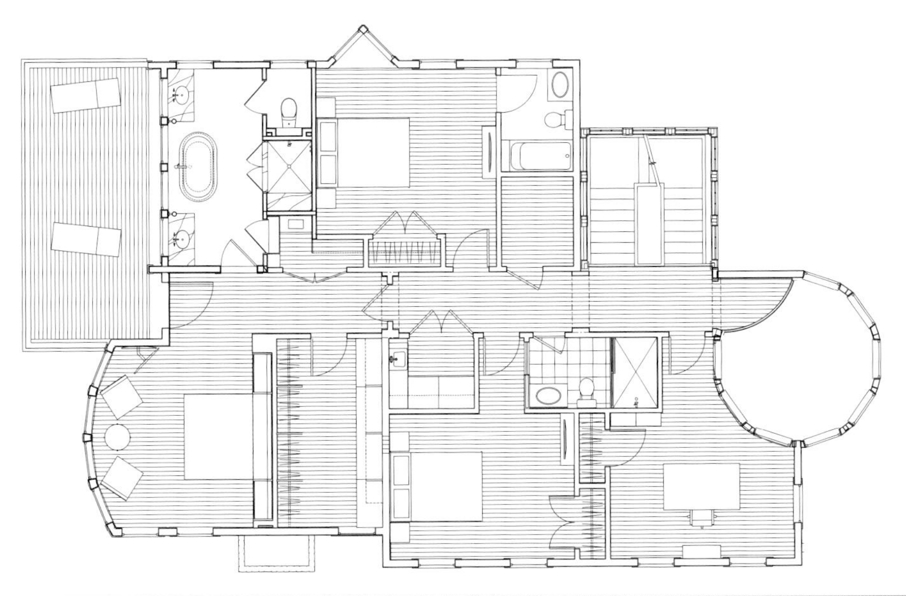

Above
Second-floor plan. The master bathroom (top left), is situated between the master bedroom (bottom left) and a private terrace (top left) that serves both spaces. This floor also accommodates two additional bedrooms, both with ensuite bathrooms, a study / office and the double-height entrance tower (right).

Left
The bathroom is flooded with natural light and enjoys expansive views over the private terrace and beyond to the waterfront. The white-painted walls and ceiling are contrasted with accents of dark timber in the joinery and translucent glass doors to the WC and shower area (right).

Michael Gallo
Builder
Gallo Contracting

This house presented many challenges, both in terms of the open design and the waterside location which is subject to prevailing winds. To deal with the conditions, the structure includes 21 steel beams and 39 steel columns in the frame of the house. These beams, once connected, create a 'wind-frame' that allows for the open-plan design on the first floor.

This open design, though beautiful, caused some major challenges for the mechanical proposal. The location of the home is in a flood zone, which meant that we couldn't install any heating or cooling equipment below the first floor. That being the case, all the pipes and ductwork had to be run from above, but with very few interior walls and a steel wind frame blocking our duct work at every turn, we had to be very creative in the mechanical delivery of air.

For the master bathroom, Kaehler Architects called for the floor to be framed five centimetres (two inches) lower than the surrounding floors. This set down would allow for a two inch bed of mortar, which would create a superior base for the tile as well as a perfect surface for the radiant heat.

In building the bathroom, we had particular concerns about the pipes feeding the bathtub. Half of the bathroom is located above an open-air porch, therefore we were concerned about the pipes freezing, especially with the cold New England winds blowing in from the water. To combat this, before setting the mortar bed we cut a portion of the floor open and dropped some of the radiant heat pipes alongside of the tub pipes to keep them from freezing during the cold winter months.

For the finishing touches, my son Joe built the custom mahogany vanities right at the site, precisely matching the window centre lines as well as matching up with the panels on the walls. The thick marble countertops were custom cut to the exact size of the vanities. Typically, counters hang over the edge of a vanity, but this design called for a 19 x 19 millimetre (3/4 x 3/4) inch recess just below the counter – a detail found in many elements throughout the house.

We have worked on many projects with the Kaehler team. We especially enjoy the challenges they bring to each project. Their 'outside the box' designs always test our skills and creativity, and they are never easy, but the sense of pride one has in building these one-of-a-kind projects is always worth the effort.

CV and Connie Ramachandran
Clients

We initially requested drawings conceptualizing the design of our new home from three different architectural firms. All firms were local and reputable, but the deciding factor in selecting Kaehler Architects was the creativity Laura Kaehler displayed in maximizing the water views while keeping the exterior design consistent with the New England neighbourhood where the project is located.

While we desired a more contemporary interior we were interested in maintaining the character of our local surroundings. Laura Kaehler and Richard Basic, the project architect for our house, were very sensitive to all of our concerns and worked to incorporate them in the design of our home. We particularly wanted a master suite that took advantage of the beautiful water views that originally prompted us to purchase the property.

We wanted the master bathroom to be full of light and views, and we also wanted to incorporate his-and-hers vanities, a freestanding soaking tub and a spacious steam shower. We worked closely with the architect in planning the layout of the bathroom. We reviewed decisions for the materials, colours, lighting, vanities, fixtures and accessories many times.

The overall design of the master bathroom is contemporary but uses traditional materials such as the white Carrara marble on the walls, floors and countertops. Multiple windows provide lots of natural light and those wonderful water views. Privacy was not much of an issue as the windows face the water and there are no buildings on either side of the house.

The custom made mahogany vanities were designed with ample storage and finished in a dark ebony stain that stands in impressive contrast to the white walls. We are very satisfied with the design and aesthetic in both the master bath and the entire house. We attribute this to the working relationship we had with the architects. Laura and Richard listened to us during frequent meetings to develop a design that we are all happy with.

Left
View of the main house (left) and the carriage house (right). Both structures replace an existing dilapidated house and a waterfront guest house which were demolished to make way for the more appropriately scaled and sensitively designed house that sits comfortably within a conservative residential neighbourhood.

Below Left
One wall of the bathroom is designed as a 'wet wall' and is clad entirely in Carrara marble. Two glass doors give access to the WC (left) and the shower (right). The door to the shower features a frosted panel at its centre to provide privacy while maintaining views out to the terrace and beyond.

Below Right
View from below of the walls and ceiling to the shower area. The Carrara marble continues into the shower where it clads all surfaces including two shelves. A centred strip of mosaic tiles in white and tones of grey perfectly complement the natural striations of the marble.

Case Study 2

Chenery House San Francisco, California, USA

Since its founding in 1992, Mark English Architects has designed numerous residential and small commercial spaces throughout California, Texas and in Mexico. The firm has a special interest in building in the urban context, with half of its work occurring in San Francisco. This project consists of a complete reorganization of the master bedroom and bathroom in an existing four-storey single-family home in San Francisco. A small space originally allotted to the master bath was maintained for the toilet and bidet, while the shower and vanity functions were extended along an entire wall of the existing master bedroom.

Mark English
Principal Architect
Mark English Architects

The project was a referral given by a former residential client in the neighbourhood. Our client is an accomplished scientist and business woman with contemporary tastes and an ability to think formally in three-dimensions. Our initial meeting was graced with a series of 'parti' drawings, made by the client to demonstrate her ideas for the massing and geometry.

A preliminary viewing of the house and its decor made clear the client's love of glass and its physical characteristics of translucency, transparency, reflection, colouration and refraction. This love of glass, coupled with a biologist's love of the artifacts of growth, led the architects to choose a variety of glass tile, block and mirror as well as natural timber as the predominant finishes.

The architects, Mark English and Maria Barmina, designed the bathroom using hand sketches and 3-D computer-rendering models. The resultant overlapping arcing and orthogonal planes were virtually tested from the vantage point of the bed, with adjustments made to accentuate the theatrical layered quality.

The hands-on nature of both the architects and the owner meant that there would be no general contractor for this project. The master tile setter, cabinet maker and carpenter were all judged to be the best in their field based on the work they had done on previous projects.

The resulting bathroom provides a bathing experience that is an integral part of the private world of the bedroom. As such, the client's original hopes were met and exceeded. Comfort, sensuality, theatre and beauty are expressed in the new space. The mutable characteristics of light playing in iridescent glass tiles and cast glass blocks, as well as in the water and wet surfaces, inspire personal contemplation. The glass tile walls, cabinet faces and mirrors are arranged in space to create a sense of layering and lightness.

Custom fabricated mirrors are cantilevered from the ceiling to allow the glass-block wall to remain complete. The curving oak cabinets are coated with a Becker Acroma Conversion Varnish finish to resist the effects of water. The colour of the veneer is in harmony with the Douglas Fir structural post and the drapery. The heated shower floor is a gently sloping plinth whose edge was determined by a thrown rope during layout. The toilet room wall-mounted fixtures float above a slab of salvaged Bay Laurel wood set into the tile floor.

Christopher 'Kit' Miller
Contractor
Amalfi Tile and Marble

I will never forget the first time I met with the client to look at Mark English's plans for her bathroom. They were elaborate, with curves and irregular transitions on most of the tiled elements. It certainly took me longer than average to process the scope of such an exceptional project.

A part of me was apprehensive that there were so many aberrant characteristics detailed for the bathroom, however the creative part of me was elated with the possibility of taking on such an endeavour. Right from the start, I began to realize the magnitude of effort building this bathroom would entail.

Conventional shower pans are usually restricted to a particular area in the bathroom. This shower pan, though, encompassed the whole room including a curved wall and stepped curb. Shower pans need to comply with applicable building codes, and without protruding curbs, this can be very difficult. It requires precise calculations for proper slopes and drain height in relation to the entrance of

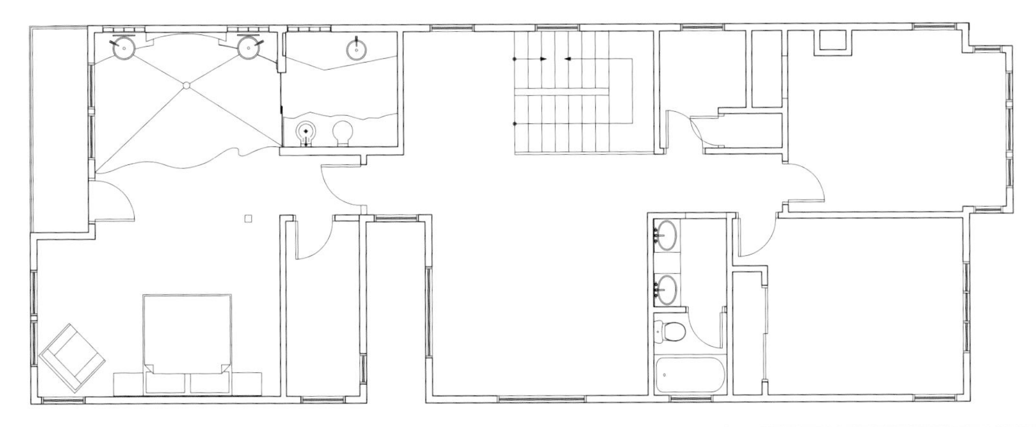

Above
The master bedroom and bathroom suite (left) has been completely reorganized. The original bathroom now contains only the WC, bidet and washbasin, while the main shower and vanity area has moved out into the bedroom space where it occupies the far wall opposite the bed.

Left
View of the shower platform and one of the vanity consoles. The WC and bidet are housed behind sliding etched glass doors. The floor of the shower, a sheet of glass mosaic tiles, slopes gently back towards the wall to ensure that water falls away from the carpeted bedroom floor.

the shower area. The outline for the curb was designed by the client and a template was used to fabricate this outline in metal. I then used this metal form to recreate the flowing curves in mortar. I also installed embedded electric radiant heating in the shower pan. I normally install these systems with mosaic floors, but never before in a shower pan.

I spoke with different vendors' technicians to ensure I used the proper products to get the optimal results without compromising the shower-pan liner. The actual setting of the tile entailed never-ending intricacies. I have worked with all kinds of glass mosaic tiles before, normally in areas that are flat and square. This bathroom, having many arcs and bends, was much more difficult. It meant cutting tiny glass tiles individually at different angles and sizes for every field of tiling. I could not use conventional levels properly and relied on a laser level.

The visual properties of the tile's iridescence were like none I have seen before. As I installed the tile it seemed as if it had come to life. It shimmered brilliantly and would change when the surroundings did. Any type of light and reflection would bring about the tile's radiance. The curved walls and angles magnified its scintillating attributes. I would catch myself just staring at the tiled areas, bedazzled.

This iridescence also made the tiles tricky to install. A tile seemingly placed perfectly in the morning would show slight imperfections in the afternoon or twilight, and so on. What's more, looking at different angles would reveal otherwise undetected blemishes. Each region of tile needed to be checked at different angles throughout the day.

Physically, the little pieces of glass were much more forgiving. It was very easy to make even very small cuts without chipping or cracking. The cut edges were almost effortless to polish, enabling me to smooth even installed tiles.

Most bathroom vanity tops I have tiled are square with either top or undermounted sink bowls. These tops boasted translucent glass bowls placed as if floating out of the curved vanity. Floating mortar and setting tiles around these circular projections proved to be a complex task. It required plenty of forethought, templates and countless readjustments. The design required incorporating a finished piece of Bay Laurel wood with its natural bark edge raised off the floor – an atypical detail involving carefully floating mortar to the irregular edge of the wood without harming it. The effect it created was as if the wood was floating in the field of tile.

The owner of the house is a dream client who was always positive and appreciative of the work I was doing. Her technical comprehension was amazing. I could talk to her about tile-specific processes in detail. It was invaluable working with a home owner who could understand and be involved on a technical level.

Mark is an outstanding architect with innovative ideas. I respect his adeptness in working with all the professions to create coherent architecture. Without my client's imagination and Mark's ingenuity the incredible vision would never have been transformed into reality. I feel very fortunate that I was included in the creation of a functional work of art. It was one of the most rewarding projects I have had the pleasure of working on.

Eve Chenery
Client

The 'bathroom remodel', that my project was very simply described as, was, in truth, a complex operation to replace a malformed and mindless central core of a structure with a new spirit and a new centre. The space was to be transformed completely to remove the mute space at the end of a passage. The mission, therefore, was to no longer tolerate dull and deadened senses at the core of the house's personal space.

I intended to transform the area by creating visual planes that were satisfying from the central vantage point of the room – a platform bed in the master bedroom. Always intriguing to me was the deliberate placement and juxtaposition of materials in ways that create a sense of calm and unity; a curve with a large radius; materials that seem to bend to the will of the senses rather than follow the expected straight cut of a saw.

I revel in the properties of light and water as they transform the appearance of glass, and so I wished to see many thousands of glass mosaic tiles to blend on large surfaces so they themselves become the canvas for light to form unexpected visual spectacles.

This display is muted by the unorthodox placement of wood – an old and very beautiful chunk of Bay Laurel was embedded into a floor of glass. The beautiful new bathing environment evoked in me a simple sense of calm and a pure sense of concentration and meditation. In delivering this new bathroom, Mark English Architects knew, listened, translated and understood, and never lost sight of the goal.

Left
In the WC, the wall-mounted fixtures float above a piece of salvaged Bay Laurel timber set into the glass mosaic floor. The effect is of a wave washing on a sandy shore.

Below
View from the bed where the glamour of this unique bathroom is apparent. The organic curves of the step to the shower platform were created by throwing a rope across the floor which was then translated into a steel template.

Case Study 3

Twickenham House London, England, UK

Paul Archer Design is a young architectural company, committed to innovative modern design and dedicated to achieving the highest level of professionalism and management. The practice recently won the AJ Small Projects 2007 Award for their project Wallace Road II, and were awarded third place for the 'Home of the Future' competition.

This project involved the renovation of an existing terraced house in Twickenham, and the addition of a pavilion-like extension opening onto the garden. Commissioned in 2005 and completed in 2007, the project includes three new bathrooms as well as a master suite, a new kitchen, dining and family room opening directly to the garden, as well as the internal reorganization of the existing house.

Paul Archer
Principal Architect
Paul Archer Design

This house in Twickenham has a fantastic east-facing garden with mature trees. Our new scheme exploits this by opening up the whole of the rear façade with five enormous sliding glass doors. These have the thinnest of mullions, allowing uninterrupted enjoyment of the garden views.

Most London town houses are so narrow that you have to choose which space has the primary relationship with the garden, for example the kitchen, the dining or the living space. In this scheme, we had the luxury of width, and hence all of these spaces have been arranged across the back of the house.

Upstairs we have created a family bathroom, a shower room for the au pair, and a large master suite with walk-through wardrobe. The master ensuite, reached via his-and-hers wardrobes to both sides, is conceived as one large space, with one simple glass panel defining the shower area. The existing house had a sloping floor, like many old buildings, and we decided to take advantage of this to arrange the slot drain of the shower at the lowest point. This meant that we did not need to step the shower floor, giving a seamless look.

The materials for the bathroom and the ground floor are kept very simple – Navarra blue-honed limestone is used throughout. It is one of the few limestones that can handle the wet environment of a shower space, and its gray patterning is extremely easy to keep clean. Back sprayed glass is used on the walls to the shower enclosures, giving a great reflective quality. Mirror is used along the wall for the double wash basins, expanding the space, but also concealing expansive storage space for bathroom paraphernalia.

The clients engaged well with the project and were clear in their requirements. We avoided some of the earlier more complex design options to focus on maximizing the internal space with a simple structure, so that there was enough budget to use good quality materials. The builders were found almost by accident – they were working on the house next door – and we have since used them many times.

Heidi and Andrew Hall
Clients

We had already met with a number of architects before Paul Archer Design. We were aware of Paul's work from a newspaper article featuring a glass box-style extension, and an architect friend had also mentioned his name. On meeting Paul Archer we felt he offered the perfect combination of very strong contemporary design with a sound attention to detail and business practice. This proved very much to be the case.

We developed a very good working relationship throughout the project. From the design process, through to tendering and selection of the right building contractors, to their on-site project management. At every stage the Paul Archer team was totally in control of every detail. Also, with a great marrying of tastes and style, we were able to follow all their design ideas and proposals.

Although we obviously provided an overall brief for the ideal layouts and requirements that we had in mind, we were able to develop and improve these through the knowledge, experience and expertise of the architects. So we followed their guidance for the detailed design of the lighting, finishes and all of the kitchen and bathroom fittings and fixtures.

In terms of the overall design we wanted clean lines and a fresh, simple colour palette. We followed the theme from the ground-floor extension through to the two main bathrooms –

Left
View of the ensuite bathroom, where limestone panels create a splashback for the twin basins. Vola taps and spouts are mounted onto the stone wall. The mirrored panels sit flush with the surrounding wall but conceal storage chased in to the wall. The glass-lined shower recess opposite the basins can be seen in the reflection.

Below
Two new bathrooms have been created on the first floor. A family bathroom (top) and an ensuite to the master bedroom (centre left). This is accessed from the bedroom via his-and-hers wardrobe areas.

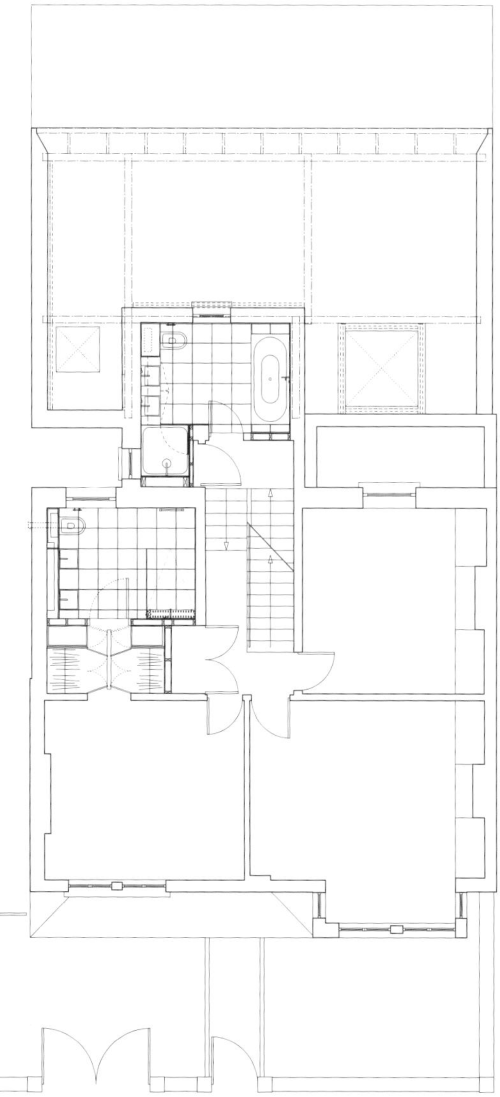

one ensuite and one family bathroom – with limestone floors and detailing, under-floor heating and jasmine white walls. We selected Philippe Starck toilets, a Kaldewei bath and Vola taps. In the ensuite bathroom we also have beautiful blue glass walls to the walk-in shower. In the top-floor bathroom, due to its smaller size, we have a slightly different style with off-white mosaic tiles to walls and floor.

Overall we could not fault Paul Archer Design, who exceeded our expectations. We were also lucky to have a good building firm. The end result is that we now have a lovely new home that we enjoy and get great pleasure from – a wonderful ground-floor living space, an ensuite dressing room and bathroom, and two further new bathrooms. We now have the perfect home which all four of us appreciate on a daily basis.

Marek Rynkiewicz
Builder
Sara Int Ltd

For this renovation project, three different bathrooms were to be built. Firstly a practical family bathroom, secondly a luxurious master suite, and finally, a compact shower room. Each bathroom had very different priorities and intended end users, and were all to be individually designed but still have a common design thread.

The bathrooms are dotted around the house and act as a link between the original house and the modern extension in that they are located within the old building, but designed using the same language as the new. A restricted and repeated palette of materials was used including stone (also used throughout the extension), tile (to give a more domestic feel as you progress up the house) and mirror. There was also a consistent range of sanitaryware used throughout, including Vola brassware and Duravit sanitaryware.

Clean lines and simple spaces were important to the client and designers, therefore all of the storage units are concealed within flush walls and cannot be read at first glance as they are hidden behind mirrors. Because the clients wanted to minimize clutter, there is an abundance of storage, little of which is apparent.

We had some difficulty with the large mirrored doors as they were extremely heavy and the hinges needed to be sturdier than usual. The back-painted glass cladding in the ensuite bathroom had to be done twice as the adhesive we first used was incorrect and burnt through the paint to create brown stains. These panels are large and costly but offer a very simple and elegant surface which is also very easy to keep clean.

The clear glass shower panel in the ensuite bathroom also caused problems as it was very large and heavy and so needed substantial support to be recessed into the wall and floor and required the addition of a bespoke stainless steel fixing bar.

The floors throughout needed careful attention as the flush shower drain and the floors had to be re-levelled as the house had suffered some subsidence in the past. The family and ensuite bathrooms had to be fitted with new joists to allow for the extra weight of the stone tiles, however this was avoided in the upstairs bathroom by using smaller ceramic tiles instead.

Left
In the ensuite bathroom, back-painted glass panels are used to line the walls, with a clear glass screen separating the shower from the rest of the bathroom.

Stone Bathrooms

Marsh Cashman Koolloos Architects

Longueville House Sydney, New South Wales, Australia

Once a dilapidated yet heritage-listed weatherboard cottage, this now much-renovated family home is located in Longueville, a leafy residential suburb some eight kilometres (five miles) from central Sydney. Longueville, a peninsula situated between Tambourine Bay and Woodford Bay, features some of the city's most expensive real estate, much of which has spectacular views due to the geography.

However, this particular house doesn't have water views so the re-design and extension of the original cottage involved turning the plan inside out so that internal views, both interior and exterior, became the focus of the living spaces. Beyond the cleaned-up Federation façade and the first two original rooms (now a study and guest room), the core of the house opens up to a series of courtyards and pools, with a void on the first floor that creates a double-height zone.

To the rear of the property is a central glass-panelled walkway, either side of which are fish ponds and large stepping stones leading to an internal courtyard. Here, an external fireplace allows the owners to maximize the time they're able to spend outdoors. To increase the sense of indoor–outdoor living, custom built glass panels completely slide away to create a seamless transition from the open-plan kitchen, dining and family area to the lawn and the pool which wraps around the house.

The master bedroom and bathroom suite are housed in a timber-clad pavilion with folding, sliding glass doors giving access to the garden. The most spectacular feature of the bathroom is a sunken combination shower and bath, accessed via steps from the main floor level. Simple, bold materials – black stone tiles and white concrete screed – create a stunning bathing environment.

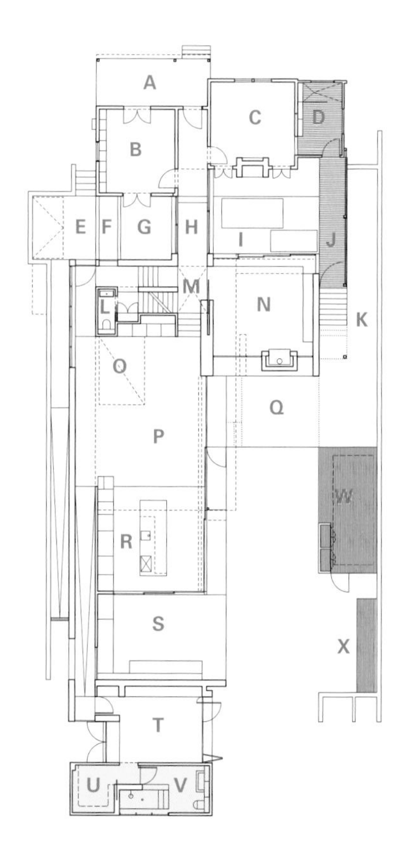

Opposite Left
The master bedroom and bathroom are housed in a timber-clad box (left). An opening of sliding glass panels opens up the bedroom to the central courtyard which unites the various parts of the programme.

Floor Plan
A Verandah
B Study
C Guest bedroom
D Ensuite
E Drying area
F Planting
G Pond
H Entry hall
I Pond
J Verandah
K Pool
L WC
M Void
N Living room 2
O Void
P Dining and living room
Q Pool
R Kitchen
S Covered courtyard
T Master bedroom
U Dressing room
V Master bathroom
W Deck
X Day bed

Left
The bathroom features robust surface treatments in a monochrome palette – dark stone tiles to the walls, and white concrete to the bath, floor and basin. The custom made combination bath and shower area is accessed by stairs leading down from the main level.

Stone

Marsh Cashman Koolloos Architects
Longueville House
Sydney, New South Wales, Australia

Bathroom Plan and Sections A–A and B–B
1:50

1 Mirror-clad cupboards with adjustable shelving
2 Stone ledge and downstand
3 Custom made concrete basin
4 Concealed WC cistern
5 WC
6 Heated towel rail
7 Pivot door to bedroom
8 White concrete cast in-situ floor
9 White concrete cast in-situ steps to bath and shower
10 Line of shower shelf
11 White concrete shower and bath
12 Glazed wall with etched panels to lower section
13 Line of skylight over
14 Sloping floor to shower and bath floor
15 Towel rail
16 Stone wall tiles

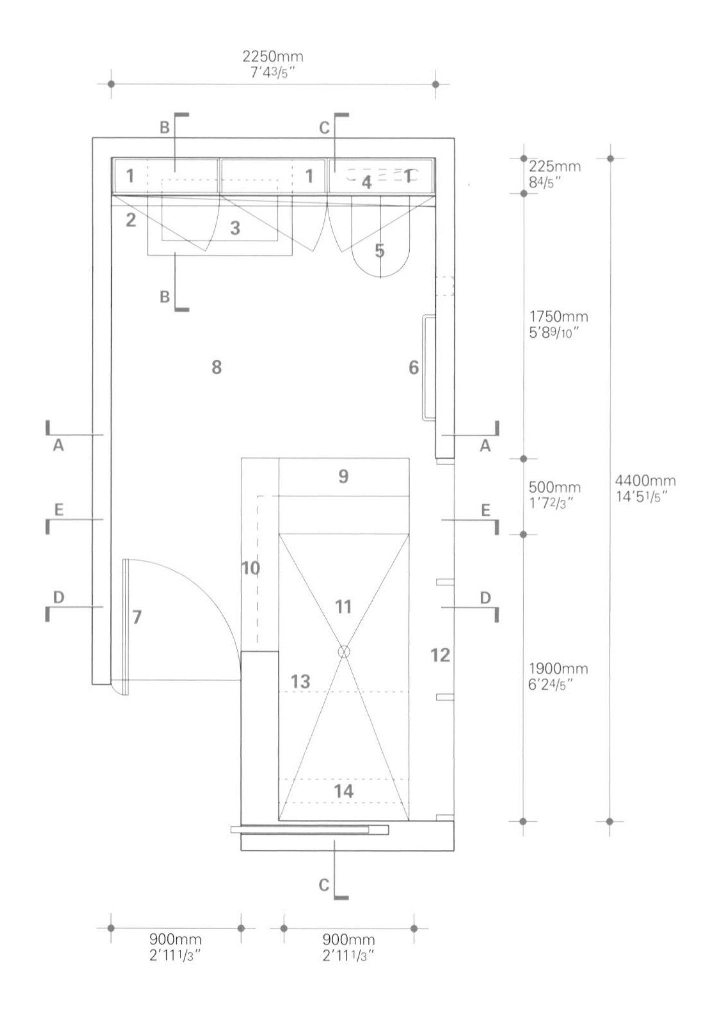

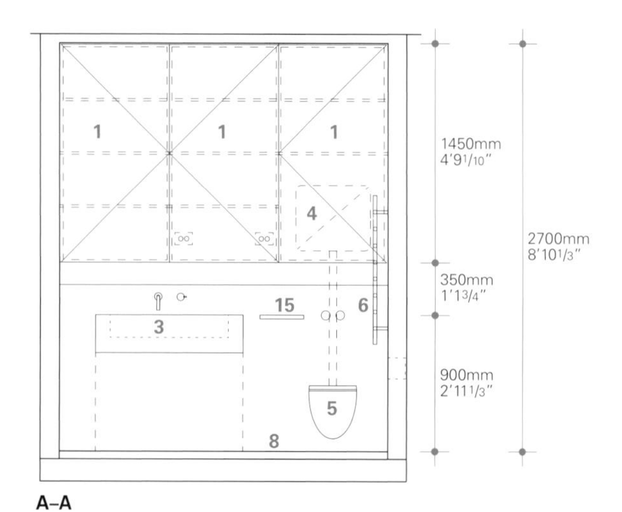

A–A

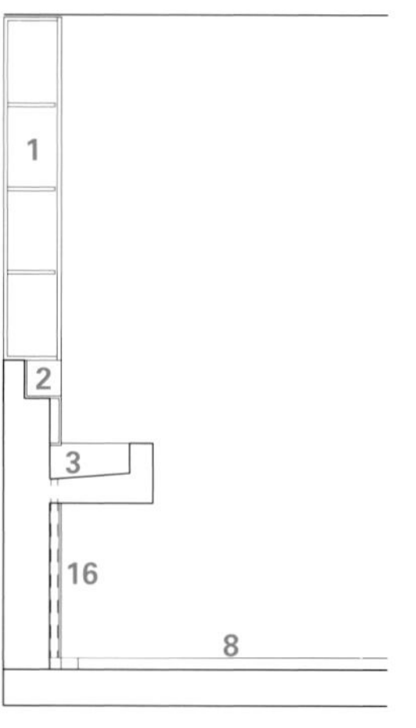

B–B

Sections C–C, D–D and E–E 1:50

1 Mirror-clad cupboards with adjustable shelving
2 Stone ledge
3 Stone-clad wall
4 WC
5 Toilet-roll holder
6 Heated towel rail
7 Clear glazed openable window
8 Etched glass fixed panel
9 White concrete cast in-situ floor
10 White concrete cast in-situ steps to bath and shower
11 White concrete shower and bath
12 Sloping floor to shower and bath floor
13 Sliding pocket door to dressing room in stone-clad wall to end of shower
14 Wall-mounted shower head
15 Mixer taps to bath spout and shower head
16 Bath spout
17 Stone-clad ledge
18 Pivot door to bedroom

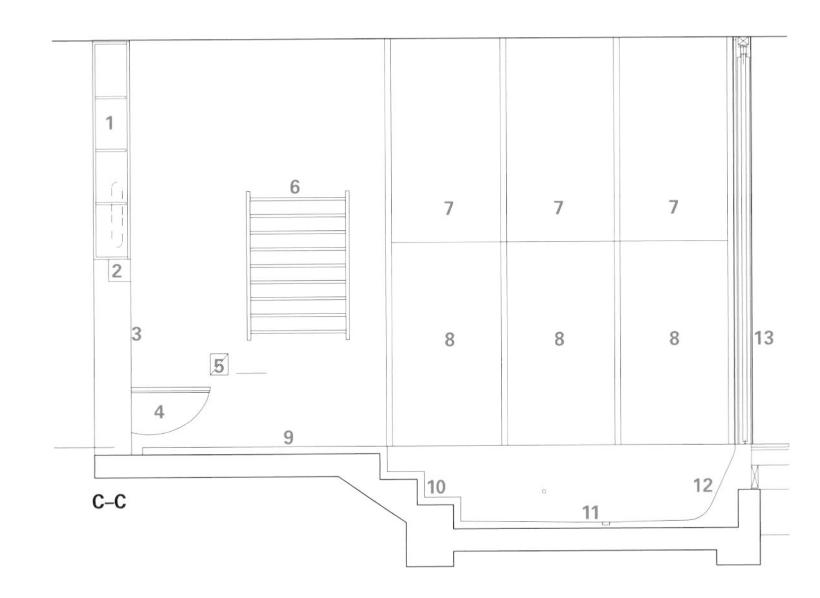

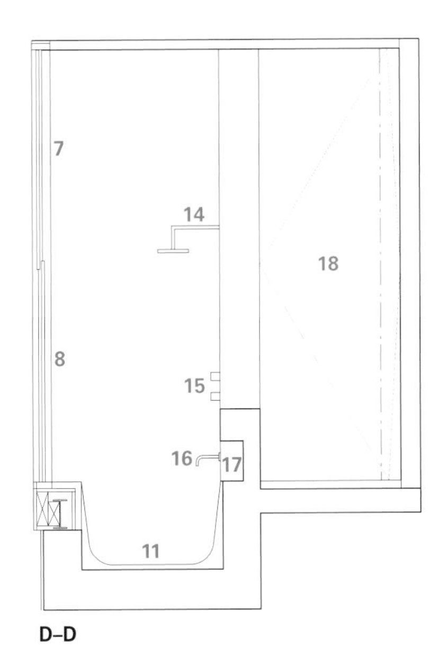

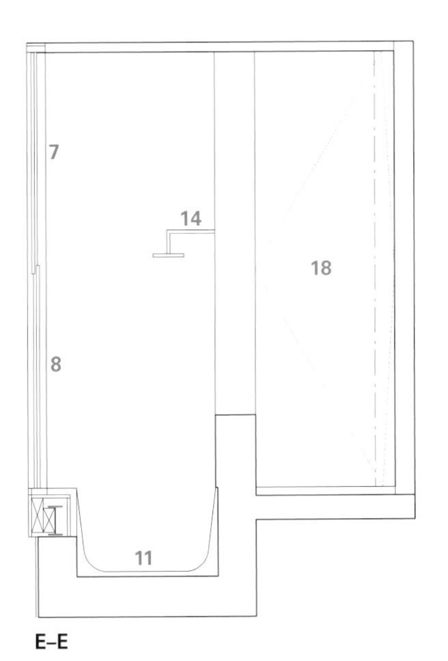

Stone

Marsh Cashman Koolloos Architects
Longueville House
Sydney, New South Wales, Australia

Ledge Detail A, Ledge Detail B, Ledge Detail C, Set Down Detail D, Packing Plan Detail E and Floor Detail F
1:5

1 Timber stud frame
2 Stone tile to ledge surface
3 CFC lining
4 Birds-mouth edge to vertical and horizontal tiles at corner
5 Stone tile to vertical surface
6 Overhead melamine cupboard carcass
7 Mirror-clad doors to overhead cupboard
8 Waterproof CFC sheet lining
9 Waterproof lining
10 Concrete screed laid to fall to drain
11 Concrete topping
12 Strip drain assembly
13 100 mm (2/5 inch) thick white melamine wall packing
14 Continuous polyurethane expansion joint
15 Shower and bath

Opposite Left
View of the combination bath and shower. The top half of the glazed wall (left) opens up to views of the garden.

Opposite Right
The basin, cast in white concrete to match the floor and bath, is cantilevered from the stone-clad wall. Above the basin, mirror-clad cupboards provide plenty of storage.

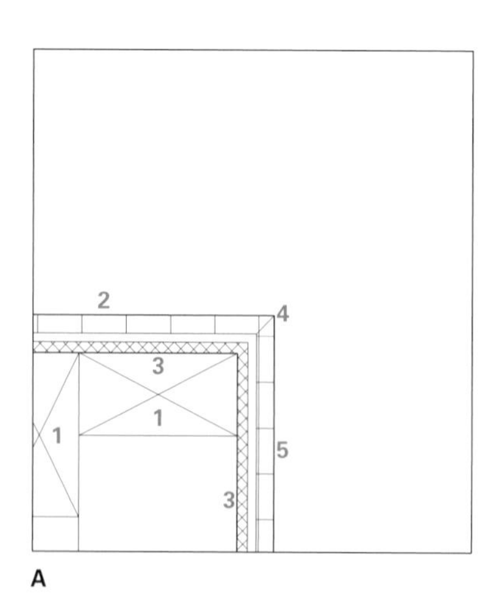

A

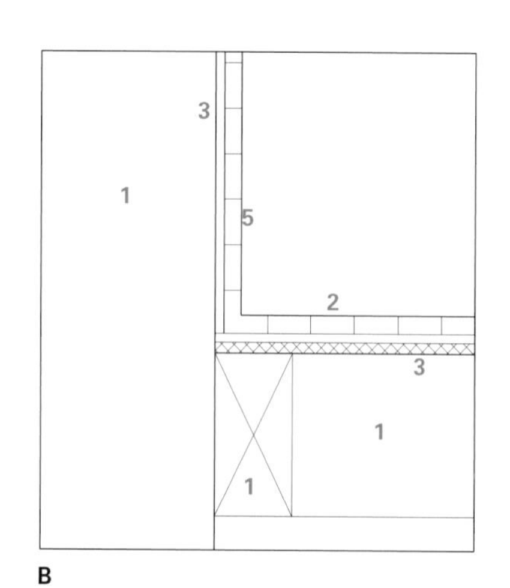

B

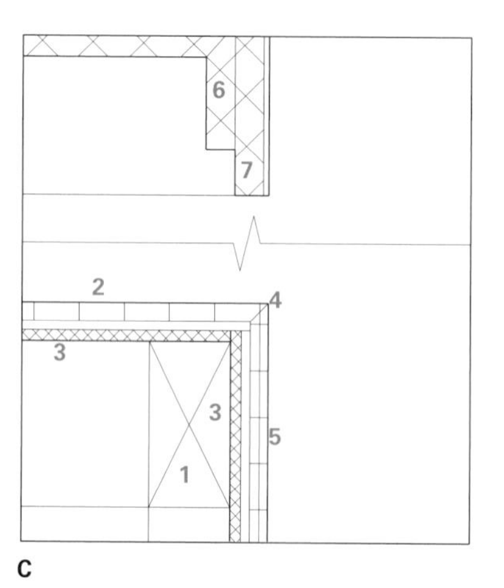

C

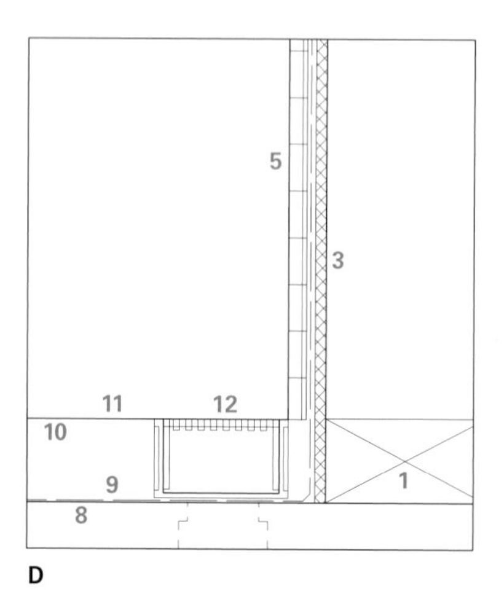

D

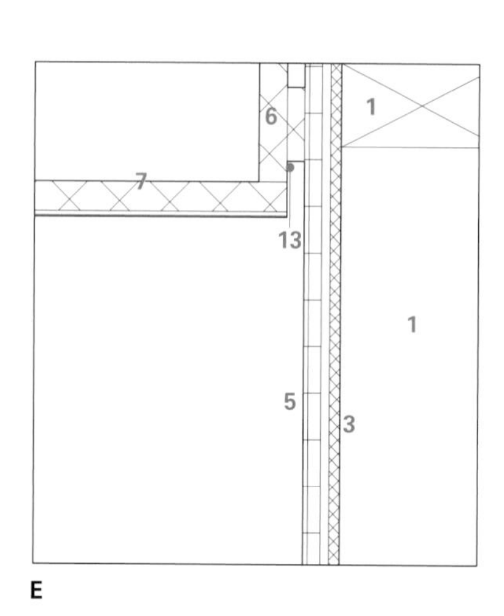

E

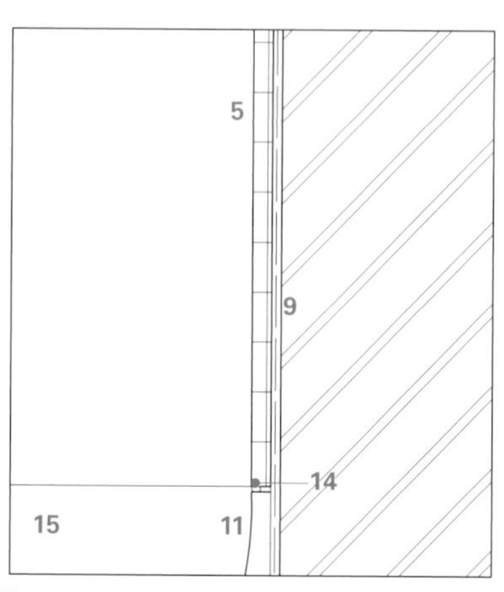

F

Materials
Countertop Custom made cast white concrete
Joinery White melamine
Floor Poured in-situ reinforced concrete with white concrete screed topping
Tiles Vitrified Oslo stone from Pazotti
Lighting Euroluce

Appliances and Fixtures
Basin Taps Logic shower mixer in chrome from Rogerseller
Basin Spout Logic wall bath outlet in chrome from Rogerseller
Basin Bespoke concrete washbasin
Shower Taps Logic shower mixer in chrome from Rogerseller
Shower 'Cafe' wall-mounted shower rose from Rogerseller
Bath Taps Logic shower mixer in chrome from Rogerseller
Bath Spout Logic wall bath outlet in chrome from Rogerseller
Bath Bespoke in-situ reinforced concrete
Towel Rails Madinoz
WC Philippe Starck Edition 3 from Duravit

Project Credits
Completion 2007
Project Architects Steve Koolloos, Mark Cashman, Alix Bond, Min Dark, Katrin Foehrenbach
Structural Engineers Simpson Design Associates
Cost Consultants QS Plus
Main Contractor Aforce Constructions
Hydraulic Engineer Acor Consultants
Landscape Architect Peter Fudge Garden Design
Pool Consultant Pride Pools
Surveyor Philip C K Hooi Pty Ltd

Tzannes Associates

Martignoni Apartment Sydney, New South Wales, Australia

This two-bedroom apartment is located on the 24th floor of the Horizon Apartments, a 43-storey tower designed by Harry Seidler and Associates in Darlinghurst, Sydney. The orientation and internal planning maximizes exposure to harbour views centred on the Opera House and the Harbour Bridge.

The client's brief was limited to the refurbishment of the kitchen and two bathrooms. In response, the architects created a layout that improved the compatibility with the existing building and complemented the client's lifestyle, which included frequent entertaining.

The kitchen and bathrooms were redesigned to provide a less cluttered visual presentation to the adjacent rooms. The existing bathrooms have low ceiling heights with no access to natural light. A conscious design decision was made to dramatize these conditions by transforming them into 'caves' with lighting that is task- and joinery-specific.

Dark-grey stone was selected as a universal finish, with large tiles applied to the walls, and smaller tiles on the floor and bath box in the guest bedroom. Downlights were employed carefully and sparingly to wash only selected surfaces with light which is then amplified, making use of the natural reflections across the stone to good effect. As a result, mirrors appear to float, back lit by concealed fluorescent lighting, often perceived as natural daylight by those new to the room.

Throughout the project, natural materials were selected in preference to applied finishes. This not only met the client's brief for durability, but also promised a timeless quality and finish which transcends fashion trends, and alleviates the need for future refurbishment and wasteful expenditure of manufactured materials.

Opposite Left
The Horizon Apartment building is an architectural icon on the Sydney skyline. Curved balconies take advantage of spectacular harbour and city views.

Floor Plan
A Balcony
B Living area
C Dining area
D Kitchen
E Laundry
F Guest bathroom
G Guest bedroom
H Entry hall
I Master bathroom
J Master bedroom

Left
In the guest bathroom, a custom made bath and shower are accessed via a bench of hard wood slats which provides both a threshold and a seat. Lighting is used judiciously to create an intimate bathing environment.

Stone

Tzannes Associates
Martignoni Apartment
Sydney, New South Wales, Australia

Guest Bathroom Plan and Sections A–A, B–B, C–C and D–D
1:50

1 Wall-hung white ceramic basin
2 Basin spout and taps
3 Mirror-clad cabinets with adjustable shelves
4 WC
5 Stainless steel toilet-roll holder
6 Stone tiles to bathroom floor
7 Stainless steel towel rail
8 Hard wood slats to bath / shower bench
9 Bath spout and tap
10 Ceiling-mounted shower head
11 Stone tiles to shower floor
12 Double-flush buttons to WC
13 Stone wall tiles
14 Tiled slope to bath end
15 Stone-clad box to conceal plumbing
16 Door to bedroom

Opposite
View of the ensuite bathroom to the master bedroom. The same finishes and approach to the detailing as the guest bathroom are employed. These include large stone tiles to the walls and smaller tiles to the floor with mirror-faced cabinets above a stone-clad wall on which the WC and basin are hung. Here, a walk-in shower is screened from the rest of the space by a large sheet of frameless glass.

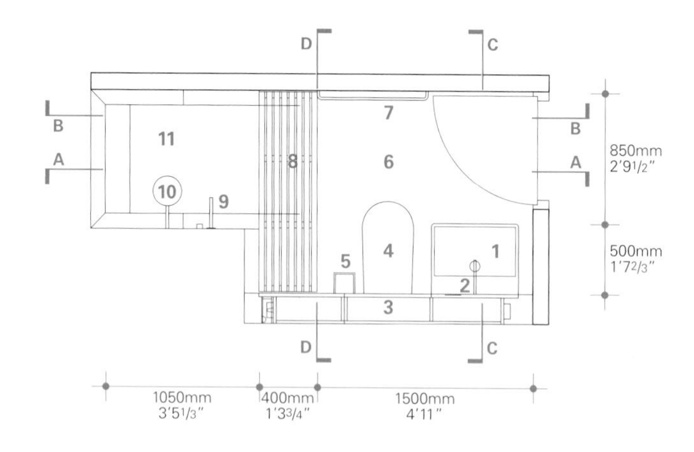

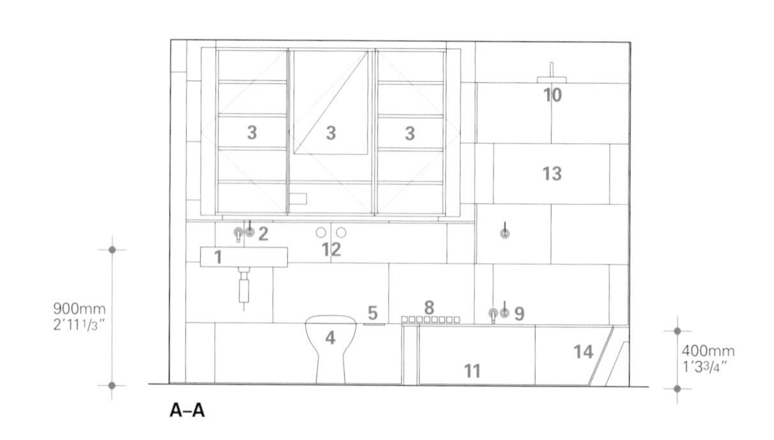

A–A

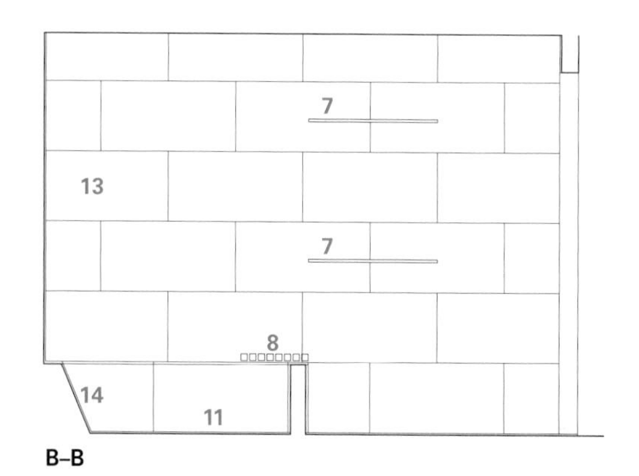

B–B

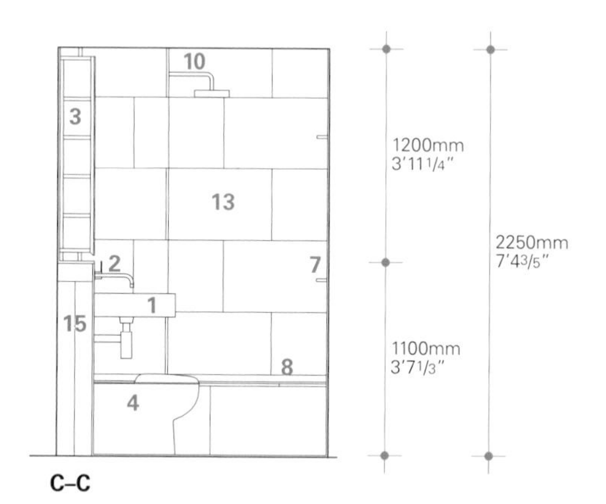

C–C

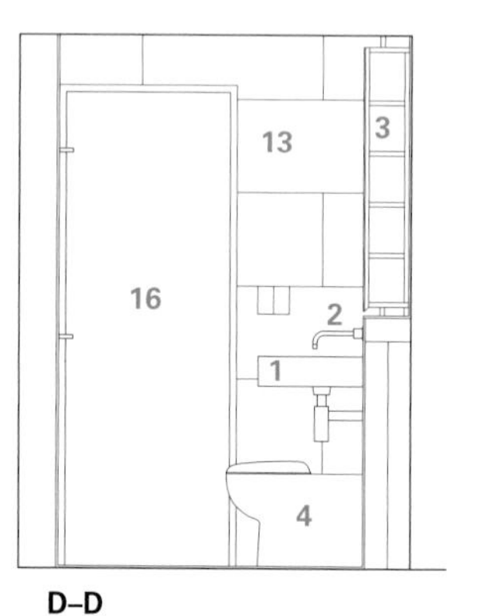

D–D

Materials
Shelf Vara Basalt stone
Floor Vara Basalt stone tiles
Wall Tiles Vara Basalt stone tiles
Lighting Concealed fluorescent fixtures

Appliances and Fixtures
Basin Taps Vola
Basin Spout Vola
Basin Duravit Special 3
Shower Taps Vola
Shower Head Waterslide
Bath Vara Basalt mosaics
WC Caroma Leda
Timber Step Unfinished Teak

Project Credits
Completion 2007
Project Architects Phillip Rossington, Mark Gazy, Allison Cronin
Structural Engineers Simpson Design Associates
Main Contractor ANT Building

Hudson Architects

The Lighthouse
Derbyshire, England, UK

Built into a hillside of the Derbyshire countryside, offering spectacular uninterrupted views of the Amber Valley, The Lighthouse is divided into three distinct zones characterized by their materiality. With its northerly side built into the rock of the hill, the building's materiality becomes progressively light towards the south elevation, moving from solid red stone (matching that quarried locally and found on the site), to timber and then glass.

A red stone boundary wall anchors the property into the landscape and runs into the interior, featuring extensively in polished form in the entrance hall. The roof of heavy slate tiles wraps around and down the north-west wall and is punctured only once with a 3.8 metre (12½ foot) diameter opening, allowing light into the central sunken courtyard.

The entrance is via an oak-panelled door into the hallway. From here are the open-plan kitchen, dining and living areas that together form the focus of the house. The living space is orientated towards a fireplace, drawing the eye to the south-west glazed elevation and the dramatic sun lounge and balconies. The lightness of the south-facing façade culminates in the spectacular two-storey sun lounge, which protrudes from the house over the grounds.

The master bathroom is part of a suite of rooms that include a dressing area, master bedroom and private terrace. The bathroom is divided into three zones. The central space, clad entirely in red stone, and which is open to the dressing area, contains a sunken bath and two basins as well as a glazed skylight. Flanking this space are a WC and a separate shower, both of which are accessed via glazed doors from the dressing area. The floor is of solid oak, as elsewhere in the house, which is interrupted only for the monolithic steps that house the bathtub and basins.

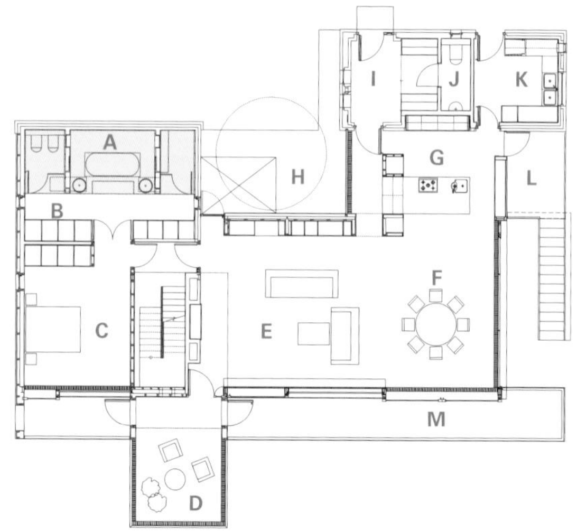

Opposite Left
The house becomes progressively light as it moves away from the solidity at the street side towards the garden, where the façade dissolves into planes of expansive glazing. Notably, a double-height sun lounge cantilevers out over the rolling landscape.

Floor Plan
A Master bathroom
B Dressing room
C Master bedroom
D Sun lounge
E Living room
F Dining room
G Kitchen
H Sunken courtyard and pool
I Entrance
J WC
K Laundry
L Balcony and stair to garden
M Terrace

Left
Red stone is used extensively in the bathroom. Stone steps have been created to provide elevated platforms for both the basins and the bath, while the walls are also clad in stone. Here, the stone has been cut in an orthogonal jigsaw to accommodate storage recesses.

Stone

Hudson Architects
The Lighthouse
Derbyshire, England, UK

Bathroom Plan and Sections A–A, B–B, C–C and D–D
1:50

1. WC
2. Bidet
3. Pivoting glass door to WC
4. Fixed glass panel
5. Fixed obscured glass window
6. Glass shelves to stone recess with folding mirrored door over
7. Basin spout and mixer tap
8. White ceramic basin
9. Red stone floor tiles
10. White ceramic sunken bath
11. Free-standing Iroko timber bench
12. Recessed ceiling light over
13. Floor-mounted shower head
14. Oak flooring to dressing area
15. WC cistern concealed behind red stone-clad panel
16. Red stone wall tiles
17. Folding mirrored door in open position
18. Openable skylight over bath tub
19. Heated towel rail
20. Pneumatic WC flush button
21. Bath tap
22. Stone-faced concealed drawers below sinks accessed from outside WC and steam room shown dotted

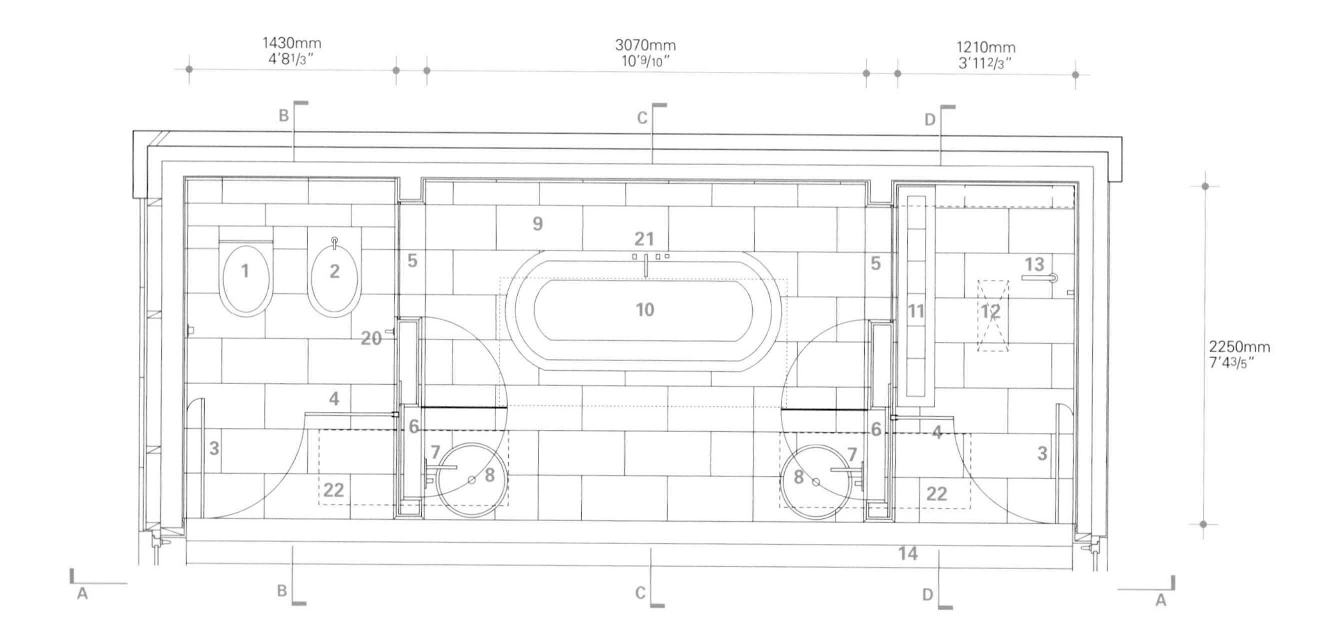

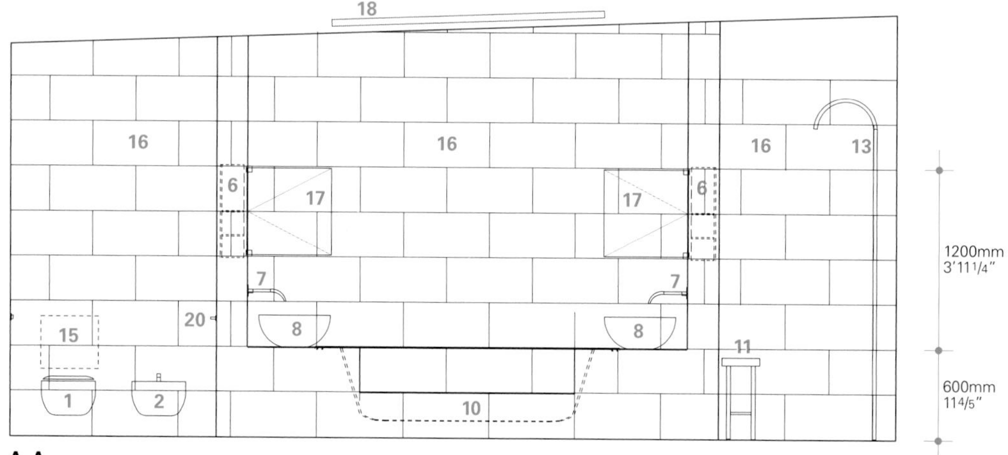

A–A

Materials
Walls, Bath Surround and Steps Farrar Red Sandstone, thoroughly seasoned and free from cracks, vents, fissures or other defects which may adversely affect appearance, strength or durability
Joinery Two-pack high-gloss factory applied paint finish to MDF supplied by Ford Joinery
Floor Solid antique oak on floating construction
Lighting Sealed waterproof downlighters by Modular Lighting

Appliances and Fixtures
Basin Taps and Spout Wall-mounted taps and spout by Aquaplus Solutions
Basin Flavia porcelain basin
Shower Shower pole and wall-mounted mixer by Aquaplus Solutions
Bath Taps and Spout Deck-mounted tap, shower head and mixer by Aquaplus Solutions
Bath DKM Designer Double-ended Bath from RAK Ceramics
Towel Rails Ashdown polished stainless steel towel rail by Plumb Warehouse

Project Credits
Completion 2006
Client Jackie Lee
Project Architects Anthony Hudson, Dieter Kleiner
Structural Engineers Techniker
Services Engineer Bridgford Construction
Quantity Surveyor Burke Hunter Adams
Landscape Designer Diarmuid Gavin

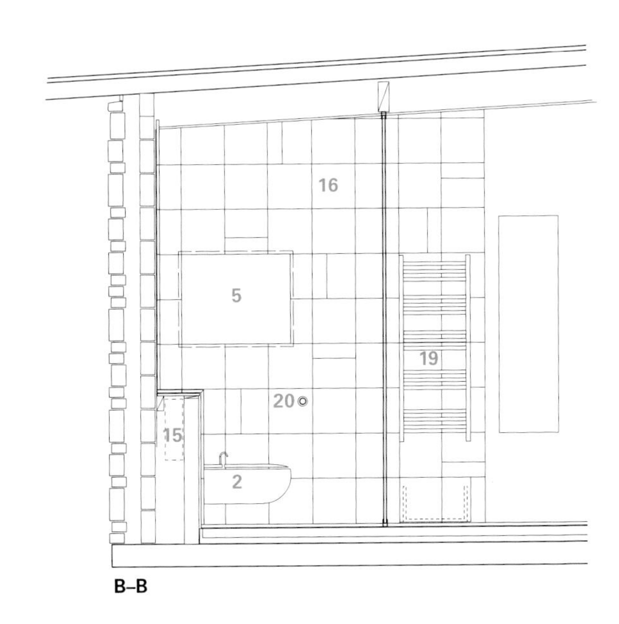

B–B

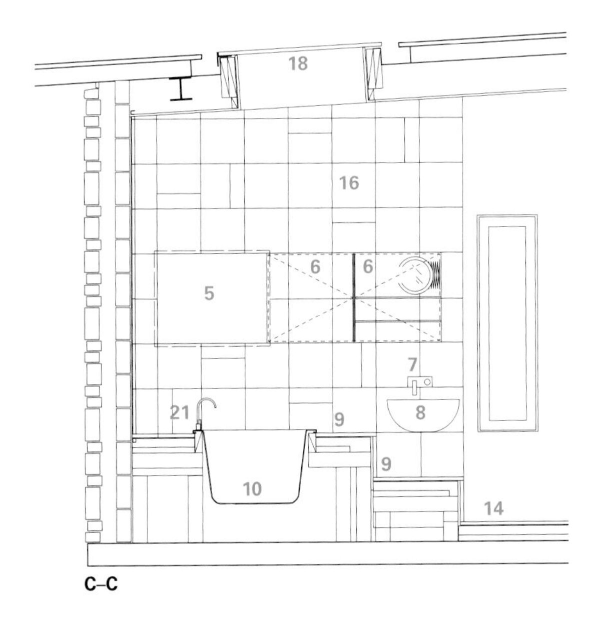

C–C

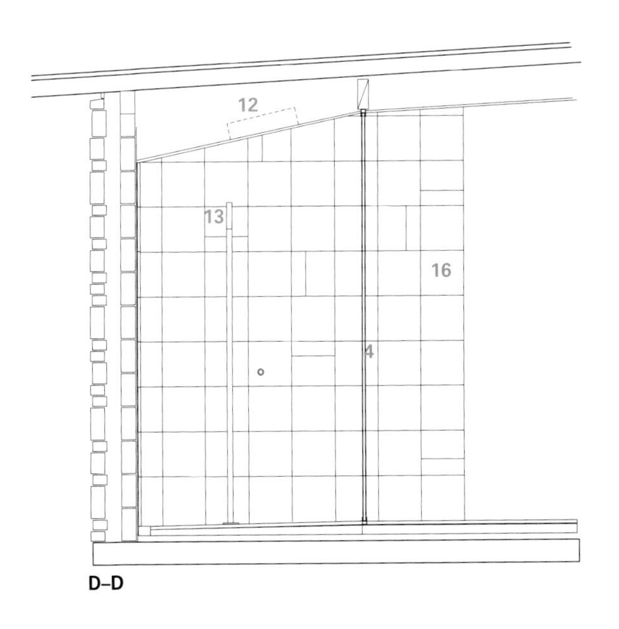

D–D

Vincent Van Duysen Architects

M–VS Residence Brussels, Belgium

This larger than average apartment was created for a retired Dutch barrister and his wife who relocated to Brussels to create their new home. Fast connections to London, Amsterdam, Paris and Antwerp, where they had lived previously and have children, plus the cultural mix of Flemish and French that permeates the city, made it the obvious choice.

A key part of the brief for their new home was the accommodation of a collection of modern furniture including pieces by Eames, Bertoia and Eileen Gray. The client purchased two apartments in a newly built complex and asked Vincent Van Duysen to design the interior from the empty shells, including connecting the two spaces.

The finished apartment features a chequerboard of Carrara marble and dark oak which forms the palette throughout the space. Sliding walls, some in glass, some in oak, carve up the penthouse in a variety of configurations, with guest quarters and his-and-hers offices on the lower floor, connected by a marble spiral staircase. Splashes of colour, partly inspired by the furniture collection, feature in every room.

The master bathroom is a large marble-clad space, divided by nib walls into three zones. At one end is the WC and a separate shower area, both separated for privacy from the main space of the bathroom. The length of the room is exaggerated by a long custom made basin and vanity unit clad in Carrara Statuario marble. Here, two large rectangular basins are recessed into a marble top with simple wall-mounted taps above.

The wall above the basins features cabinet doors that are clad in the same marble as the walls and appear seamless in the closed position. When open, the inside face of mirror is exposed. At the far end of the bathroom is a marble-clad bath tub, lit from behind by a full-height wall of glazing.

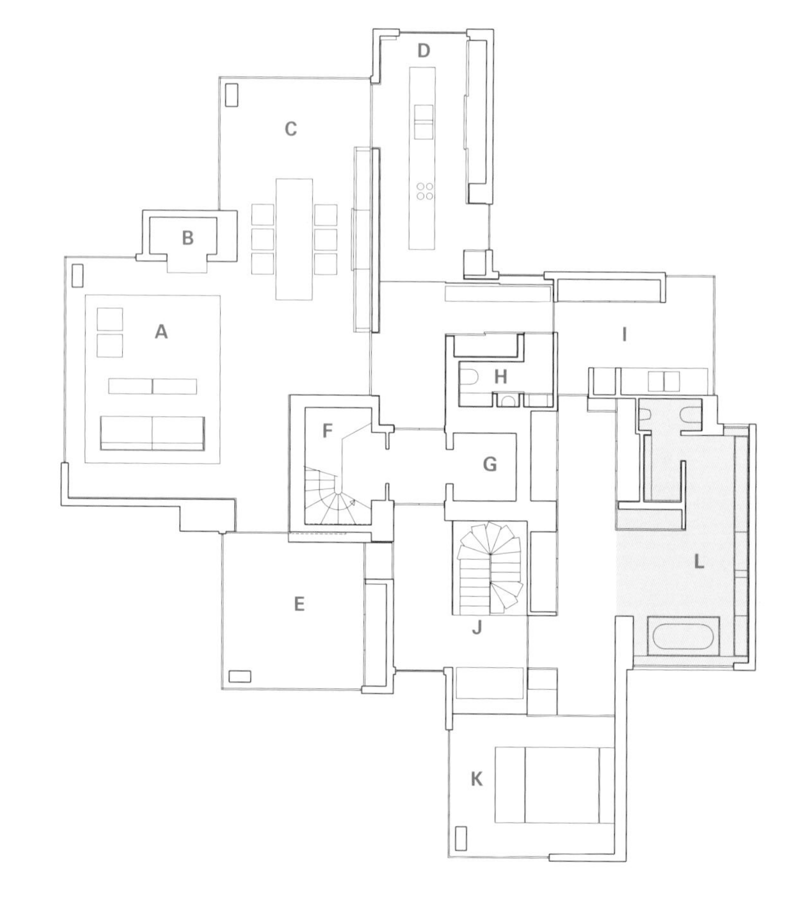

Floor Plan

A Living room
B Fireplace
C Dining room
D Kitchen
E Library
F Fire stair
G Lift
H WC
I Laundry
J Stair to lower floor
K Bedroom
L Dressing and master bathroom

Opposite Left
View of the kitchen. Like the bathroom, the island bench and the custom made extractor housing above are also clad in Carrara Statuario marble.

Left
The bathroom is an essay in minimalism. All of the main components, including the free-standing stone bath tub, the basin cabinetry and the wall are clad in luxurious white marble. The only accents are the two mirror cabinets which, when closed, present a seamless face of the same marble.

Below Left
The basin cabinetry extends the full length of the room. An abundance of storage is concealed behind door and drawers with handle-less push catches.

Stone

Vincent Van Duysen
M-VS Residence
Brussels, Belgium

Bathroom Plan and Sections A–A, B–B and C–C
1:50

1 WC
2 Bidet
3 Shower recess
4 Stone-clad ledge
5 Towel rail
6 Marble countertop with storage below
7 Line of open drawers below marble countertop
8 Custom made marble basin
9 Marble-clad mirror cabinet
10 Marble-clad bath tub
11 Stainless steel grille cover to floor heating
12 Full-height linen cupboard with adjustable shelves
13 Laundry bins
14 Concealed spotlights in painted plasterboard ceiling
15 Carrara Statuario marble wall cladding
16 Ceiling recess for concealed lighting and roller blind housing
17 Full-height glazed exterior window with roller blind
18 Carrara Statuario marble cladding to bath tub
19 Shower head
20 Carrara Statuario marble floor to shower recess laid to fall

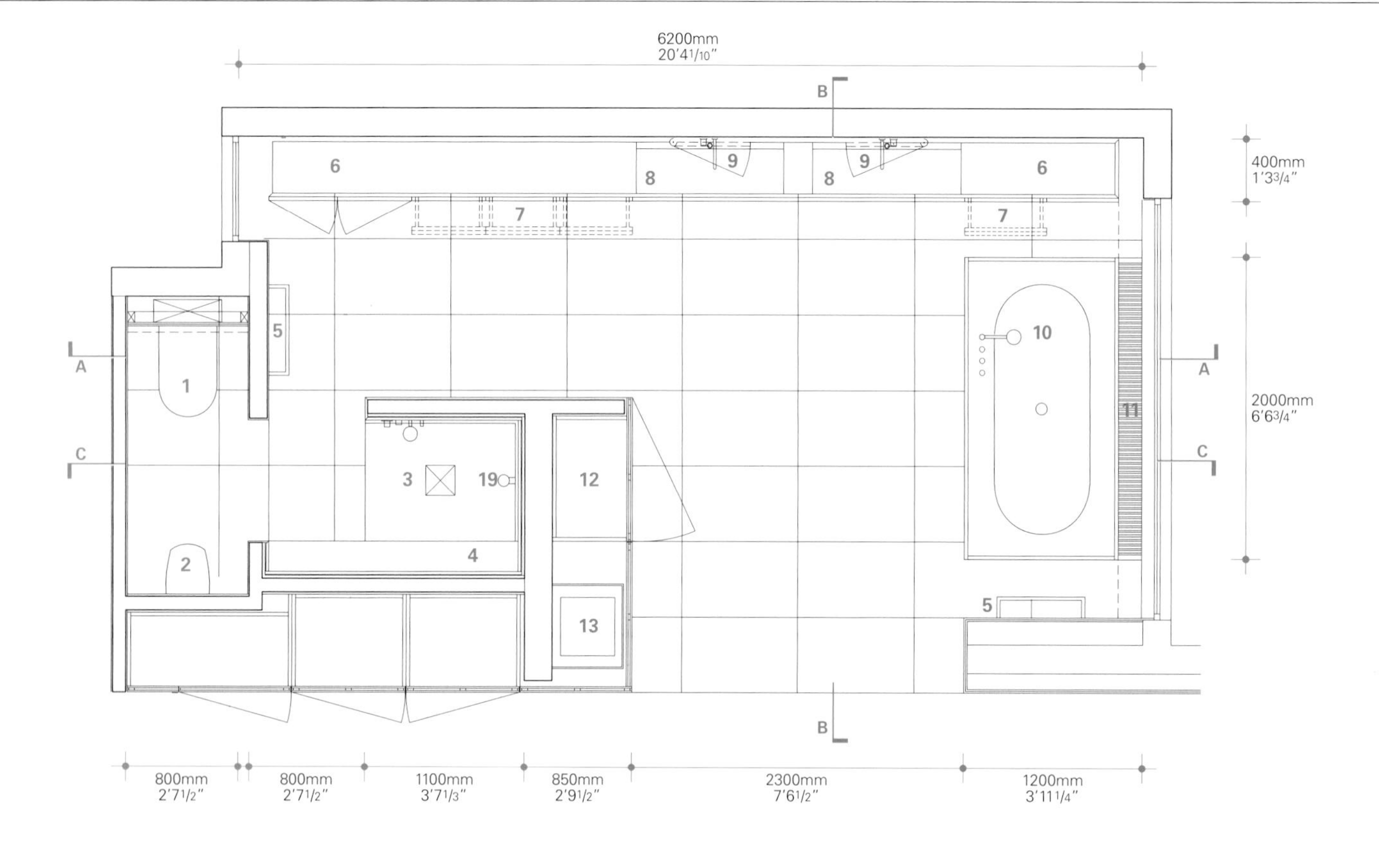

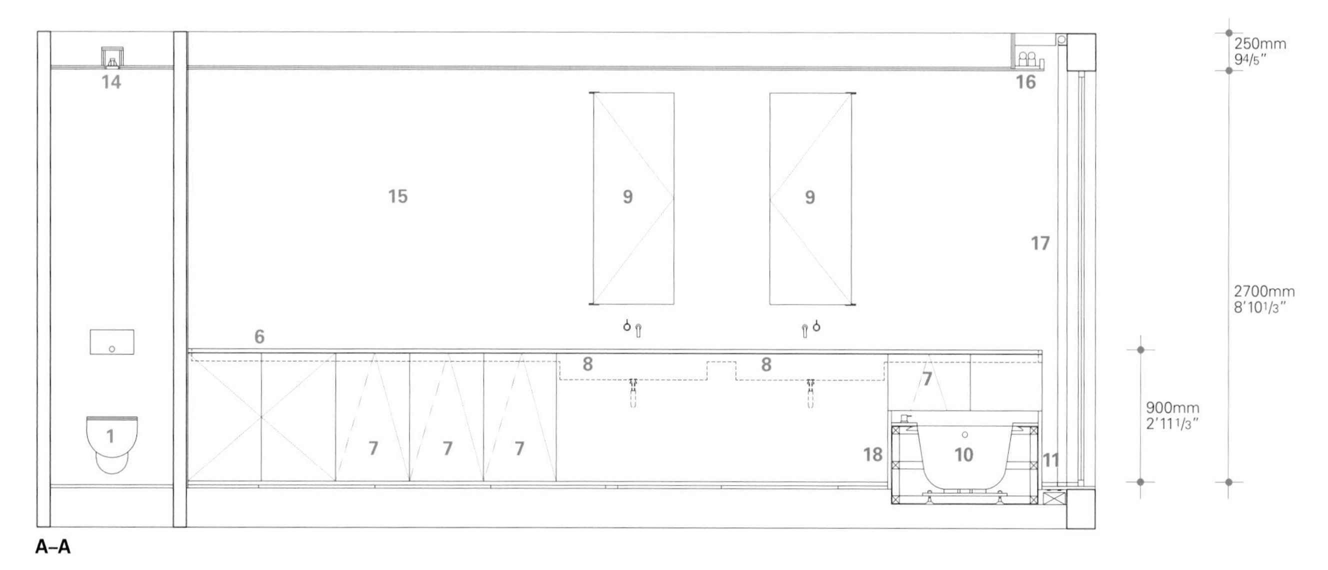

A–A

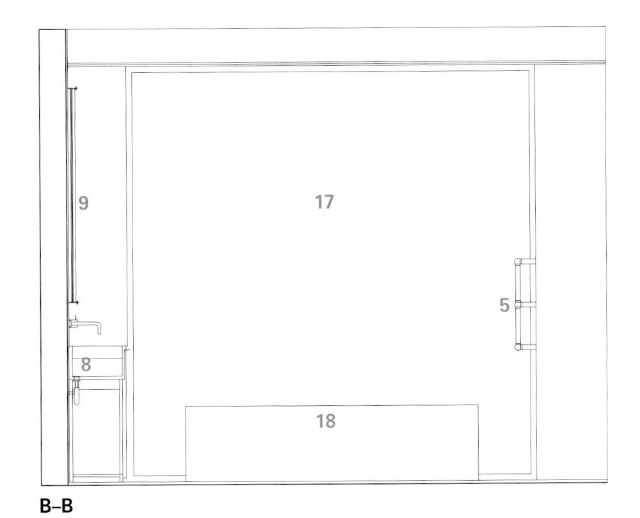

B–B

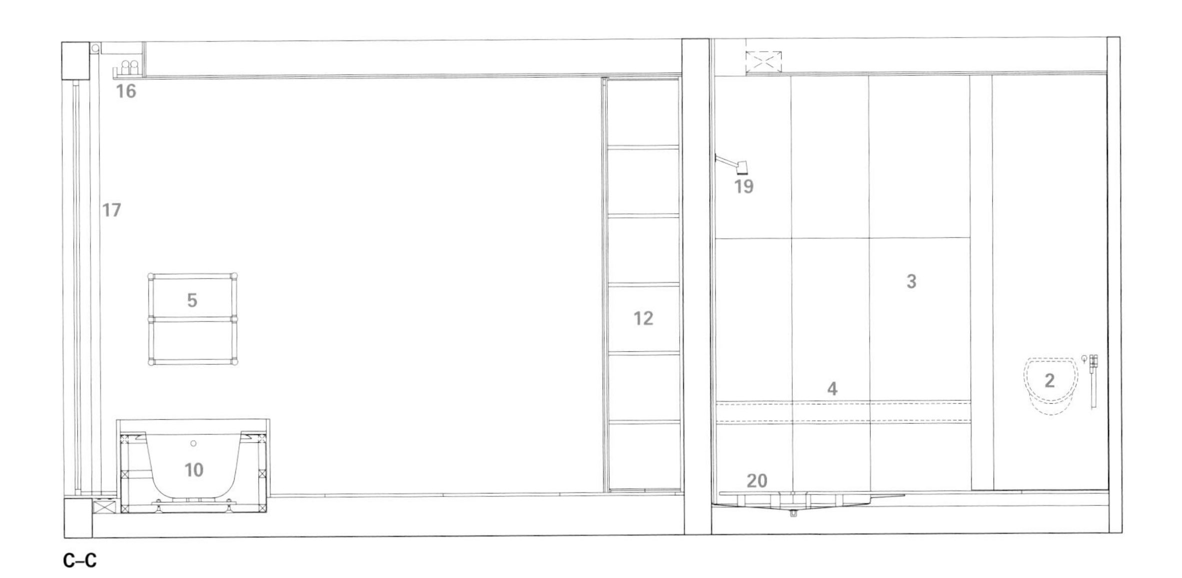

C–C

Stone

Vincent Van Duysen
M-VS Residence
Brussels, Belgium

Bath Plan and Elevations A and B and Sections A–A and B–B
1:20

1 Bath surround side panels in Carrara Statuario marble
2 Hand shower
3 Bath spout
4 Mixer tap and drain closer set
5 Top to bath surround in Carrara Statuario marble
6 White ceramic bath tub
7 Timber batten structure to marble bath surround
8 Steel strap to support bathtub bolted to concrete floor structure
9 Carrara Statuario marble floor tiles
10 Reinforced concrete floor

Shower Elevation Details
1:20

1 Carrara Statuario marble cladding to shower recess
2 Concealed spotlights in painted plasterboard ceiling
3 Painted plasterboard ceiling with waterproof finish
4 Wall-mounted shower head
5 Custom made under-floor shower tray laid to fall
6 Shower head with flexible hose
7 Shower mixer tap
8 Carrara Statuario marble floor to shower recess
9 Under-floor shower drain
10 Reinforced concrete floor
11 Sliding glass door

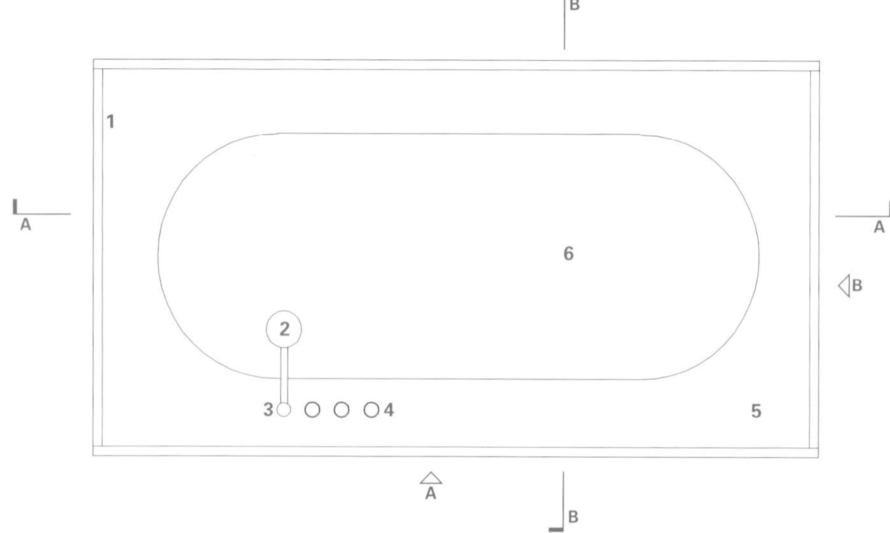

A

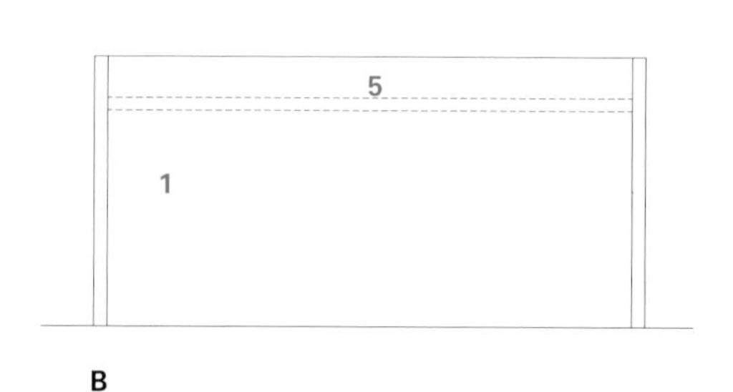

B

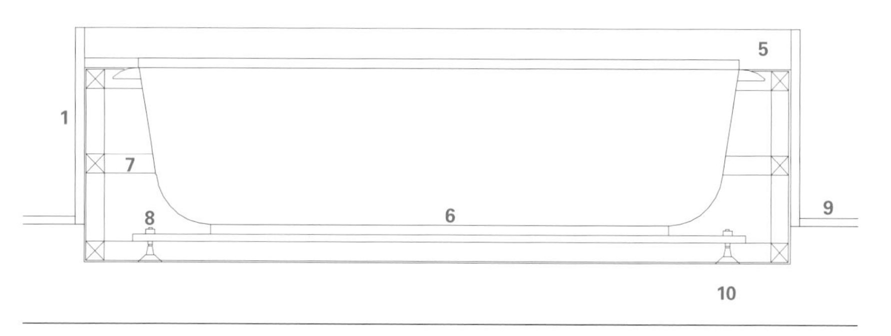

A–A

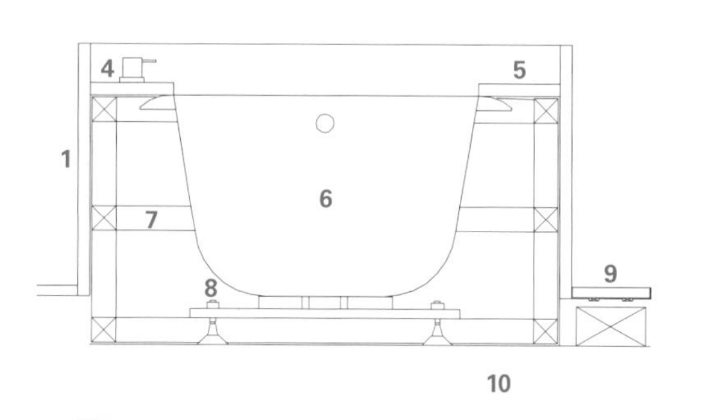

B–B

Materials
Countertop Carrara Statuario marble with integrated basins
Joinery Lacquered timber cupboard and drawer fronts
Floor Carrara Statuario marble

Appliances and Fixtures
Basin Taps Vola with chrome matte finish
Basin Spout Vola with chrome matte finish
Basin Custom made integrated marble
Shower Taps Vola with chrome matte finish
Shower Head Vola with chrome matte finish
Bath Taps and Spout Vola with chrome matte finish
Bath Duscholux Ancona with custom made marble casing
Towel Rails Custom made in stainless steel
Toilet Keramag Mango

Project Credits
Completion 2001
Project Architects Vincent Van Duysen, Stephanie Laperre
General Contractor De Coene Decor
Structural Engineers Bouquet-Deloof
Lighting Consultant Tekna bvba

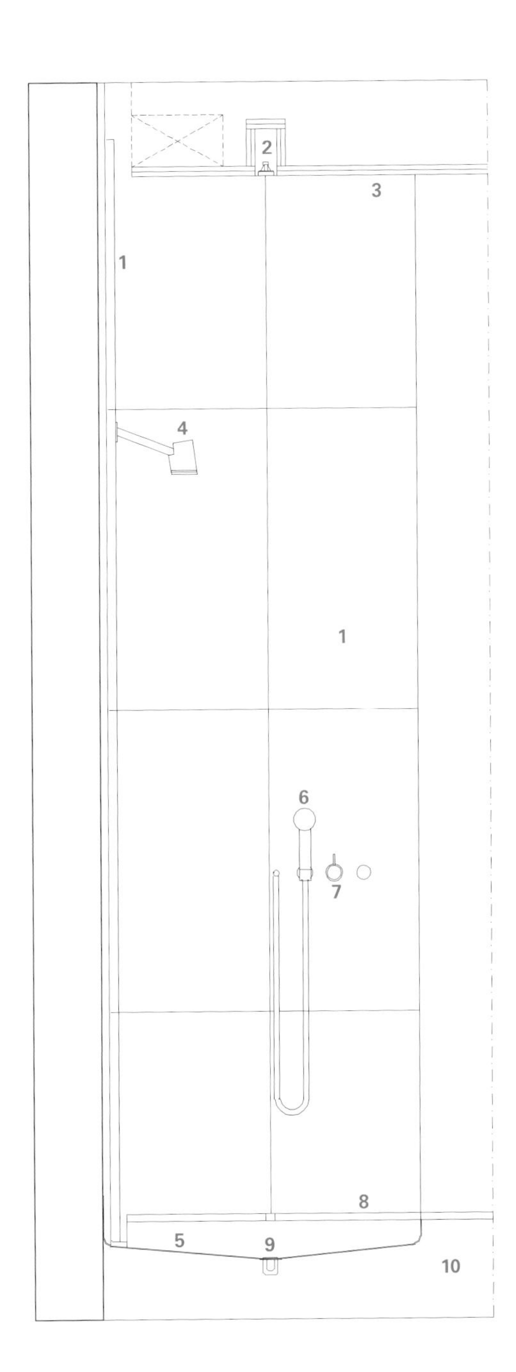

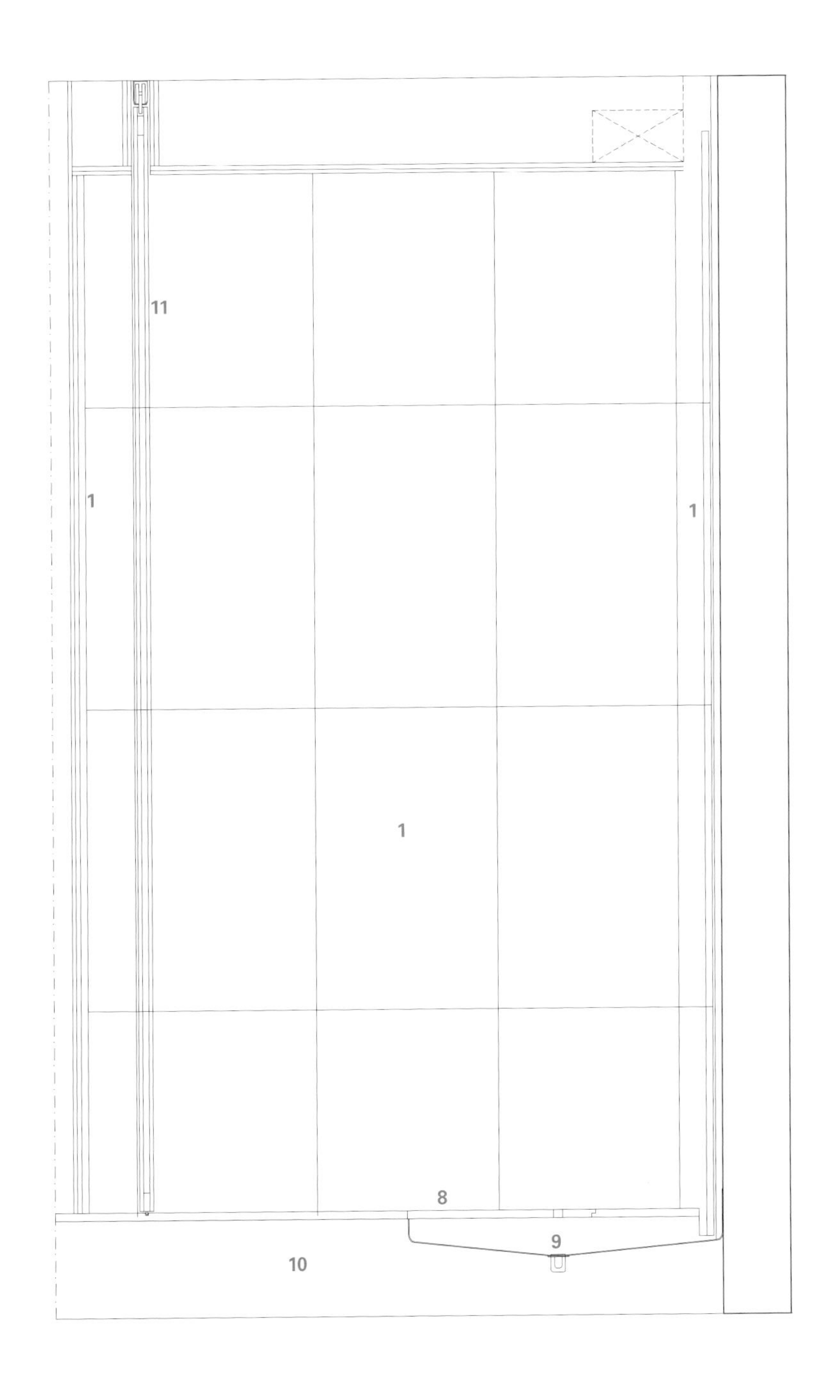

Coy + Yiontis Architects

Berkley Dobson House Melbourne, Victoria, Australia

Perhaps because of the historic neighbourhood in which this house is situated, the majority of this residence, in particular the new extension, is invisible from the street. The new building spreads low to all corners of the site to remain concealed, which also heightens its privacy and the inherent 'surprise' upon entering a contemporary residence through a humble Victorian worker's cottage façade.

The building is essentially made up of three separate pavilions, each with a distinct function. The first is a study and guest bedroom housed in the original cottage, the second contains the living, dining and kitchen spaces, and the third, separated from the living spaces by a courtyard with pool, contains the garage and laundry on the ground level and the master bedroom, ensuite bathroom and dressing room above.

The transition between each pavilion is intended to be a distinct experience, marking the change in environment and leading the visitor into the new space. Upon entry, the house is completely transparent – the eye is drawn through to the end of the house, giving the impression of one large, continuous yet divided space rather than a series of individual chambers.

Inside and outside merge through the use of sliding glazed panels and the continuity of building materials. In the kitchen, the two living rooms, the workshop, the master bedroom, and the downstairs guest bathroom, translucent external walls slide away to allow the inhabitants to enjoy the elements. In the master ensuite bathroom, the entire ceiling is glazed. In the study, the fully glazed southern aspect overlooks the pond and the courtyard. In each case, the sixth side of the space has been consciously omitted to forge a link with the outside.

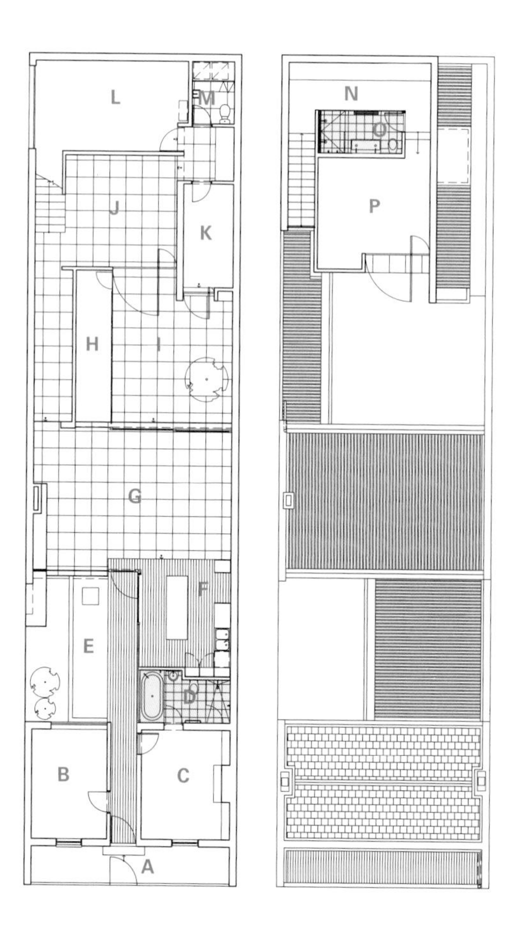

Opposite Left
View of the dining area and kitchen from the master bedroom on the upper level of the pavilion at the rear of the site. The bedroom also overlooks the pool and courtyard.

Floor Plan
A Entrance and verandah
B Study
C Guest bedroom
D Guest bathroom
E Pond
F Kitchen
G Living room 1
H Pool
I Courtyard
J Living room 2
K Workshop
L Garage
M Laundry
N Dressing room
O Master bathroom
P Master bedroom

Left
The guest bathroom is clad entirely in Carrara marble. Simple white fixtures and stainless steel fittings, and a frameless glass screen to the shower ensure a calm bathing environment. Full-height timber-framed sliding doors slide away from the marble-clad bath, opening up the whole space to the open air and views of the pond.

Stone

Coy + Yiontis Architects
Berkley Dobson House
Melbourne, Victoria,
Australia

Guest Bathroom Plan and Sections A–A, B–B and C–C
1:50

1 Shower head
2 Shower mixer tap
3 Carrara marble floor tiles to shower enclosure
4 Frameless glass door to shower enclosure
5 WC
6 Stainless steel towel rail
7 Basin spout
8 Wall-hung white ceramic basin
9 Mirror-clad cabinet over basin
10 Carrara marble floor tiles
11 Door to guest bedroom
12 Carrara marble bath surround
13 Bath spout
14 White ceramic bathtub
15 Full-height sliding glass door
16 Basin mixer tap
17 WC flush button
18 Carrara marble-covered access panel to shower

Opposite
The master bathroom is detailed in the same manner as the guest bathroom, employing Carrara marble throughout. The roof light floods the bathroom with natural light while a wall of etched glazing (right) brings light into the adjacent dressing room.

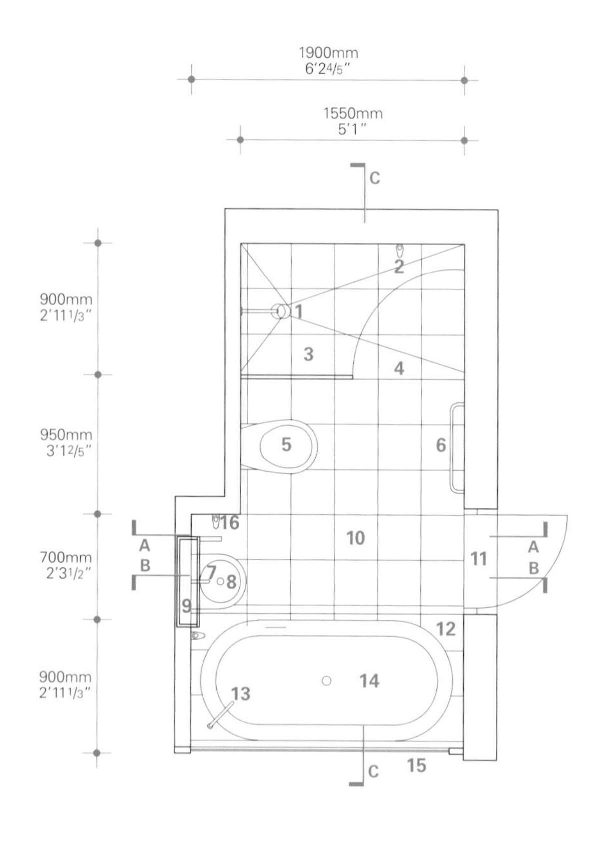

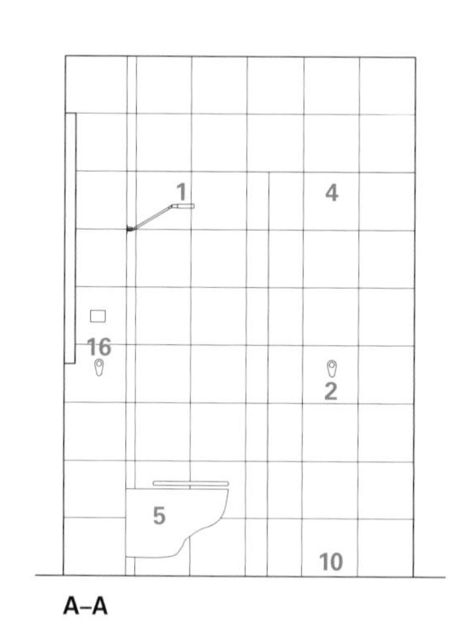

A–A

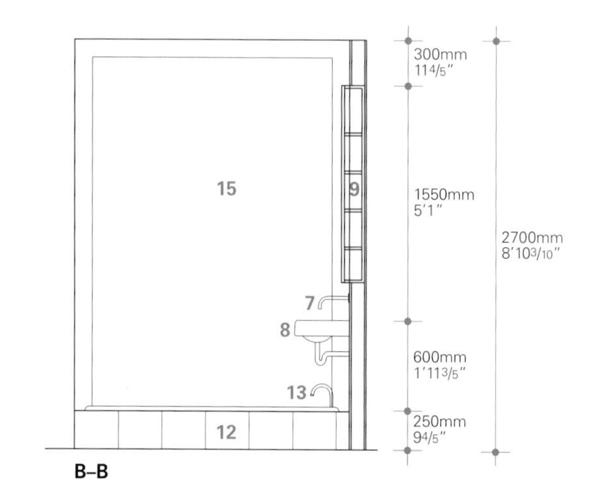

B–B

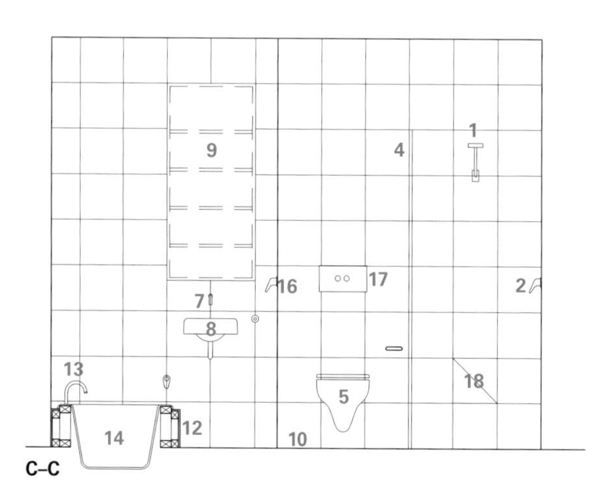

C–C

Materials
Joinery MDF with two pack paint finish
Floor Carrara Marble tiles
Splashback Carrara Marble tiles
Wall Tiles Carrara Marble tiles
Lighting Megalit Rastaf

Appliances and Fixtures
Basin Taps Fantini Isola
Basin Spout Vola
Basin Custom made stone basin
Shower Taps Fantini Isola
Shower Head Dornbracht Tara
Bath Taps and Spout Fantini Isola with custom made spout
Bath Kaldewei with spa
WC Villeroy & Boch Subway

Project Credits
Completion 2005
Project Architects Rosa Coy, Byron George, Paul Quang
Structural Engineers Ross Greer and Associates
Cost Consultants Geoffrey Moyle
Services Engineer Thomas Consulting Group

Kengo Kuma and Associates

Lotus House Kanagawa, Japan

A chequerboard façade of travertine panels hung on a flexible stainless steel frame, alternating with rectangular openings, forms a delicate screen that veils the Lotus House, a vacation home west of Tokyo. The architect intended this porous stone screen 'to flutter like delicate lotus petals', and integrate the building with the landscape.

The house is comprised of two wings linked by a central courtyard and a terraced pond that generously spreads over the front of the complex. The pond is dotted with lotus flowers, one of the symbols of enlightenment in Buddhism. The courtyard, almost empty apart from a few pieces of antique furniture, functions as a transitory space, separating the activities of the everyday, such as cooking, washing and sleeping, from the more refined, leisurely activities of reading, playing the piano and watching films.

The main bathroom is located on the first floor and includes enclosed areas for bathing, showering and dressing, as well as a matching bathtub outside on the deck overlooking the lotus pond below. The space features calming dark grey polished Shirakama stone for the floor, walls and the tubs, both of which are partly sunken into the floor.

Elsewhere, floor-to-ceiling glazing and multiple entrances link the house to the landscape. Mediating between the home and its setting, the chequerboard veils parts of the front, sides, and almost the entire back of the painted-concrete structure. Though the travertine wrapper filters, without completely eliminating, views in and out of the house, sliding glass walls open every major room to the lotus pond.

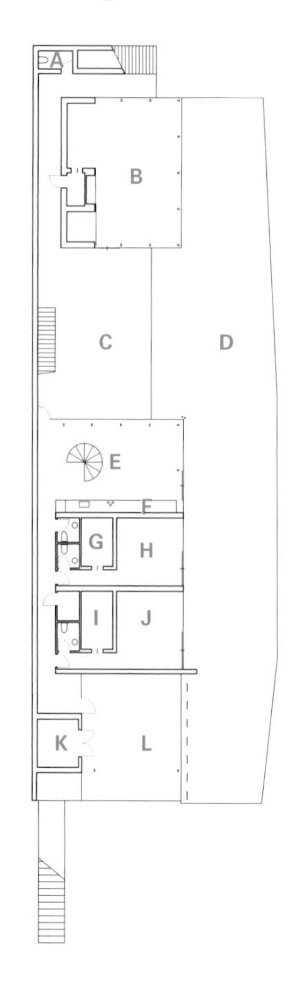

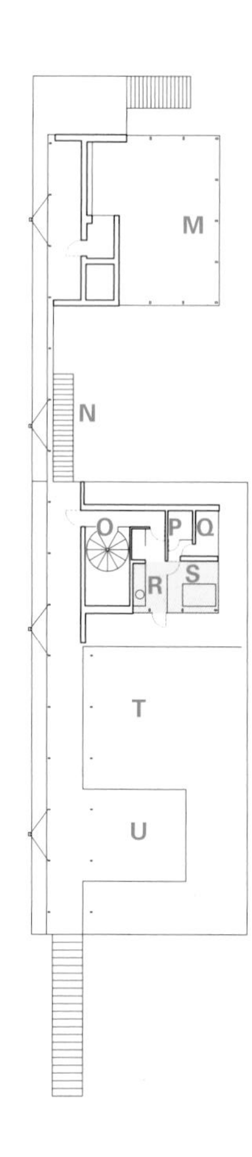

Opposite Left
The main bathroom is located on the first floor, overlooking the lotus pond. Below, the dining room (foreground), and courtyard have direct access to the landscape via full-height sliding glass doors.

Floor Plan
A WC
B Living room
C Courtyard
D Lotus pond
E Dining room
F Kitchen
G Bathroom
H Bedroom
I Bathroom
J Bedroom
K Utility room
L Garage
M Void over living room
N Stair from courtyard below
O Stair from ground floor
P WC
Q Shower
R Bathroom
S Soaking tub
T Reflecting pool
U Deck

Left
View of the covered courtyard that links all of the major spaces in the house, including the living room, seen here. The travertine, used for the floors and the screen façade, contrasts with exposed timber beams in the double-height spaces of both the courtyard and living room.

Bottom Left
The bathroom features two monolithic stone bathtubs – one on the deck overlooking the lotus pond below. The travertine screen partially screens bathers, but open sections allow views straight into the mature trees of the landscape.

Stone

Kengo Kuma and Associates
Lotus House
Kanagawa, Japan

Bathroom Plan and Sections A–A, B–B and C–C 1:50 and 1:20

1 Glass wash basin
2 Tempered glass countertop
3 Mirrored wall
4 Medicine cupboard
5 Washing machine behind plywood doors with polyurethane paint finish
6 Sauna behind plywood doors with polyurethane paint finish
7 Shirakama stone bathtub on cinder block structural frame and asphalt waterproofing
8 Shirakama stone floor
9 Shower head
10 Roller blind in concealed ceiling niche
11 Shirakama stone wall tiles with water-repellent treatment
12 Shirakama stone niche with concealed lighting
13 Waterproof plywood with insulation
14 Glazed wall between dressing room and bathroom
15 Drainage channel with stainless steel grate
16 Mixer taps
17 Plywood door with polyurethane paint finish
18 Stainless steel towel rail
19 Concealed lighting
20 Mixer tap and spout to wash basin

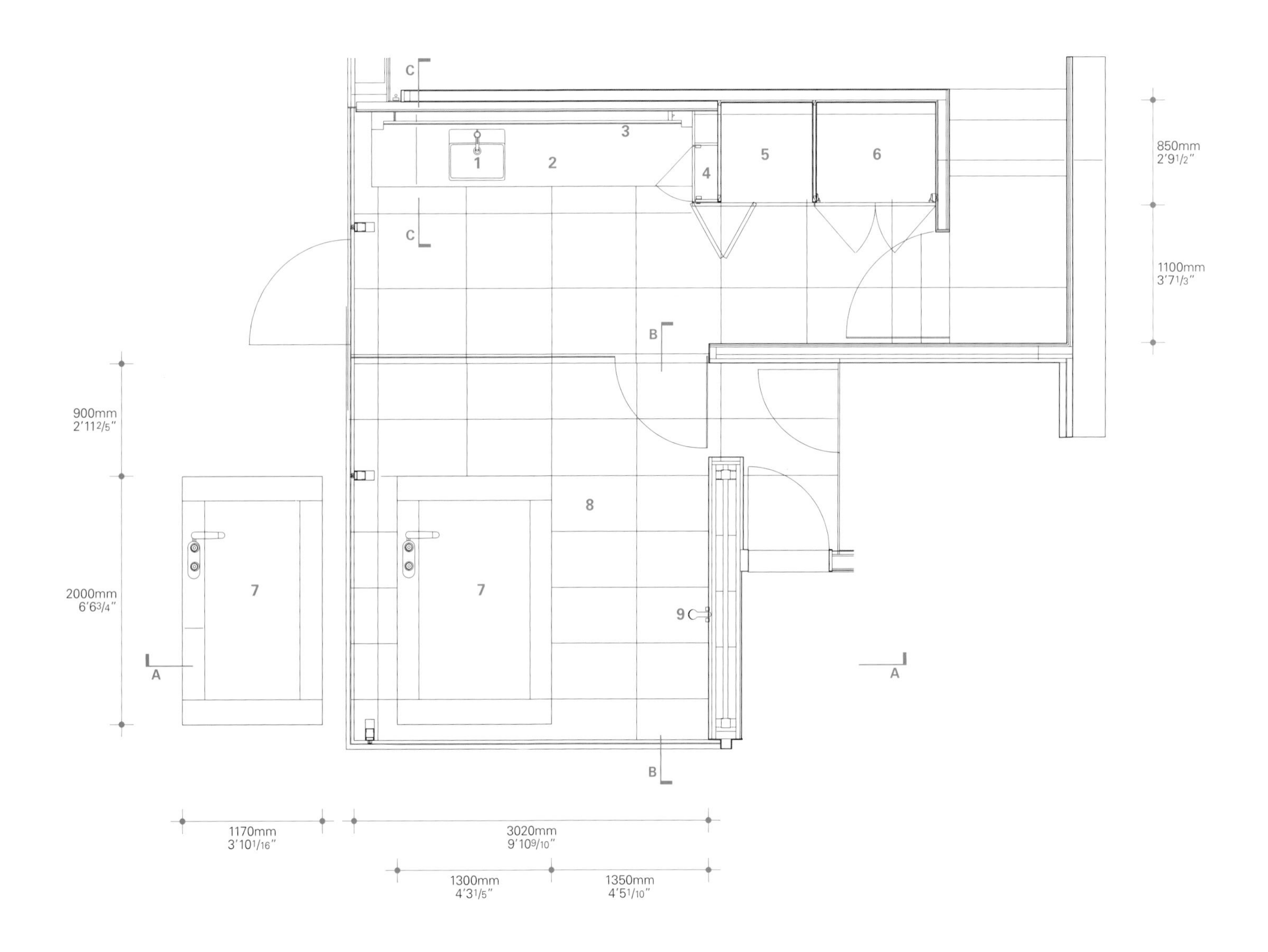

Materials
Vanity Bench Tempered glass
Joinery Plywood carcasses and doors with polyurethane paint finish
Floor Polished Shirakama stone

Fixtures
Taps and Spout INAX
Basin INAX
Bath and Jacuzzi INAX
WC INAX
Shower Head INAX
Lighting Xenon, fluorescent light tubes, halogen downlights and Halogen underwater lights from Erco

Project Credits
Completion 2005
Project Architects Kengo Kuma, Minoru Yokoo, Yuki Ikeguchi
Structural Engineers OAK Structural Design Office
Mechanical Engineers P.T. Morimura & Associates
Landscape Architect Takashi Shirai and Associates
Lighting Consultant EPK Corporation

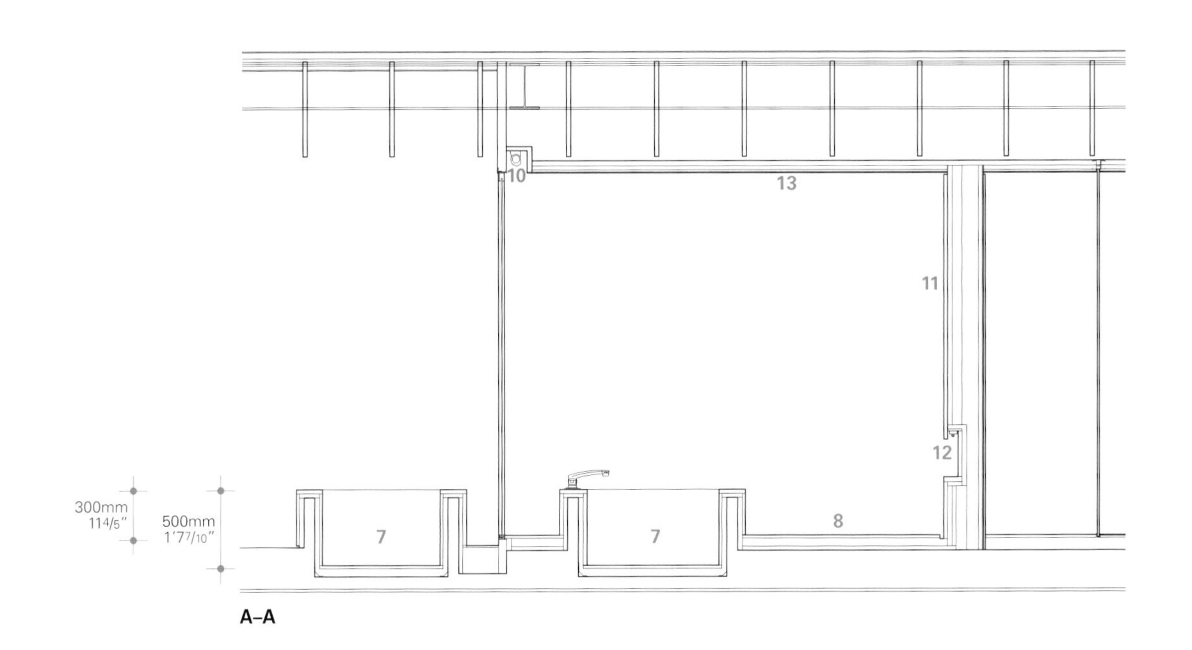

A–A

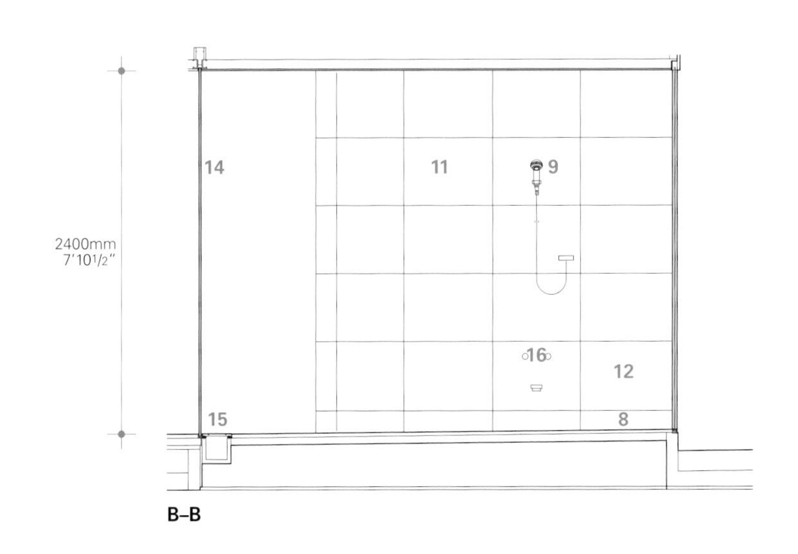

B–B

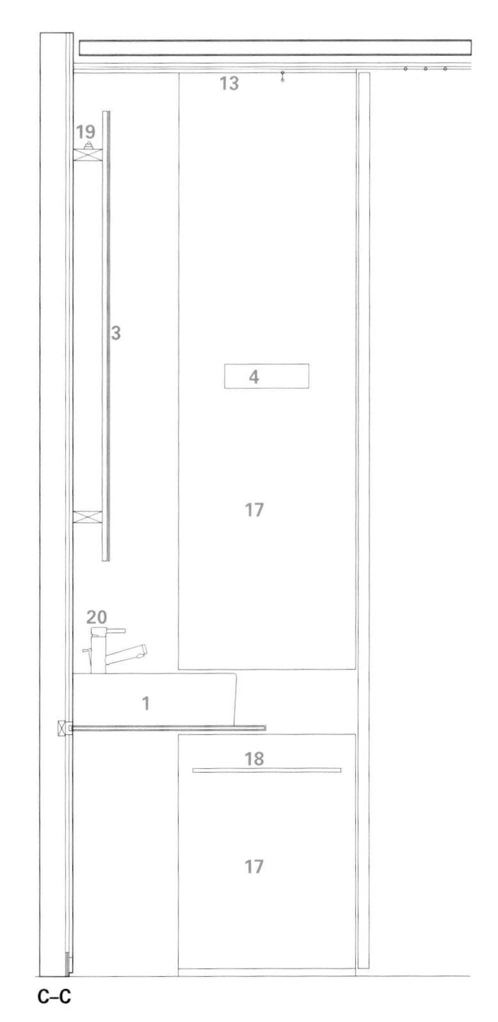

C–C

BAAS Jordi Badia / Mercè Sangenís, Architects

CH House
Barcelona, Spain

This vacation house is located in La Garriga near Barcelona, a town long associated with holidays thanks to its location between the plain of Vallès and the foothills of the Montseny mountains.

The longitudinal floor plan allows for access from both ends of the building, which is a response to the fact that the house sits on a sloping site between two streets. The principal entrance is on the upper street, while next to the lower one is the garage that, together with the swimming pool, bridges the slope and so creates a horizontal platform for the house and landscaped spaces that act as extensions of the domestic spaces within.

On one side of the house are ranged three children's or guest bedrooms, each with an ensuite bathroom, and a study. The house is then bisected by the main entrance and a courtyard, on the other side of which the spaces are arranged as three parallel zones separated by walls of pale timber cupboards.

One of these spaces accommodates the master bedroom suite, complete with dressing room and bathroom, while the central space contains the living room which is defined on one side by the stair up from the garage. On the other side of this wall are located the dining room and kitchen, both of which have access to a generous west-facing terrace.

The ensuite master bathroom sits between the bedroom area and the dressing room, which opens on to the courtyard. Natural lighting is via a large skylight over the shower area and a shift in the façade that allows the sunken bathtub to project out over the landscape with slots of glazing at either end. A minimal palette of pale stone, green painted walls and accents of warm timber in the cabinetry lend a calm atmosphere.

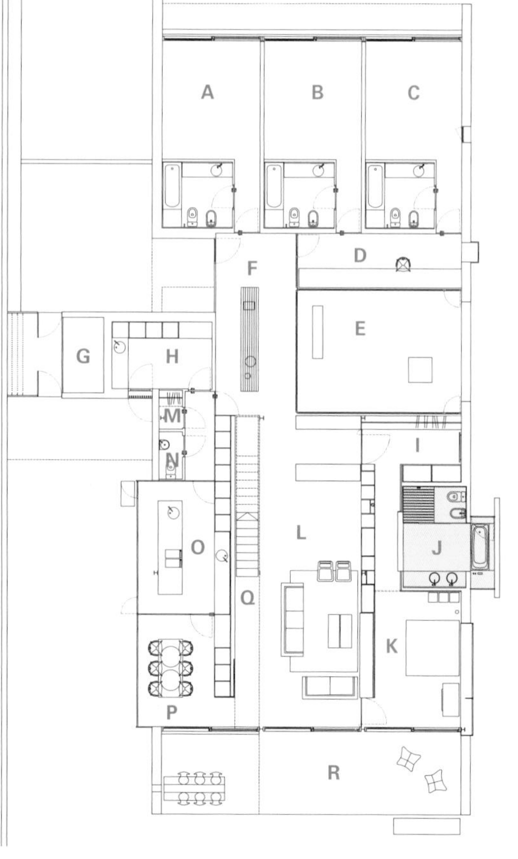

Opposite Left
View of the west terrace (left), access from the living and dining spaces, and the south façade (right) which features a projecting glazed box that houses the bathtub to the master bedroom.

Floor Plan
A Guest bedroom and bathroom
B Guest bedroom and bathroom
C Guest bedroom and bathroom
D Study
E Courtyard
F Entrance
G Utility / store
H Laundry
I Dressing room
J Master bathroom
K Master bedroom
L Living room
M Cloak room
N WC
O Kitchen
P Dining room
Q Stair from garage
R Terrace

Below
View of the master bathroom. A sunken stone bathtub is recessed into the floor. The room is flooded with natural light by two glazed panels to the south and north and by a skylight above. The twin vanity bench is complemented by mobile timber storage units.

Stone

BAAS Jordi Badia / Mercè Sangenís, Architects
CH House
Barcelona, Spain

Bathroom Plan and Sections A–A and B–B
1:50

1 Dressing room
2 Storage
3 WC
4 Bidet
5 Shower
6 Glazing to bath enclosure
7 Bath tub
8 Stone surround to bathtub
9 Basin
10 Stone vanity bench
11 Mirror-faced cupboards
12 Terrazzo floor tiles
13 Recessed wall lights
14 Terrazzo wall tiles
15 Concealed masonry structure to under-bath area
16 Skylight over bath
17 Dressing room mirror
18 Timber veneer cupboards to dressing room
19 Skylight over shower
20 Timber duck board to shower recess
21 Shower drain

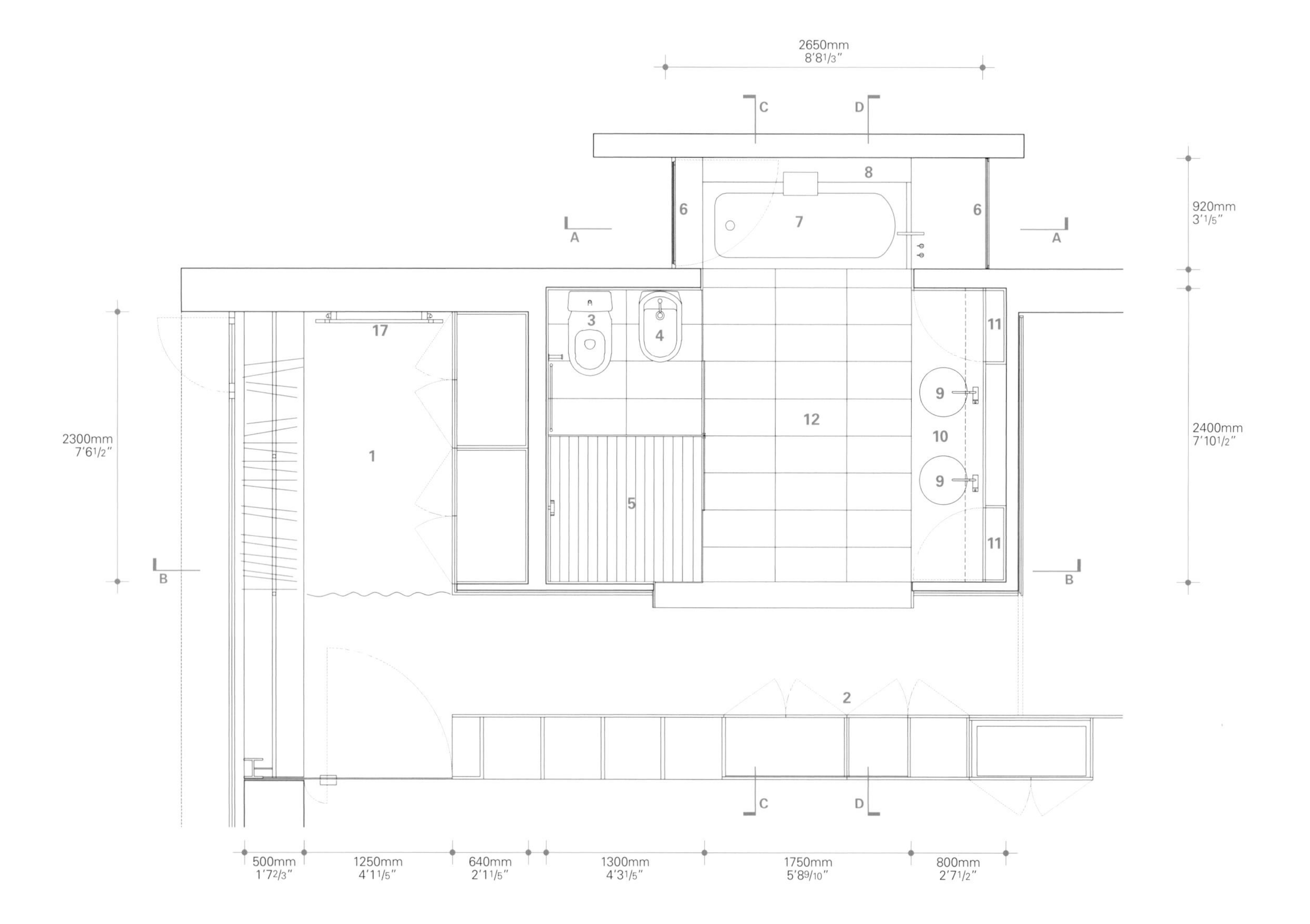

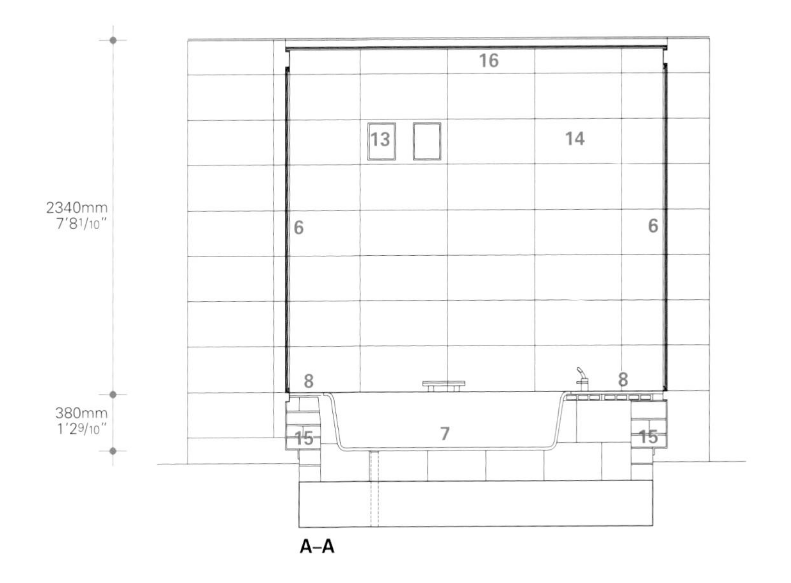
16
13
14
2340mm
7'8 1/10"
6
6
8
8
380mm
1'2 9/10"
15
7
15
A–A

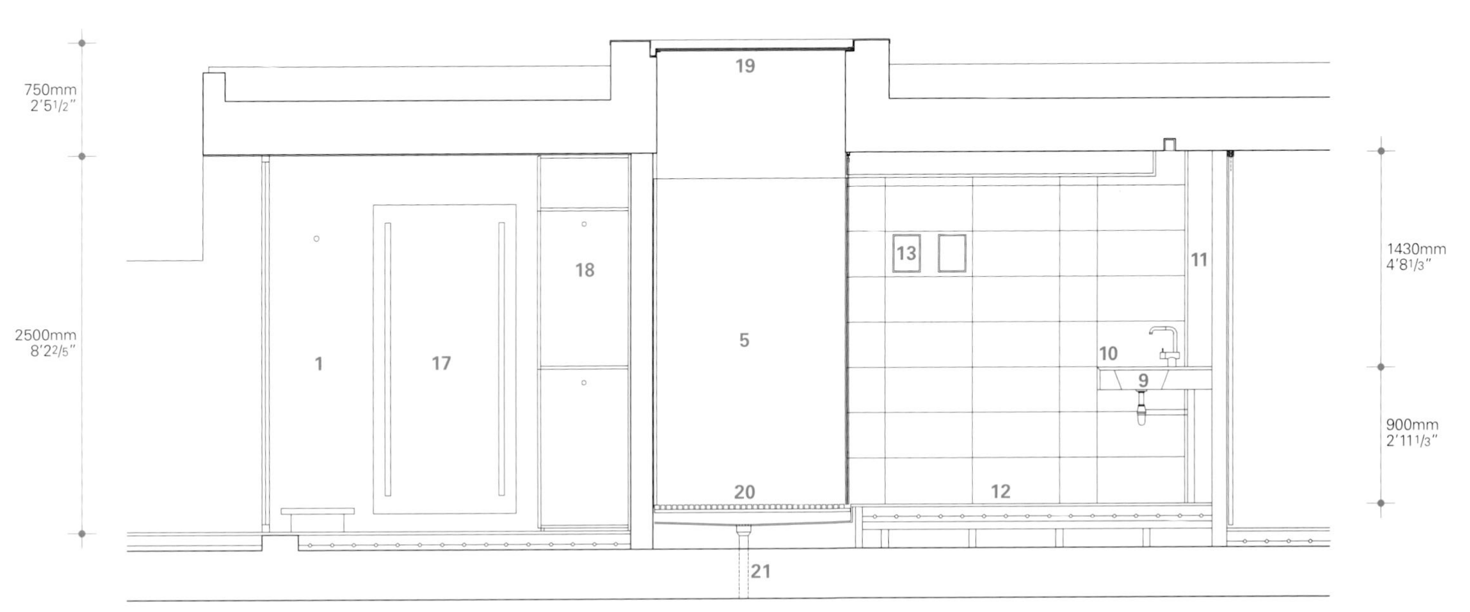
750mm
2'5 1/2"
19
18
13
11
1430mm
4'8 1/3"
2500mm
8'2 2/5"
1
17
5
10
9
900mm
2'11 1/3"
20
12
21
B–B

Stone

BAAS Jordi Badia / Mercè Sangenís, Architects
CH House
Barcelona, Spain

Bathroom Sections C–C and D–D
1:50

1 Timber veneer cupboards to dressing room
2 Dressing room
3 Glass panel to shower enclosure
4 Glass panel to WC and bidet enclosure
5 Skylight over bath
6 Glazing to bath enclosure
7 Stone bath tub
8 Stone surround to bath tub
9 Mirror-faced cabinets over vanity bench
10 Fixed mirror
11 Spout and mixer tap to basins
12 Stone vanity bench
13 Terrazzo wall tiles
14 Terrazzo floor tiles

Opposite Left
The sunken bathtub (left) is bathed in light from full-height glazed panels to both ends of the bath, and by a skylight above.

Opposite Right
The shower enclosure, like the bath, features a glazed ceiling. Access is via translucent glass doors. The timber duck-board floor is matched by a timber shelf to hold shower products.

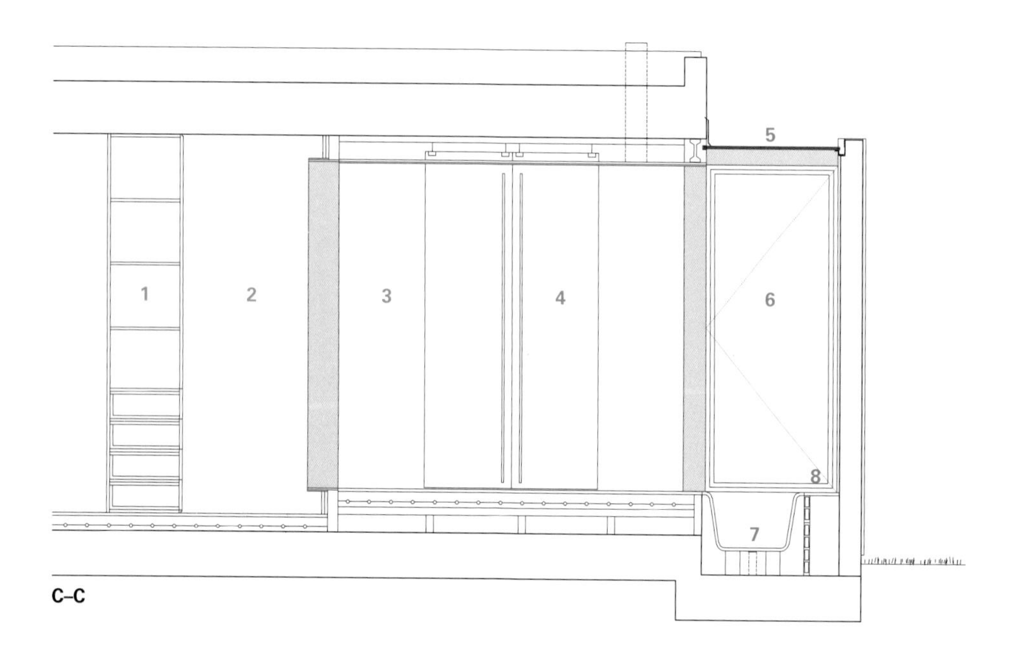

C–C

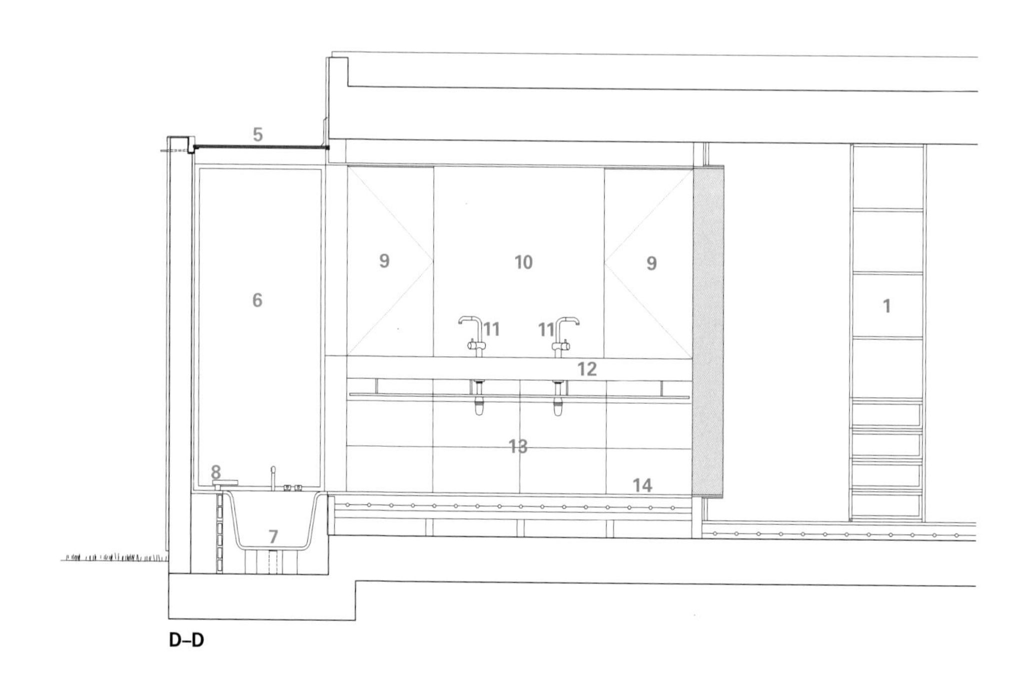

D–D

Materials
Vanity Bench Timber frame with Cabra stone countertop
Joinery Timber frame with wenge veneer
Floor and Wall Tiles 300 x 600 mm (1 x 2 foot) polished Cabra stone tiles

Fixtures
Taps and Spout R-27306328 by Roca
Basin Custom made circular stainless steel
Bath Continental bath by Roca
WC Meridian by Roca
Bidet Meridian by Roca
Shower Head Vola Monomando KV1
Lighting Hoffmeister / Simes spotlights in ceiling

Project Credits
Completion 2000
Project Architects Jordi Badia, Ignacio Forteza, Marcos Catalán (interior designer), Elena Valls, Tirma Balagué, Albert Cibiach, Rafael Berengena, Sergi Serrat
Structural Engineers Eduard Doce
Main Contractor Germans Pujol S.A

Schneider + Schumacher Architects

House F
Germany

Charmed by an urban villa dating from around 1910, the client nevertheless wanted to transform the house with minimalist detailing and modern aesthetics. The result is a lovingly restored house with a new two-storey annexe. The new 3.5 metres (11 foot) by 17.5 metres (57 feet) block rests on a folded structure of solid steel plates, and is clad with aluminium panels. Extremely slim profiles are used for the frosted and clear glass sliding elements that run the length of the extension.

The existing villa remains unchanged in character, carefully restored to its former glory. New elements, such as built-in wardrobes and bathrooms follow the aesthetics of the annexe. The bathroom shown here is the largest of the new, individually designed bathrooms. The juxtaposition of old and new, the harmony between old villa and annexe, is repeated here in the detailing and in a more subtle form – high-gloss smooth surfaces contrast with silky matt traditionally-crafted timber cladding and rendered surfaces.

The new elements appear as modern objects placed into an old shell due to their large-scale timber and stone formats. Floor and walls are clad in Coimbra limestone slabs and, thanks to a rebate along the lower rim of the wall tiles, the technically necessary silicone seam between floor and wall remains invisible. The natural stone slab holding the sink rests on a wall-hung drawer cabinet made of dark stained oak. Further storage is behind the mirror above.

The largest single piece of stone is the cladding of the bathtub, made from a 30 millimetre (11/10 inch) thick stone slab. The generously dimensioned shower niche renders any form of shower enclosure unnecessary. A recessed shelf, also made of stone and incorporated into the wall cladding, offers space for showering products.

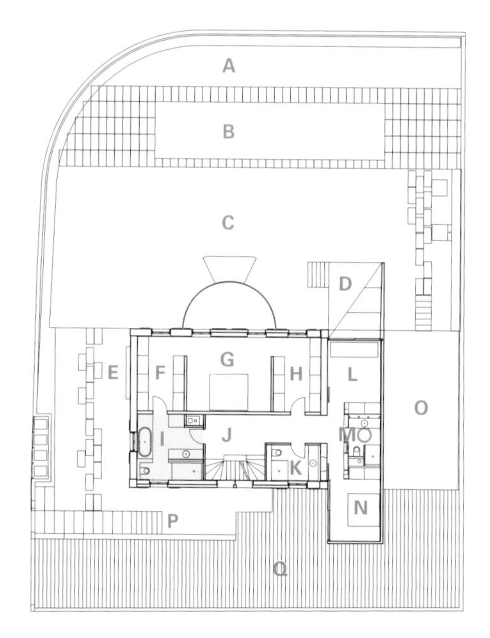

Opposite Left
The dramatic extension cantilevers over the garden and features large sliding doors that open up the first floor kitchen to the landscape.

Floor Plan
A Hedge
B Pool
C Meadow
D Terrace
E Perennial planting
F Dressing room 1
G Master bedroom
H Dressing room 2
I Master bathroom 1
J Master suite lobby
K Master bathroom 2
L Guest bedroom
M Guest bathroom
N Guest bedroom
O Terrace
P Main entrance
Q Courtyard

Left
Much of the bathroom is clad in Coimbra stone slabs which are also used for the benchtop and bath surround. Elsewhere, dark timber joinery and brushed stainless tapware provide detail accents.

Below
The simple bath area is lit naturally by windows with plain white roller blinds and with overhead spotlights. A large stone recess at the end of the bath allows plenty of space for towels and products.

Stone

Schneider + Schumacher Architects
House F
Germany

Bathroom Plan and Sections A–A, B–B, C–C, D–D and E–E
1:50

1 Stone ledge behind WC
2 WC
3 Coimbra stone floor tiles
4 Shower recess
5 Stone-lined ledge for shower products
6 Taps and spout to bath
7 White ceramic bathtub
8 Coimbra stone bath surround
9 Door to dressing room
10 Storage cupboards
11 Coimbra stone countertop
12 Under-mounted white ceramic basin
13 WC flush panel
14 Roller blind covered window
15 Wall-hung timber drawers to vanity bench
16 Mirror-faced cabinets above vanity bench
17 Shower head
18 Wall-mounted radiator
19 Recessed wall lights

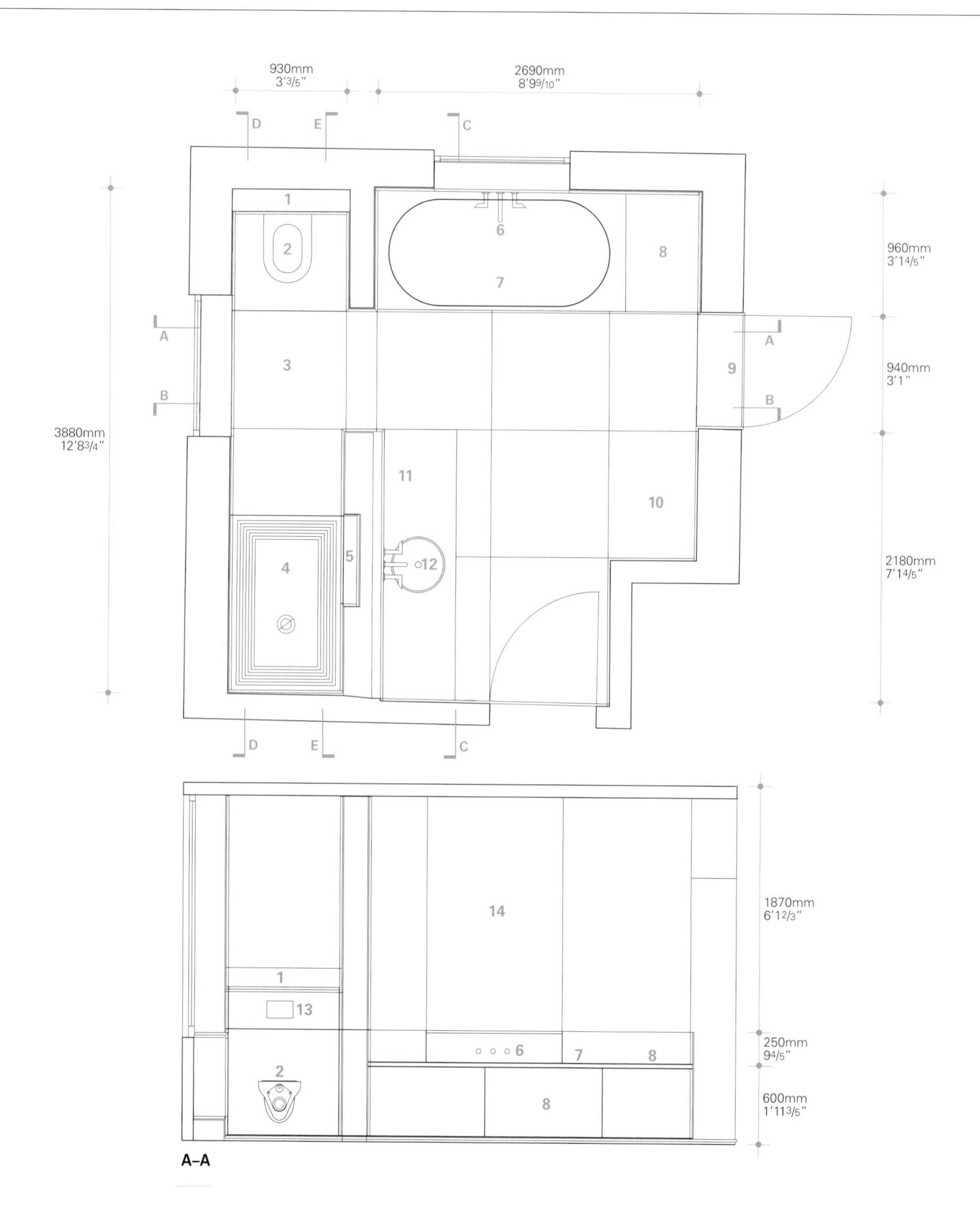

Materials
Benchtop Coimbra stone
Joinery Timber veneer
Floor Coimbra stone tiles

Fixtures
Taps and Spout Sam Eileen
Basin Duravit Architec
Bath Bette Starlet
WC Duravit Starck 2
Shower Head Dornbracht Regendusche
Lighting Kreon

Project Credits
Completion 2004
Project Architects Astrid Wuttke, Esther Hagenlocher, Ralf Seeburger, Brian Ginder, Christian Schmidkowski, Kai Otto, Michael Schumacher
Structural Engineers B+G Ingenieure / Bollinger + Grohmann
Services Engineers Planungsgemeinschaft DUO / Schüler und Meisel
Environmental Engineer Trümper Overath Heimann Römer
Landscape Architect Ulla Schuch Gärten und Landschaften
Surveyor Ingenieurbüro Wittig

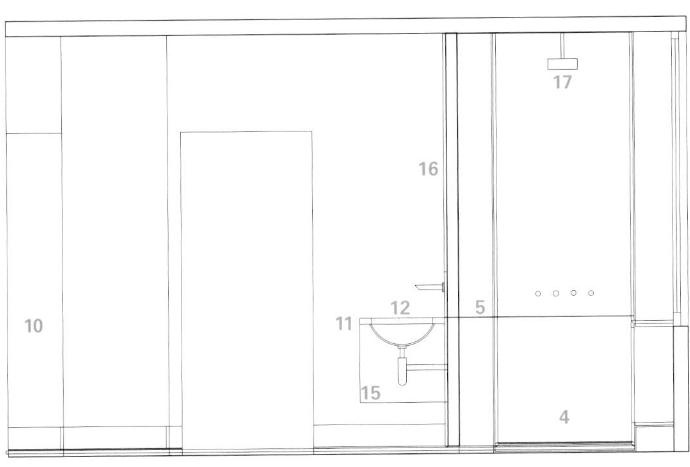

B–B

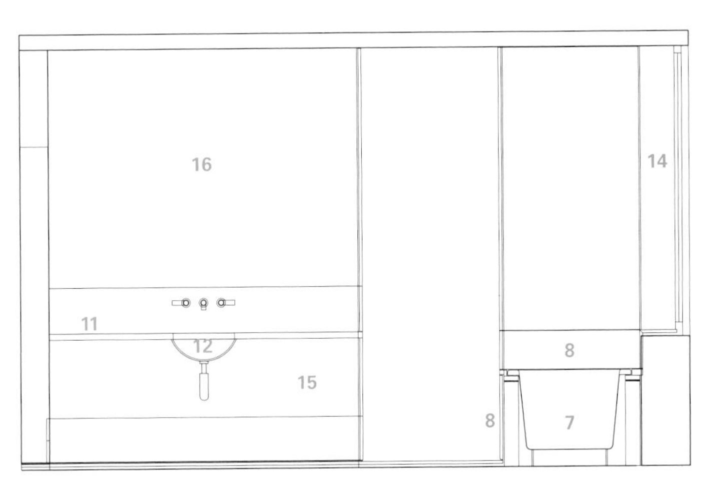

C–C

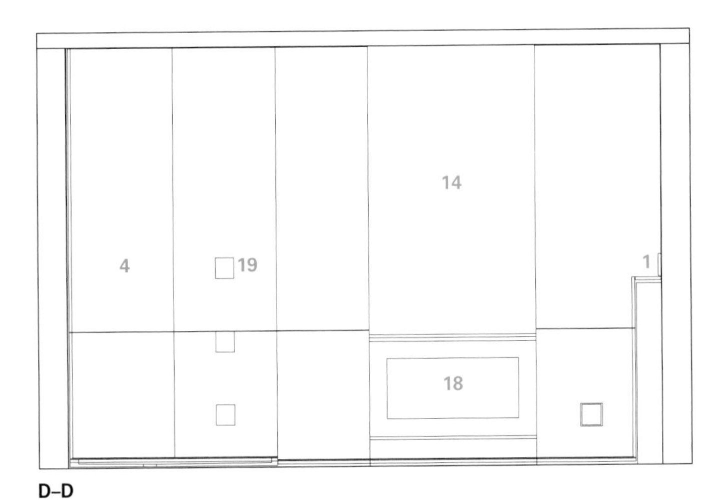

D–D

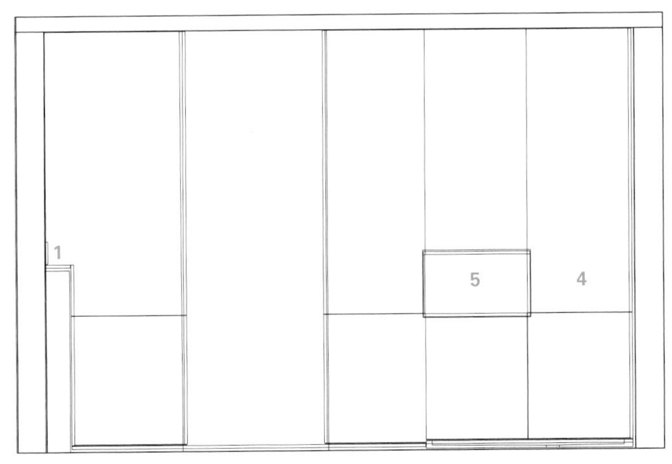

E–E

Turner Castle

Opal House
London, England, UK

When the client was looking to commission an architect for his new house in London, he appointed the architects of his former apartment who, through an extended and productive collaboration, had developed a heightened sensibility to their client's requirements.

The property is a four-storey semi-detached Victorian town house, which has been stripped back to its load-bearing walls and completely remodelled inside. Externally, the original brickwork and window surrounds have been retained and a modern glazed pavilion has been added to the rear. The real transformation is an assembly of spacious volumes carved out of the original architecture. At the front of the house, a cantilevered timber and glass open-tread staircase rises through a stupendous triple-height volume. The main entertaining space, with living room, dining area and kitchen, is a double-height space with polished concrete floor, which runs the full length of the extended lower-ground floor.

A palette of muted neutral colours (pinks, greys and corals) and rich natural materials was chosen to heighten the flow of interconnected spaces. The study shelving and cupboards, stair treads and kitchen island are all finished in dark oak, which is used for the flooring throughout. Colour, shape and texture are added with specially selected and bespoke furniture as well as the client's collection of paintings, books and artefacts. The upper floor is reserved for the principal bedroom which features a series of gargantuan floating cupboards, cantilevered from the wall, which are finished in dusty pink and lined with a deep aubergine. Unusually, the bathroom is located within the open space of the bedroom floor (a door set flush in the wall leads to a separate WC), delineated only by a change in the floor finish from timber to limestone. A large, free-standing stone tub, a shower area and cantilevered basin area are also clad in limestone.

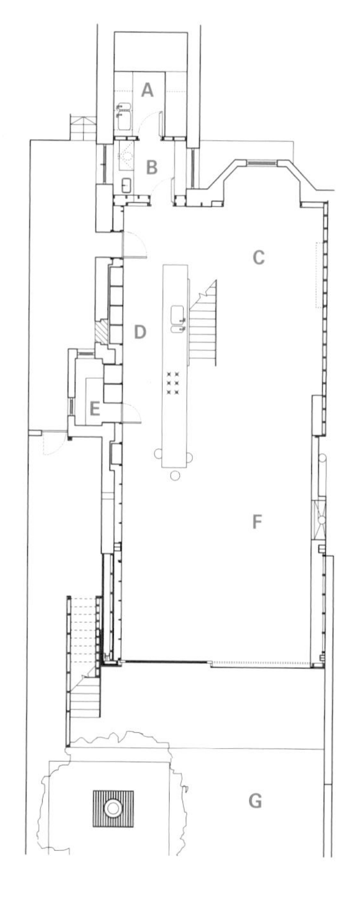

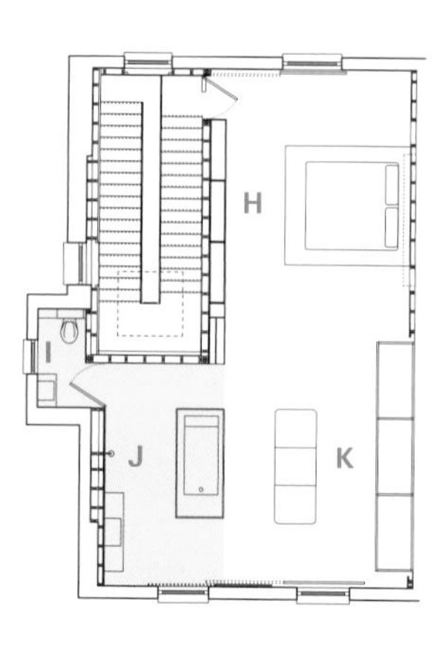

Opposite Left
The original brick façade and windows of the Victorian house were restored, while a glass and steel extension to the ground floor give an indication that the interior of the house has been entirely remodelled.

Floor Plan
A Utility room
B WC
C Dining room
D Kitchen
E Pantry
F Living room
G Garden
H Master bedroom
I WC
J Bathroom
K Dressing area

Above
The bathroom, dressing area and master bedroom occupy one continuous space. A monolithic stone bathtub takes centre stage, while a floating basin and wall-mounted shower almost disappear in a wall of pale limestone cladding.

A chocolate brown leather chaise-longue adds an element of comfort to the dressing area as do walls of storage cupboards painted in a warm dusky pink.

Stone

Turner Castle
Opal House
London, England, UK

Bathroom Plan, Elevation A and Section A–A
1:50

1 WC
2 Basin
3 Polyurethane-painted door to WC
4 Polyurethane-painted cupboard doors to dressing area
5 Shower head
6 Stone basin counter
7 Basin
8 Custom made stone bathtub
9 Mirrored doors to cabinet
10 Limestone shelf below basin counter
11 Stone surround to bathtub
12 Shower valve
13 Stone floor tiles
14 Wall-mounted basin taps
15 Concealed lighting behind stone panelling to shower wall

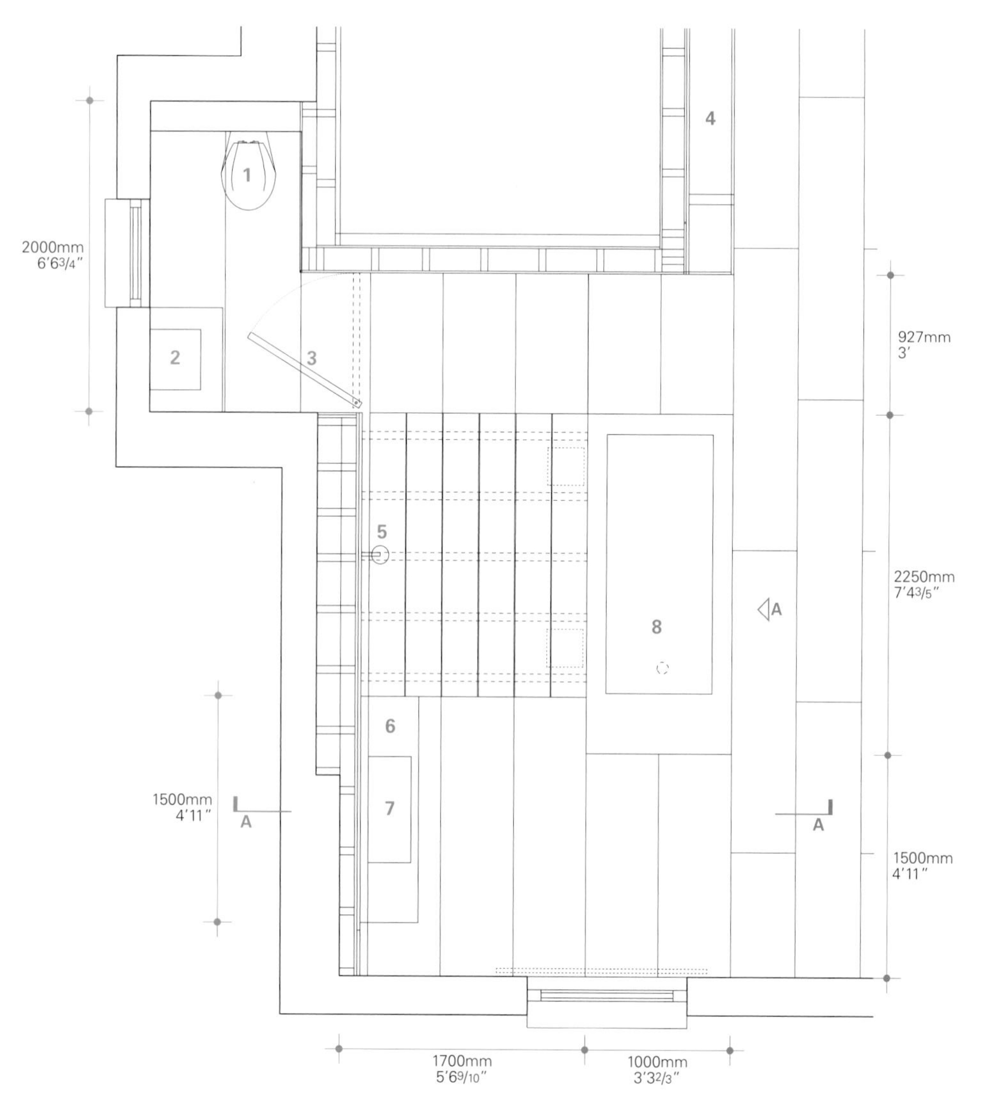

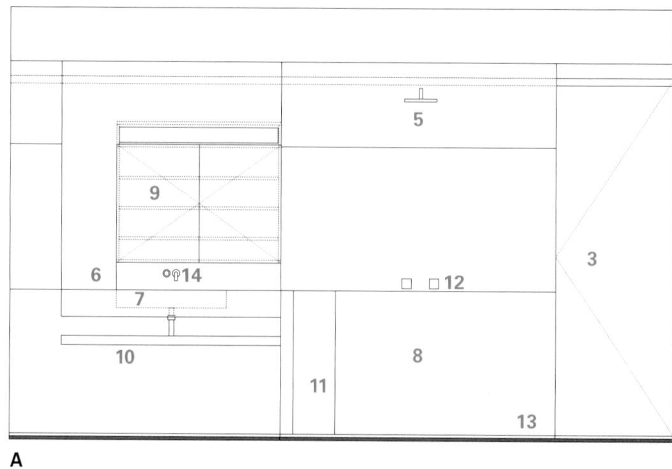

A

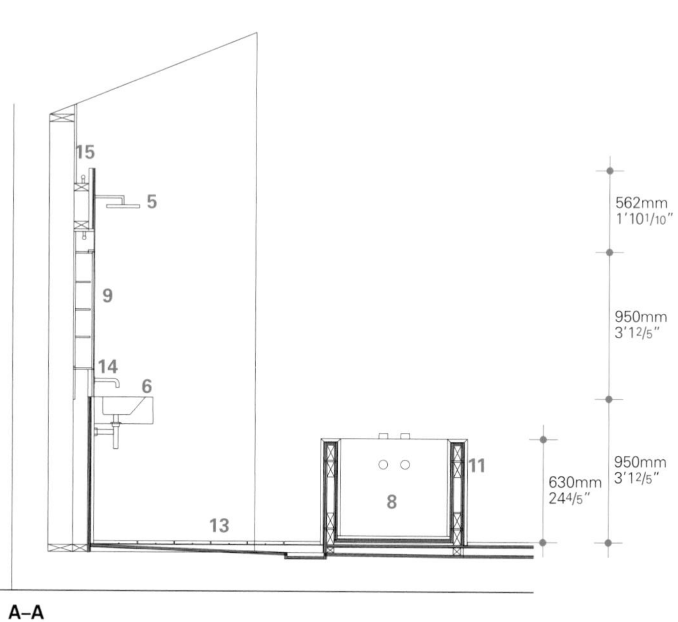

A–A

Detail Bath Plan and Sections A–A and B–B 1:20

1 20 mm (3/4 inch) thick stone cladding to bath surround and ledge on timber frame
2 Stainless steel taps and spout
3 80 mm (3 inch) diameter circular stone plug with rubber seal
4 Stone lining to bath
5 20 mm (3/4 inch) thick stone cladding to bath surround on timber frame
6 50 mm (2 inch) diameter overflow drilled in stone lining
7 Plug with outlet below connected to 100 mm (4 inch) pipe
8 Floor waste under stone flooring
9 20 mm (3/4 inch) thick stone cladding to bath laid to fall to waste
10 20 mm (3/4 inch) thick sloped stone cladding to bath end

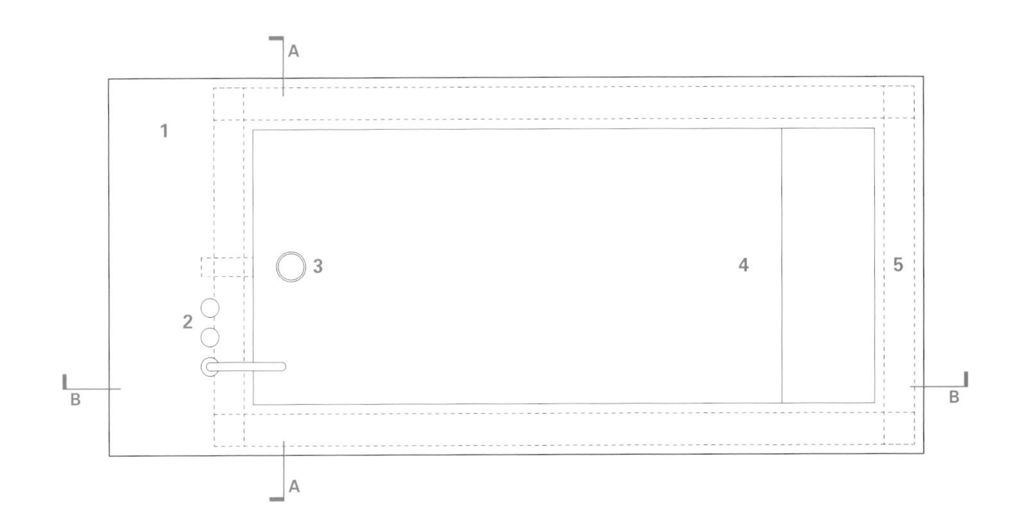

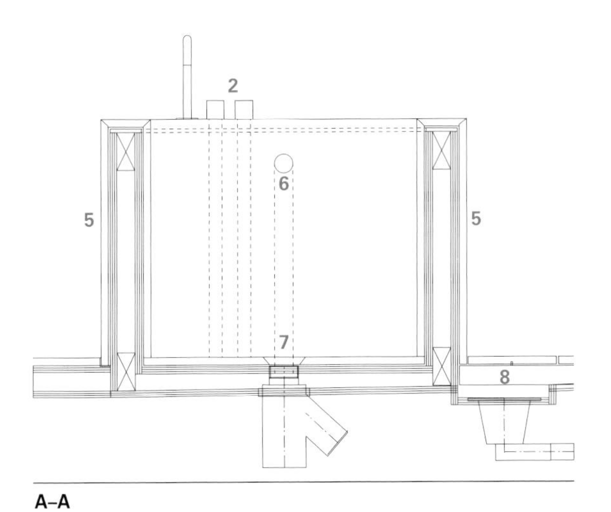

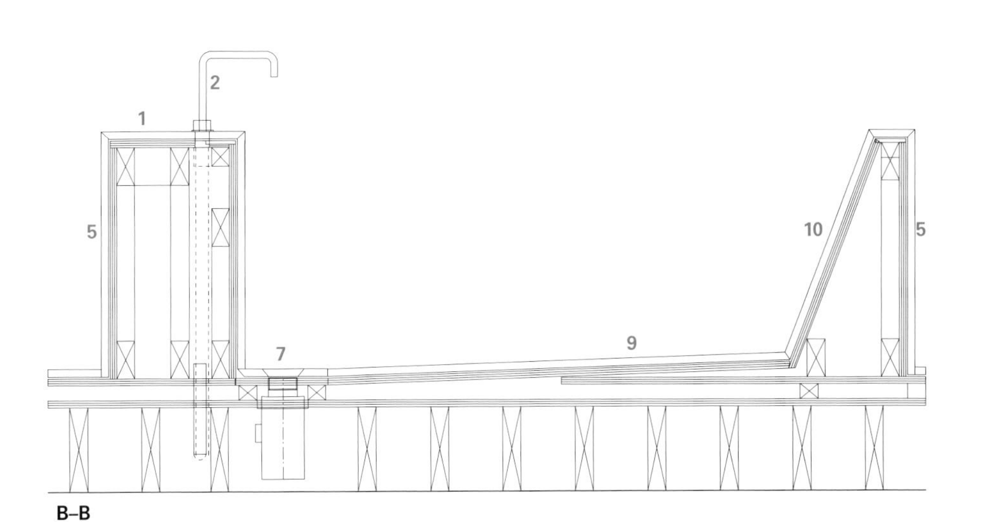

Stone

Turner Castle
Opal House
London, England, UK

Basin Elevation and Plan Details
1:10

1 Mirror to cabinet doors
2 Stainless steel tap
3 Stainless steel spout
4 Stone basin with pencil round corners to all internal corners
5 Outlet hole drilled through stone to allow for waste fitting
6 Stone countertop
7 Invisible fixing for cantilevered basin and stone-clad wall

Opposite Left
View of the cantilevered cupboards with concealed lighting behind from the stone bathtub.

Opposite Right
View of the bath and dressing area from the bed. Extra large timber floor boards lend a sense of luxury and scale to the open-plan master suite.

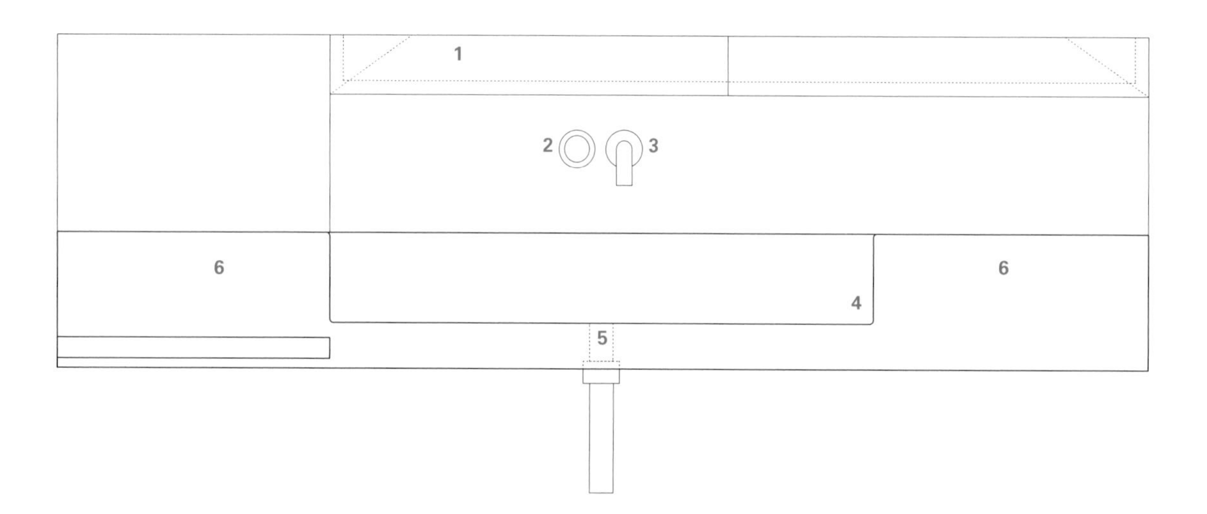

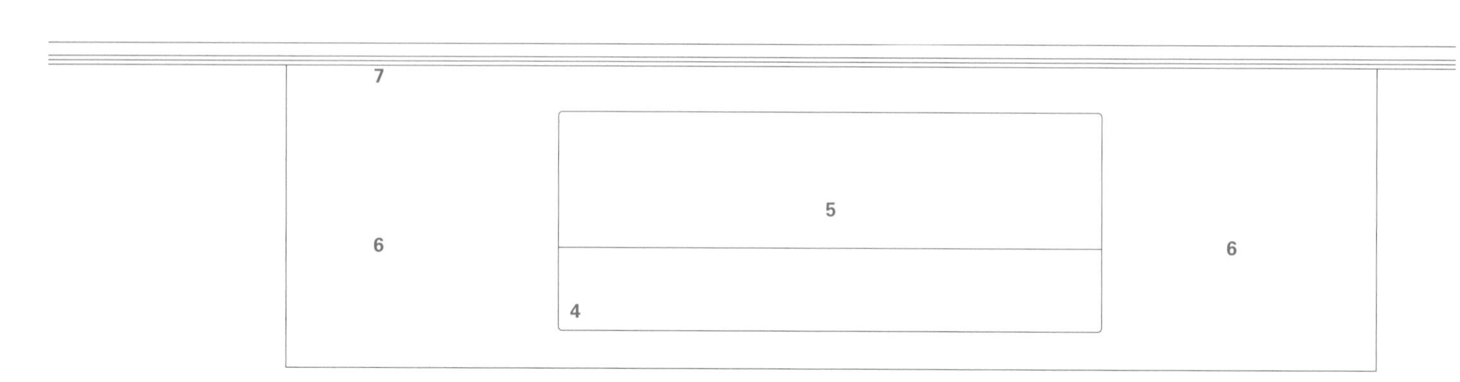

Materials
Countertop Limestone
Joinery Gloss-finish sprayed MDF
Floor Lime-washed larch
Tiles Limestone
Lighting Cold cathode tubes

Appliances and Fixtures
Basin Taps Vola
Basin Spout Vola
Basin Ideal Stone Interiors
Shower Taps Vola
Shower Head Hansgrohe
Bath Taps Vola
Bath Spout Bespoke design by Turner Castle
Bath Bespoke design by Turner Castle
Towel Rails MRG Fittings
Toilet Hansgrohe

Project Credits
Completion 2007
Project Architects Cassion Castle, Carl Turner, Lizzie Castle, Susie Hyden, Anna Tenow, Hannah Schneebeli
Structural Engineers Wright Consultancy Group
Main Contractor Turner Castle
Bespoke Furniture Fabrication Turner Castle

Ramón Esteve

El Carmen Residence
Valencia, Spain

This residential building is knitted into the historical fabric of the El Carmen district of Valencia. The building accommodates the studio and apartment of architect Ramón Esteve over its four storeys. The open, light-filled office is located on the first floor, with access for clients and guests via a black marble staircase from the ground floor.

The upper two levels are occupied by the residential quarters which include the master bedroom and bathroom as well as two guest bedrooms, each with its own ensuite bathroom. Above are the living spaces, kitchen and dining area, with direct access to a large terrace with sweeping views over the city. The apartment is deliberately devoid of clutter or excessive ornamentation, with expanses of white-painted walls and ceilings remaining uninterrupted by light fixtures and switches, which are concealed. An element of contrast is introduced in the black Ulldecona stone floor which is laid in large slabs to appear virtually seamless.

The bedrooms are similarly minimal – frameless floor-to-ceiling white-gloss wardrobe doors integrate them into their all-white surroundings. A touch of glamour and texture is introduced in the bathrooms which feature basins carved from slabs of black stone and fitted with stainless steel accessories. The two guest bathrooms provide walk-in shower areas, while the master bathroom features a monolithic stone bathtub carved from a single slab of marble weighing 300 kilograms (660 pounds).

Throughout the building, traditional glass double doors in the exterior envelope allow the interior to be lit naturally, while slatted timber sliding screens allow a high degree of lighting control, privacy and insulation in response to the often sweltering Mediterranean climate.

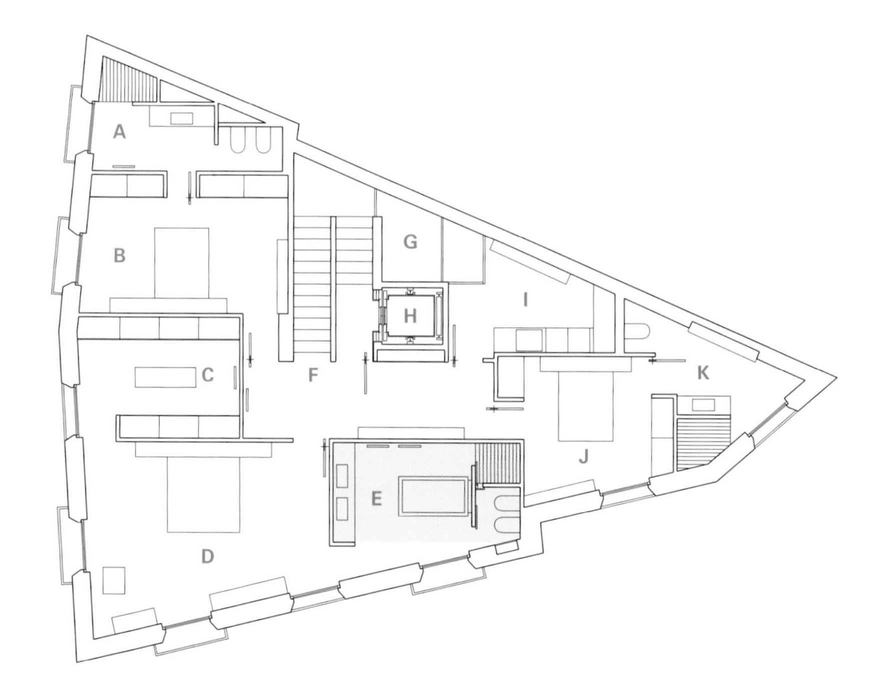

Opposite Left
The façade incorporates a section of an historic stone wall (left). All of the new double doors are protected by timber screens that allow each room to respond to changing environmental conditions.

Floor Plan
A Guest bathroom
B Guest bedroom
C Dressing room
D Master bedroom
E Master bathroom
F Stair
G Void
H Lift
I Laundry
J Guest bedroom
K Guest bathroom

Left
In the master bathroom, the custom made black marble floor, countertop with integrated basins and the bathtub are paired with plain white painted walls, white joinery and mirrored cabinets to create a serene and minimal bathroom.

Stone

Ramón Esteve
El Carmen Residence
Valencia, Spain

Bathroom Plan and Sections A–A, B–B and C–C 1:50

1 Entrance to master bedroom
2 Black marble countertop
3 Black marble basin
4 Stainless steel towel rail
5 Full-height double doors with timber screen
6 Black marble bathtub
7 Cupboard with white-sprayed door
8 WC
9 Bidet
10 Sliding-door pocket
11 Shower enclosure
12 White-painted plasterboard wall
13 Mirror-faced wall-hung cabinets
14 Stainless steel basin spout and tap
15 Open towel-storage ledge below counter
16 White-sprayed drawer fronts
17 White-sprayed cupboard fronts
18 Translucent door to shower enclosure
19 Translucent door to WC and bidet enclosure
20 Bath spout and taps

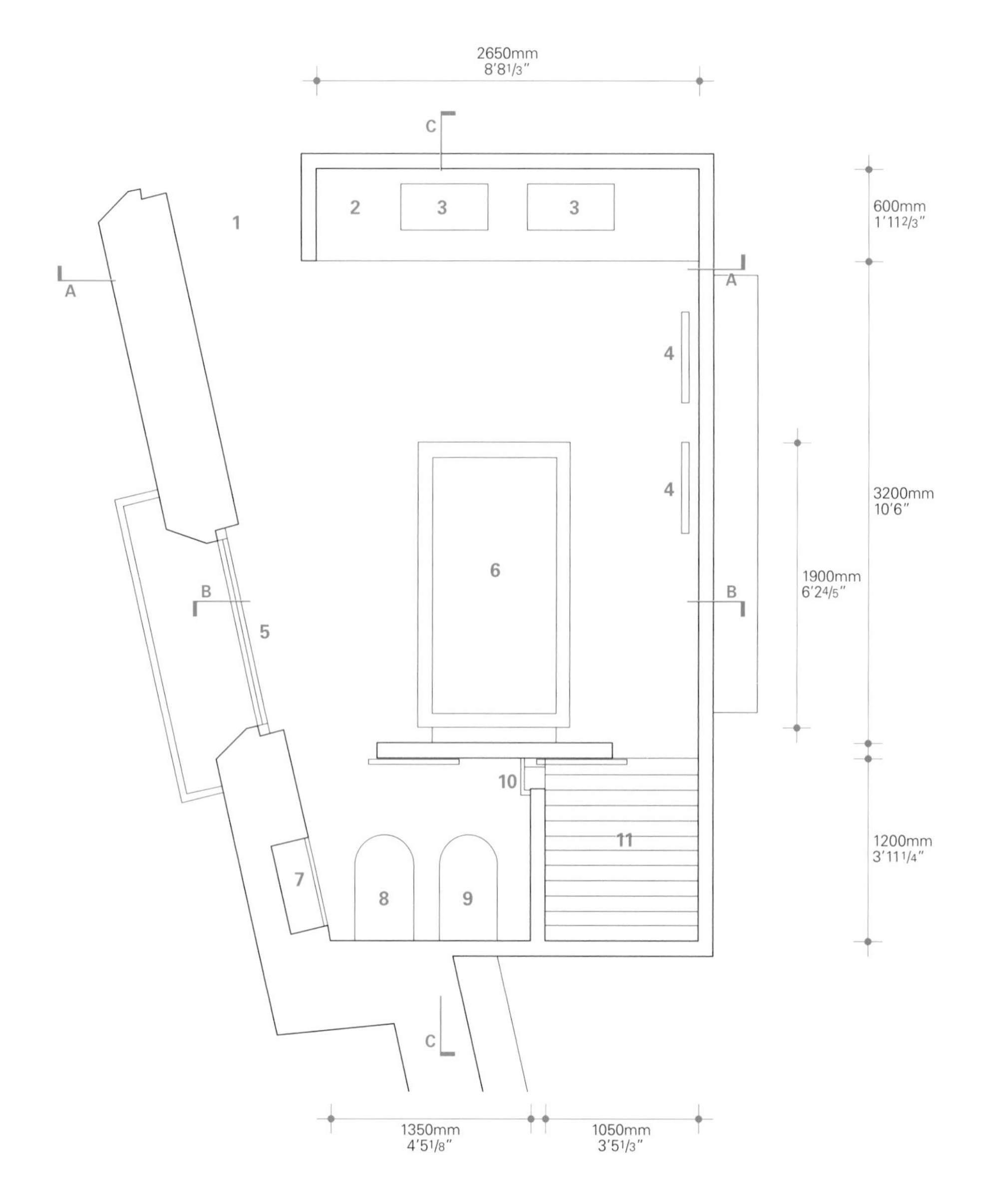

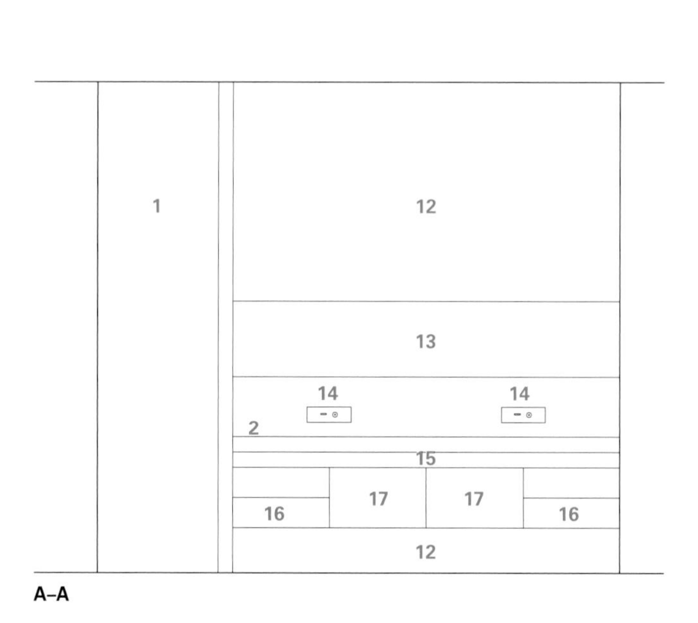

A–A

Materials
Countertop Black marble, custom designed and made by Ramón Esteve Design
Joinery White gloss polyurethane spray to MDF carcasses
Floor 1000 x 1000 mm (3 1/3 inch) black marble
Splashback White-painted plasterboard with waterproof sealant
Lighting Fluorescent fittings

Appliances and Fixtures
Basin Taps and Spout Permeso by Progetti
Basin Custom designed and made by Ramón Esteve Design
Shower Taps Permeso by Progetti
Shower Head Permeso by Progetti
Bath Taps and Spout Permeso by Progetti
Bath Custom designed and made by Ramón Esteve Design
WC SA02 from Galassia
Bidet SA02 from Galassia
Towel Rails Custom designed by Ramón Esteve Design

Project Credits
Completion 2005
Client Ramón Esteve
Project Architects Ramón Esteve, Sonia Rayos, Angels Quiralte, Juan A. Ferrero, Silvia Martínez, Emilio Pérez, Antonio Morales, Rafael Esteve
Structural Engineers Ramón Esteve Estudio de Arquitectura
Mechanical Engineers Ramón Esteve Estudio de Arquitectura

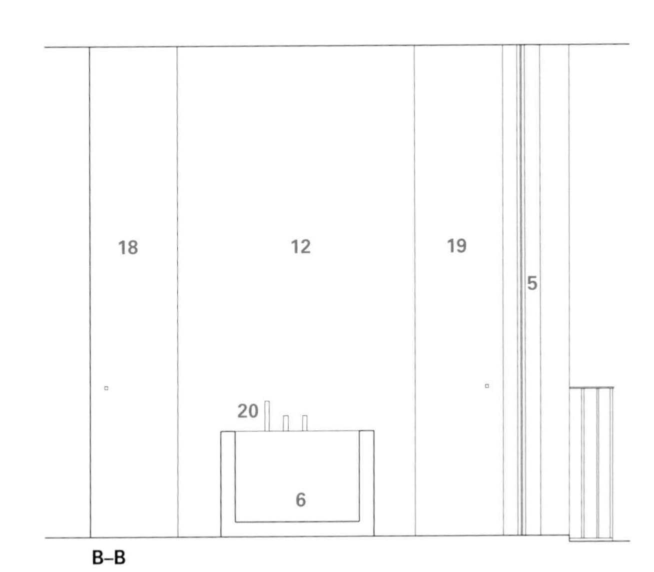

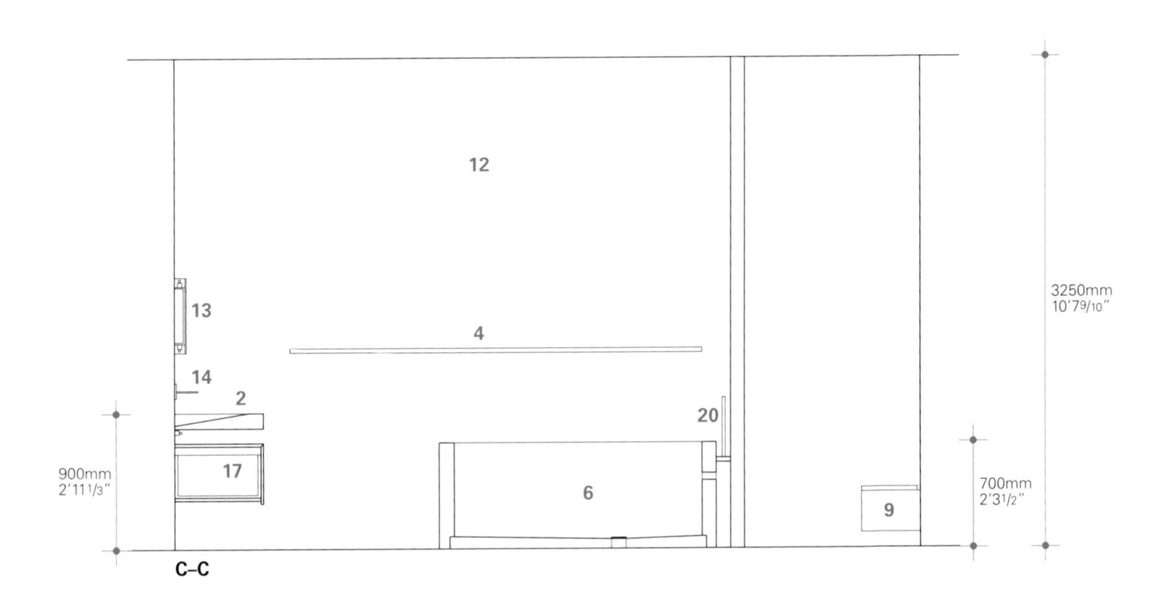

Vincent Van Duysen

VDD Residence
Dendermonde, Belgium

This two-storey family home is designed as a compact rectangular prism, with rough red brick forming a carapace around the exterior. Three of the façades are virtually blank, protecting the house from neighbouring properties. However the fourth façade is relieved by a double-height colonnade with large swathes of glazing that open up the house to views over the swimming pool and a field of poplar trees in the distance.

The programme is arranged as two parallel zones within the rectangular envelope. To the north-east, a double-height entrance hall, courtyard patio and service zones (storage, bathroom and cloakroom) are arranged. In contrast, the primary living spaces and master bedroom and bathroom upstairs, are placed across the south-western façade to take advantage of natural light and views. Upstairs, the main bedroom, bathroom, dressing room and a sun terrace are arranged as a luxurious private suite.

The bedroom, located in the centre of the plan, opens on to a large terrace to one side via full-height sliding glass doors, and on the other side, to a landing where storage cupboards and the WC are located next to the bathroom. Adjacent to the bathroom, a large dressing room is equipped with custom designed joinery.

The bathroom, in particular, is a haven of calm. The walls, floor and a monolithic bathtub are clad in Belgian Bluestone with the space divided into two zones, one for bathing and one for showering, by a sheet of frameless fixed clear glazing. Along the façade, full-height frameless glazing allows uninterrupted views over the landscape.

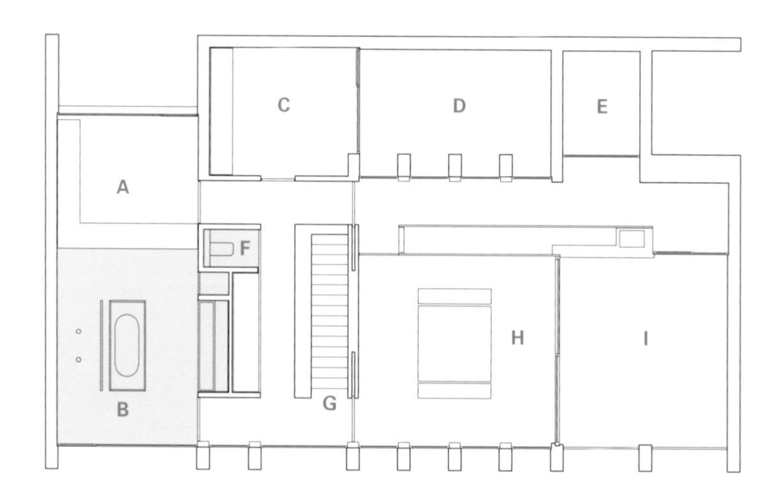

Opposite Left
A two-storey brick colonnade acts as a transition space between the living spaces, which are arranged along the length of the ground floor (and the master bedroom and bathroom above), and the simply landscaped terrace, pool and garden.

Floor Plan
A Dressing room
B Bathroom
C Bedroom
D Patio
E Void
F WC
G Stair from ground floor
H Master bedroom
I Terrace

Left
A detailed view of the bathtub and shower where Belgian Bluestone is used extensively for the floor, walls, bathtub and a ledge in the shower. Two ceiling-mounted shower heads allow two people to use the shower simultaneously.

Stone

Vincent Van Duysen
VDD Residence
Dendermonde, Belgium

Bathroom Plan and Sections A–A and B–B 1:50

1 Wardrobe joinery to adjacent dressing room
2 Shower recess
3 Glass blade wall between bath and shower
4 Belgian Bluestone bath surround
5 White ceramic under-mounted bathtub
6 Belgian Bluestone floor tiles
7 Stainless steel grille for under-floor heating
8 Mirror-faced cabinets above vanity
9 Belgian Bluestone vanity bench
10 Towel storage cupboard
11 WC
12 Broom cupboard
13 Storage cupboards to hallway
14 Bookcase / balustrade to stair
15 Timber veneer cupboards beneath Belgian Bluestone benchtop
16 Shower head

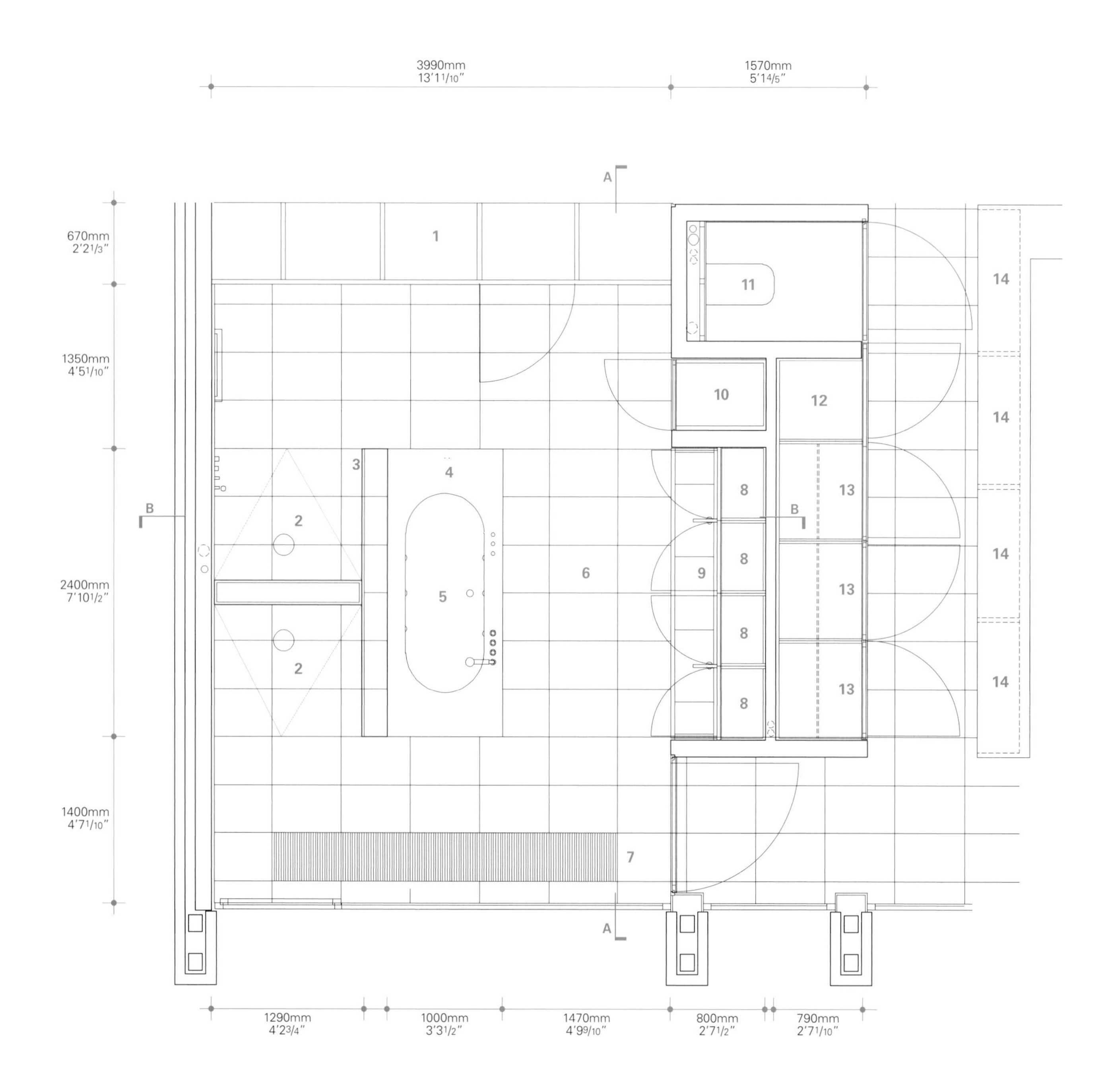

Materials
Benchtop Custom made in Belgian Bluestone
Joinery Timber veneer
Floor Belgian Bluestone tiles

Fixtures
Taps and Spout Vola chrome matte
Basin Custom made in Belgian Bluestone
Bath Duscholux Ancona with custom made Belgian Bluestone casing
Shower head Dornbracht rain shower
Lighting Tekna bvba
Shower Screen Helioscreen

Project Credits
Completion 2002
Project Architects Vincent Van Duysen, Sophie Laenen
Structural Engineers Bouquet-Deloof
Main Contractor Bouwkantoor Dedeyne
Lighting Consultant Tekna bvba

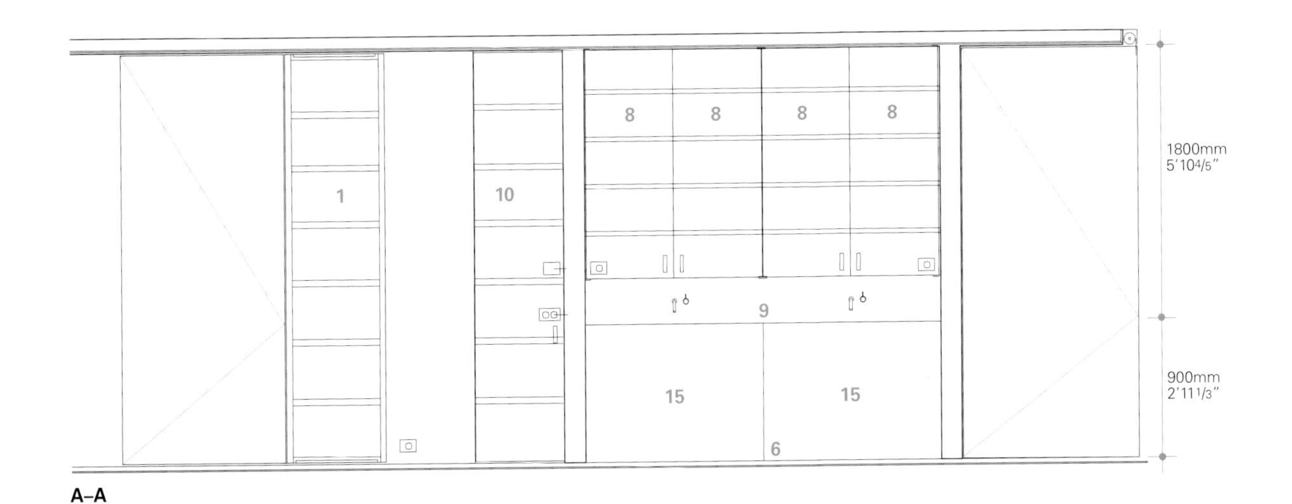

A–A

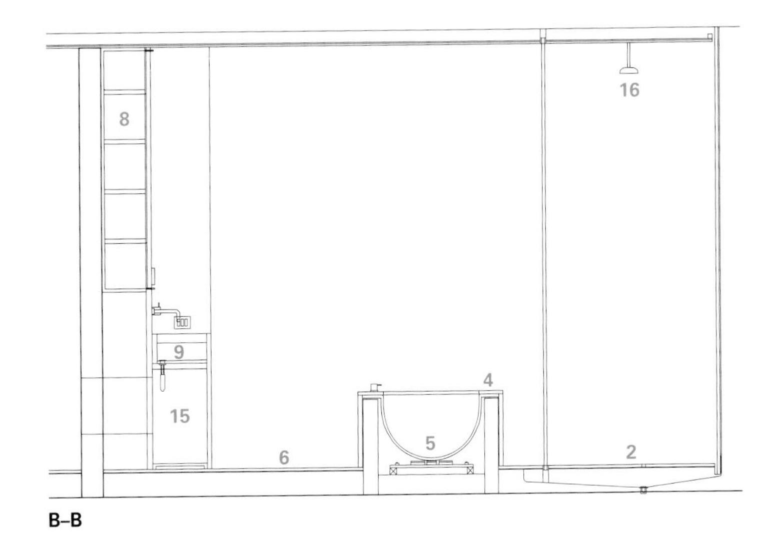

B–B

David Nossiter Architects

Pye Barn Moulsford, Oxfordshire, England, UK

The existing building, an eighteenth century barn, had been converted to a dwelling fifty years ago and was in desperate need of modernization. The architects wanted to provide a contemporary family home without compromising the rural setting and oak structure of the original barn.

The barn is situated on 12,140 square metres (three acres) of land with direct access to the village green beyond. It was therefore important to exploit the connection with the landscape. The garden elevation is characterized by opening glazed strips along both the ground-floor living areas, and first-floor master bedroom suite. On summer evenings the family can slide open the full-height windows and enjoy the spectacle of the original structure above them, views of the garden below and of the village green beyond.

At the centre of the house is an eight metre (26 foot) high galleried hallway which characterizes the strength and scale of the oak structure. However, the upper gallery led to a dead end and as a consequence was under-utilized. Therefore, key to the design was the re-organization of the first floor plan so that all the bedrooms were accessed via the gallery.

The design was a process of subtraction rather than addition. Open-plan spaces and ceilings reach to the apex of the roof and the proportions of the original barn are celebrated. The new interventions are treated as stand-alone units and detailed accordingly.

The master bathroom, with family proportioned bath, sits between and around the massive oak-framed structure. Surfaces fold so that the stone countertops become splashbacks. With the exception of selected areas of vivid colour, materials and finishes are natural and a counterpoint to the scale and hewn surface of the oak.

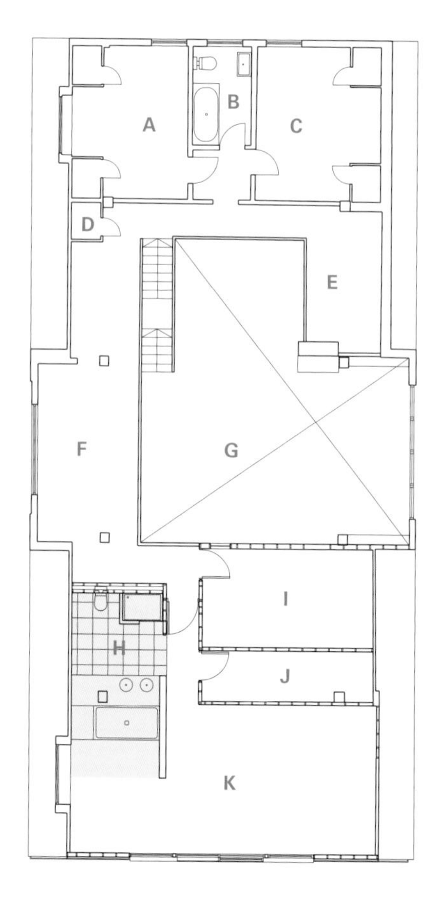

Opposite Left
The original barn is a handsome structure, with its rustic brick walls and red clay-tiled roof. The interior has been transformed with sensitive intervention into a beautiful and functional family home.

Floor Plan
A Bedroom
B Bathroom
C Bedroom
D Store
E Gallery
F Gallery
G Void over living area below
H Master bathroom
I Guest bedroom
J Dressing room
K Master bedroom

Above
The bathroom is divided into two zones. The bathing area (foreground) is open to the bedroom, while a second area, which features a stone-clad vanity unit, also accommodates the WC and shower enclosure.

Stone

David Nossiter Architects
Pye Barn
Moulsford, Oxfordshire,
England, UK

Bathroom Plan, Sections A–A and B–B and Elevation A
1:50

1 Shower enclosure
2 WC
3 Line of existing skylight over
4 Marble countertop
5 Under-mounted white ceramic basin
6 Marble top to storage unit and end of bath surround
7 Steel bathtub
8 Oak capping to ceramic-tiled low stud wall
9 Radiator
10 Partition wall to shower
11 Adjustable shelves to storage unit
12 Existing timber beam
13 Existing timber strut
14 MDF shelving unit with mirror bonded to back face
15 Existing timber column
16 White sprayed MDF cupboard doors
17 Marble cladding to rear of basin counter
18 Removable MDF side panel to bath
19 Radiator recessed into low stud wall
20 Wall-mounted bath spout and taps
21 Existing skylight

Opposite
This bathroom is essentially a clever composition of rectangular prisms of varying materials and finishes, sensitively inserted between the existing timber structure.

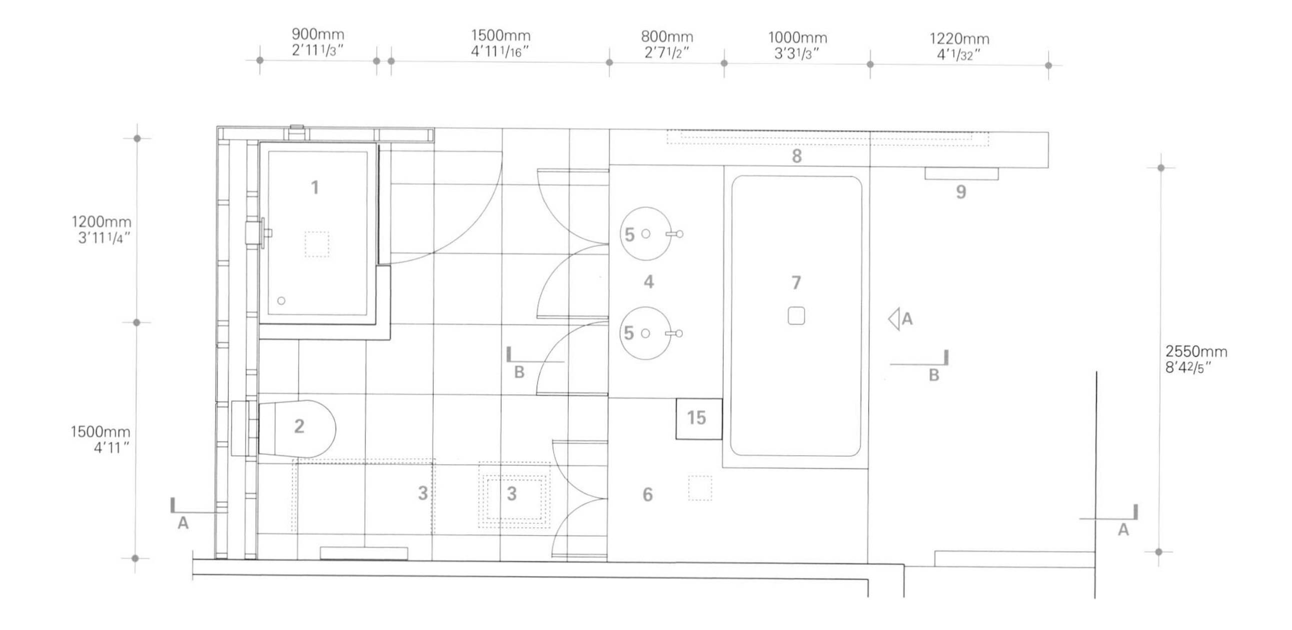

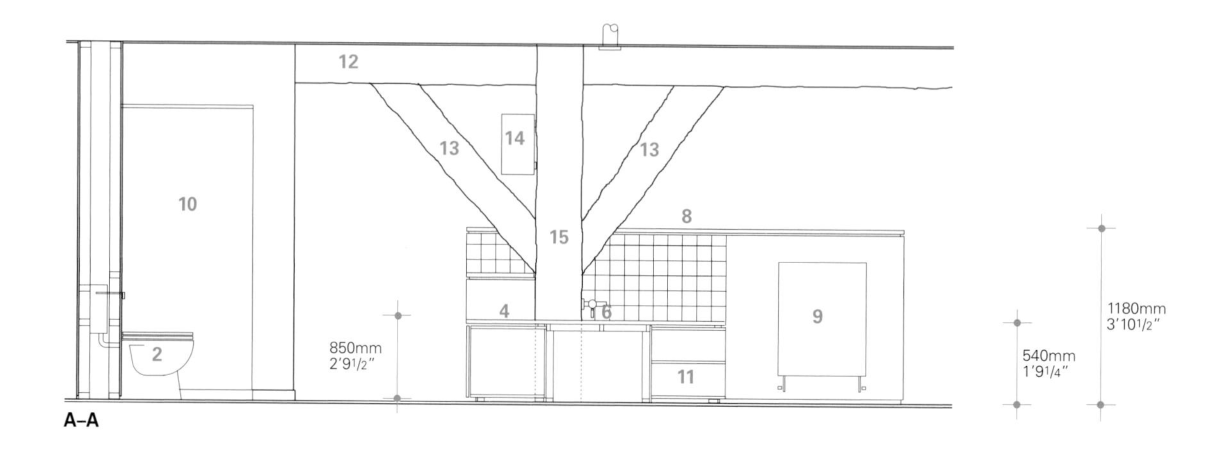

Materials
Countertop Azul Cascais limestone
Joinery Spray-painted moisture-resistant MDF
Floor 450 x 450 mm (17 3/4 x 17 3/4 inch) 'Fontainebleau' ceramic tiles
Tiles 97 x 97 mm (3 4/5 x 3 4/5 inch) Amazon Green glass tiles
Lighting Dimmable recessed downlights in ceiling and LED wall-mounted lights within shower cubicle

Appliances and Fixtures
Basin Taps Grohe 'Essence' range mixer with pop-up waste
Basin Aston Matthews under-mounted basin
Shower Mixer Grohe 'Grotherme' 2000 with diverter
Shower Head Grohe 'Rainshower Modern Jumbo' with projection arm and 'Sena' hand held shower with hose
Bath Taps and Spout Grohe 'Essence' range bath / shower mixer with hand shower and hose
Bath Kaldewei 'Condoduo' bath
WC Ideal Standard 'Space' range back-to-wall WC and concealed cistern

Project Credits
Completion 2007
Clients Justin and Larissa Hardy
Project Architects David Nossiter, Will Garner, Adam Rothwell
Structural Engineers Hardman Structural Engineers
Cost Consultants Bonfield Construction Consultants
Main Contractor John R Luck Ltd

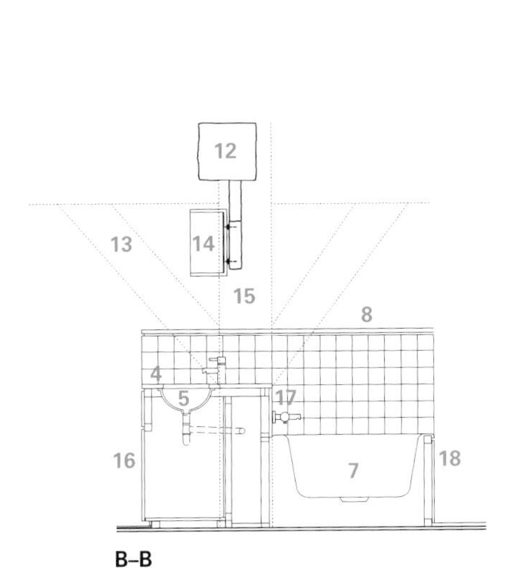

B–B

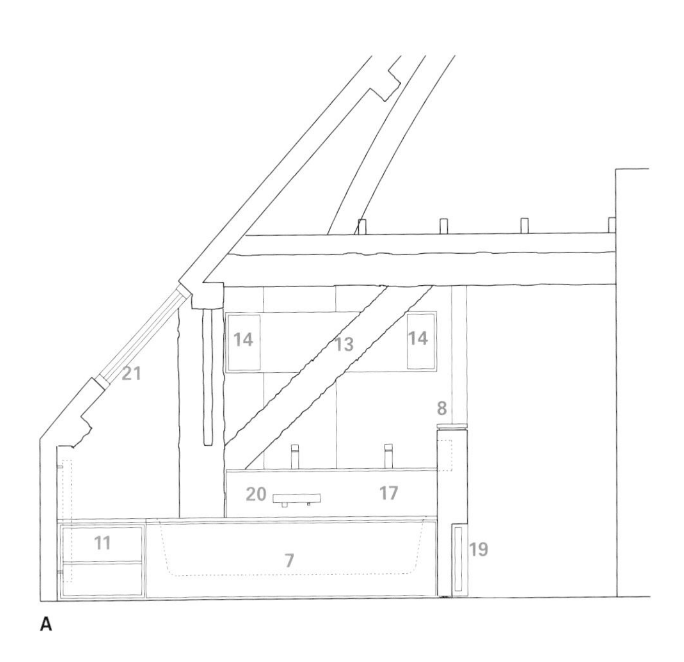

A

Ullmayer Sylvester Architects

Falkland House Apartment London, England, UK

The original apartment, located on the ground floor of this beautiful red brick mansion block in the heart of Kensington, West London, was characterized by a rather utilitarian and cellular room layout and antiquated services. The apartment is not particularly large, but a long service corridor integrated into the apartment gave it the potential to feel much more spacious.

The new design opens up the apartment, working with the rhythm of existing and new openings of consistent height that are punched into internal and external walls. Upon entry it is now possible to see nearly 17 metres (56 feet) from the entrance to the rear façade. Natural light enters at regular intervals along one side of this corridor via the existing windows and new internal openings. Similar viewing corridors are introduced elsewhere, most notably along the rear façade and between the kitchen and the living area. These give the illusion of coherent 'arcades' that add grandeur whilst individual rooms remain distinctly defined. These long views revolve around the spatial heart of this home – the kitchen and dining area.

New materials introduce further clarity and hierarchy – sandblasted glass, limestone, painted joinery, islands of green slate in the wet areas and a stained-ash herringbone parquet with a silky satin-sheen finish which features throughout the apartment.

The bathroom, the WC and the bedrooms are the result of rigorous planning in confined areas. The bathroom is tailored to suit the standard size Montauk slate tiles without cutting, whilst elsewhere bespoke joinery and wall panelling is fitted snugly into niches and corners.

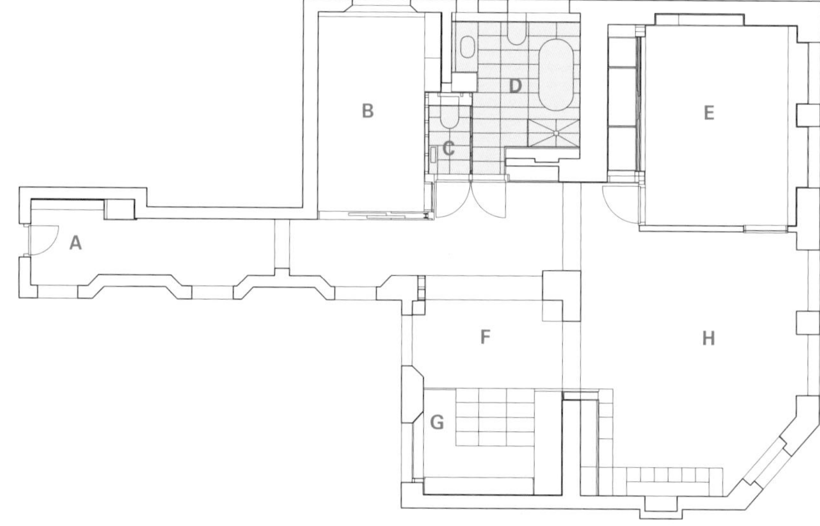

Opposite Left
View of the exterior of this handsome red brick mansion block in Kensington. The newly refurbished interior strikes a confident note of modernity within the historic Victorian envelope.

Floor Plan
A Entrance
B Bedroom
C WC
D Bathroom
E Master bedroom
F Dining area
G Kitchen
H Living room

Above Left
A free-standing bathtub is separated from the shower area by a screen of clear glazing. Clean simple white fittings, panelling, walls and window frames are contrasted with large slate tiles on the floor and wet area walls.

Above Right
A custom made niche was tailored to accommodate a large ceramic sink, which is cantilevered from the wall to create more space. General storage is in the form of mirror-faced cupboards, above.

Stone

Ullmayer Sylvester Architects
Falkland House Apartment
London, England, UK

Bathroom Plan and Sections A–A, B–B, C–C and D–D
1:50
1 White laminate ledge
2 Integrated basin in Corian countertop
3 Full-height storage cupboard with adjustable shelves
4 White laminate panel with concealed cistern behind
5 WC
6 Existing window with sandblasted glass
7 Montauk slate floor tiles
8 White ceramic free-standing bathtub
9 Shower recess separated from room by fixed glass screen
10 Service duct
11 Mirror-faced storage cupboards
12 Stainless steel WC flush panel
13 Bath control valve
14 Hand held shower hose
15 Montauk slate wall tiles
16 White laminate panel
17 White laminate panel to conceal plumbing
18 Door to bathroom
19 Concealed, recessed lighting
20 Wall-mounted radiator

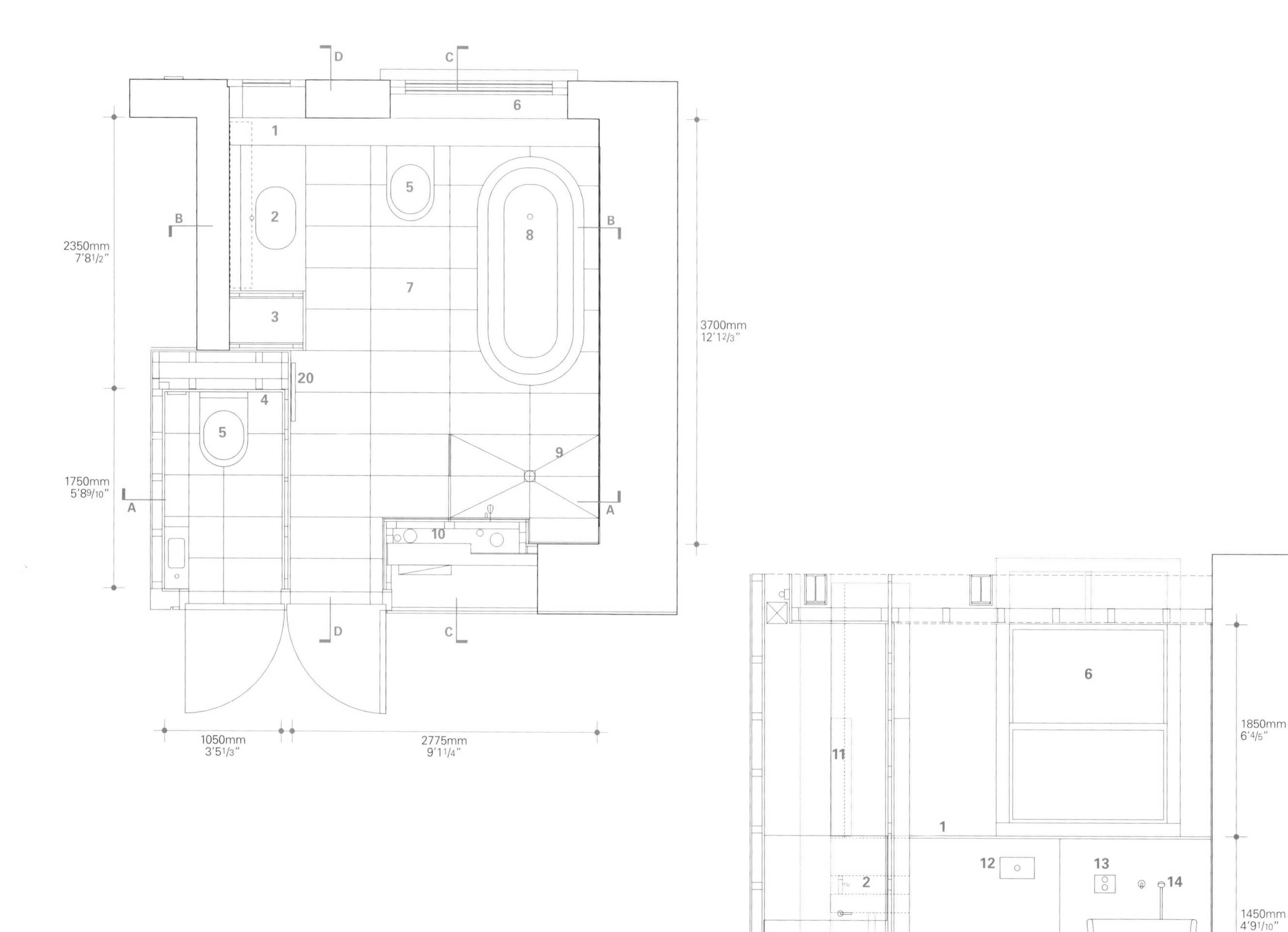

A–A

Materials
Countertop White Abet Laminati on plywood substrate
Joinery White Abet Laminati on plywood substrate
Floor 600 x 300 mm (2 x 1 foot) Montauk green slate tiles
Lighting Concealed incandescents

Appliances and Fixtures
Basin Taps and Spout Hansgrohe Metris S monoblock tap
Basin White Duravit Vero furniture washbasin with overflow and tap platform
Shower Hansgrohe Rainbow Set overhead shower
Shower Head Hansgrohe Raindance shower head S 150 Air 3jet
Bath Taps and Spout Hansgrohe Raindance S shower head, XXL100, Hansgrohe Isiflex XXL Metal Effect shower hose and Stillness wall-mounted bathspout
Bath Etruscan bath with integral overflow system
WC White Duravit Starck 3 wall-mounted compact toilet

Project Credits
Completion 2007
Client Joan Spiekermann
Project Architects Silvia Ullmayer
Structural Engineers David Akera Structural Engineers
Building Control Consultants Butler and Young
Main Contractor Artpol Construction
Specialist Kitchen Contractors Biofarben
Specialist Joinery Contractors RogerRoger

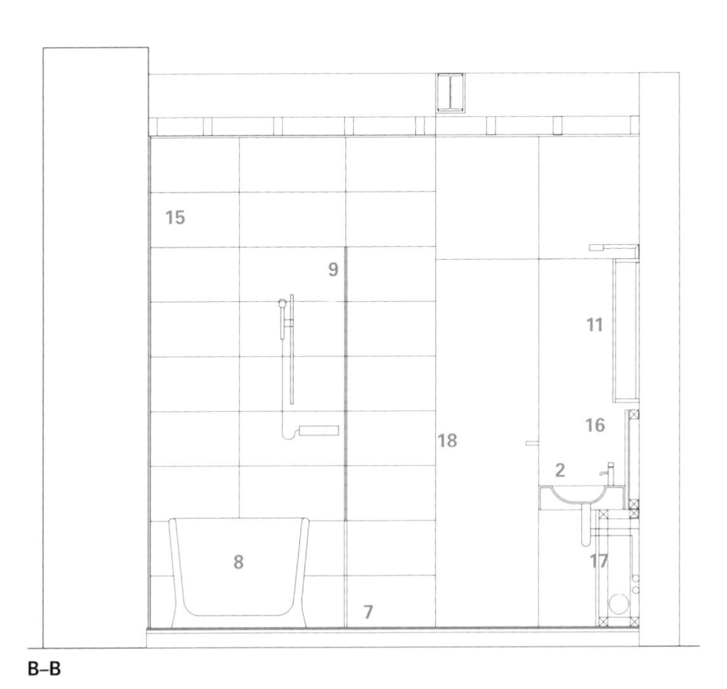

B–B

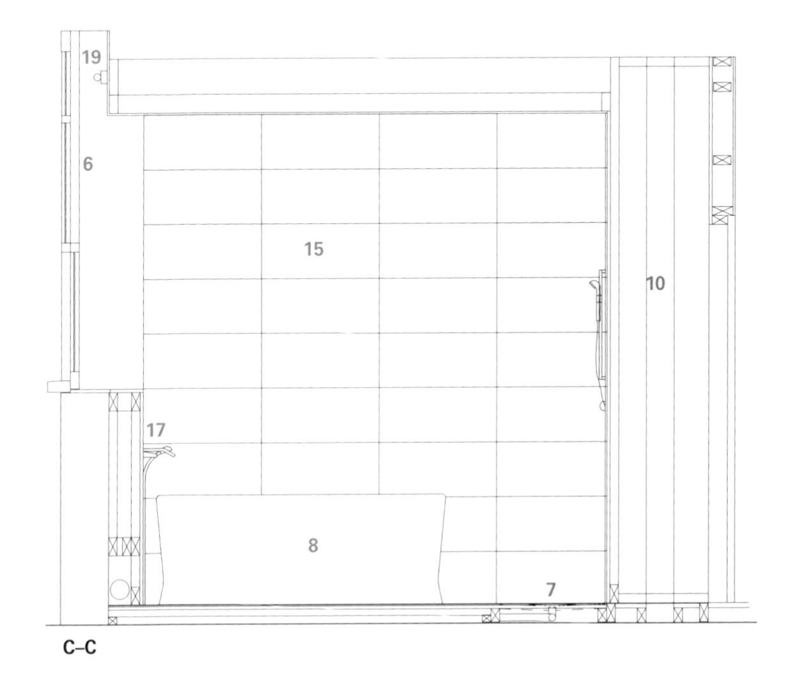

C–C

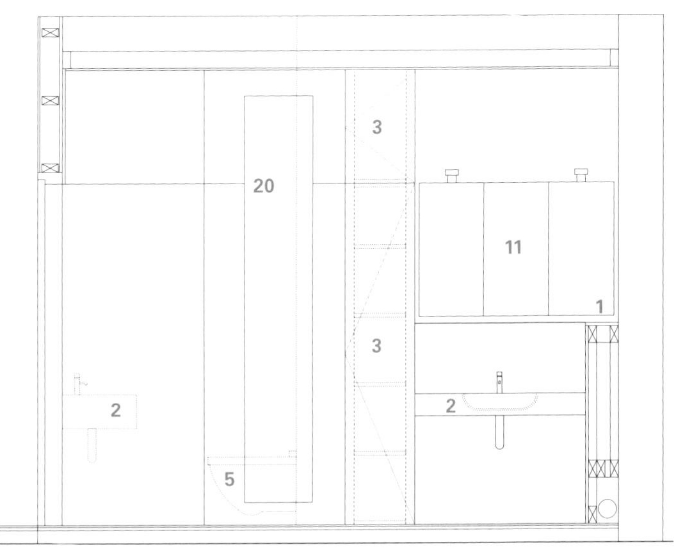

D–D

Wingårdhs Architects

Villa Astrid
Gothenburg, Sweden

This house has taken its cue from the dramatic west Swedish landscape in which it stands. The difficulties of the site, the oblique angle of the steep cliff in relation to the view, were challenges that informed the design. In addition, the development regulations that apply to the area stipulated a roof pitch of between 14 and 30 degrees and an eaves height of three metres (10 feet), both of which conditions had to be incorporated into the design.

However, in a dramatic departure from the way nearby sites have been tackled, the rock with which the house is united is exposed on the interior and forms one wall of the deep courtyard, admitting daylight into the living spaces. The plan is arranged as two long angled wings in a scissor-like formation, with a shorter arm to one side to create a sharply-angled U-shape with the rocky courtyard at its centre. The upper floor – overlooking the courtyard below but directly accessing a ground-level terrace on the other side of the building – accommodates all of the living spaces in an essentially open plan, while the lower floor – partially built into the bedrock – has bedrooms and utility areas (laundry and storage) arranged with direct access to the courtyard.

The master bathroom, in particular, incorporates the rock face into the room. The bathroom is arranged as a simple wet room with a timber vanity bench with twin basins and a WC ranged against one wall, and a shower against the other, with only a frameless glass screen separating it from the rest of the space. Dramatically, one wall of the slate-lined room disintegrates into the naturally faceted face of the warm gold and red-hued rock.

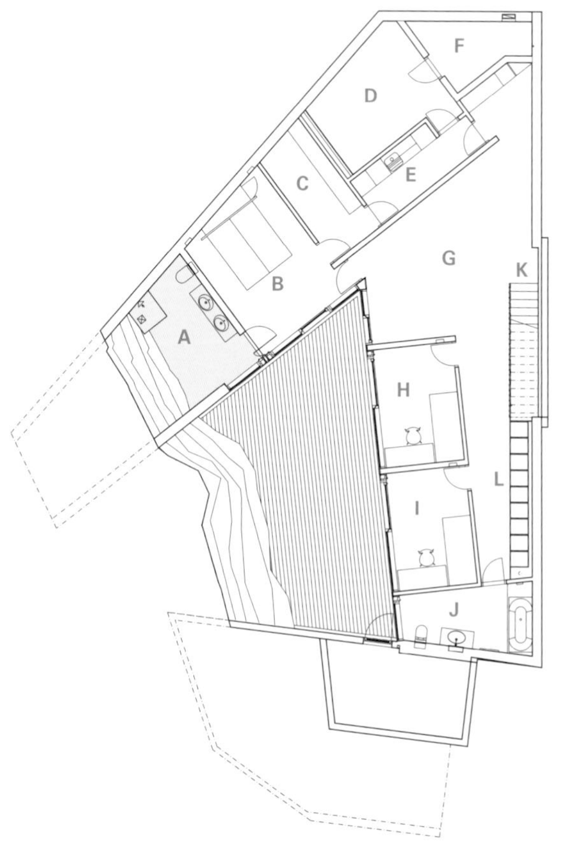

Opposite Left
The house opens up to an expansive terrace on one side of the building. The exterior is clad in copper panels that have aged to a dark patina.

Floor Plan
A Master bathroom
B Master bedroom
C Dressing room
D Storage
E Laundry
F Storage
G Play area
H Bedroom
I Bedroom
J Bathroom
K Stair up to ground floor
L Cupboards

Left
View of the interior courtyard, which starts as a timber deck accessible from the bedrooms arranged around its perimeter, and transforms into a solid wall of rock (left).

Below
In the master bathroom, a timber countertop echoes the warm tones of the bedrock, which has been left exposed as a sculptural feature of the slate-lined wet room.

Stone

Wingårdhs Architects
Villa Astrid
Gothenburg, Sweden

Bathroom Plan, Elevations A and B and Sections A–A and B–B
1:50

1 WC
2 Solid oak countertop and side panels to vanity unit
3 White ceramic basin
4 Window to courtyard
5 Towel rail
6 Clear glazed door to shower enclosure
7 Wall-mounted adjustable shower head with hose fitting
8 Floor drain to shower
9 Full-height fixed glass shower screen
10 Slate floor tiles
11 Existing rock face
12 WC flush to concealed cistern
13 Wall-mounted up-lighter over mirror
14 Mirror over vanity unit
15 Spray finish to drawer fronts
16 Glass pivot door from master bedroom

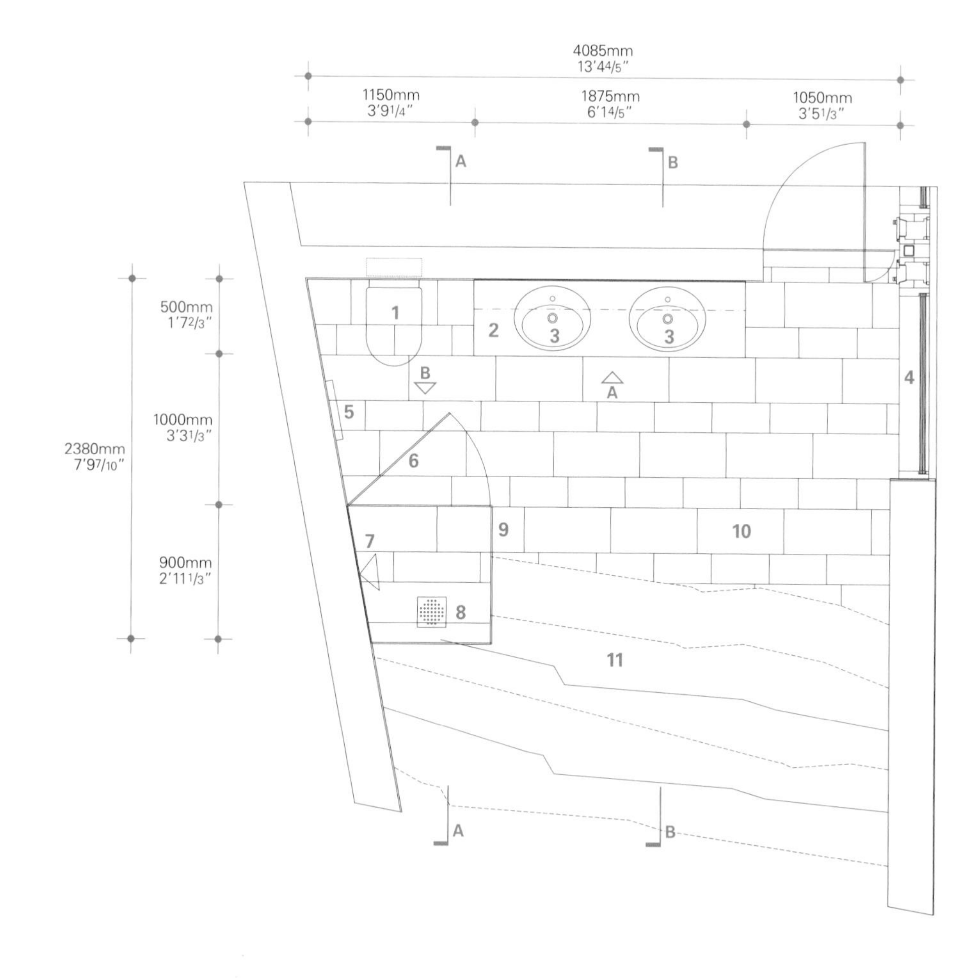

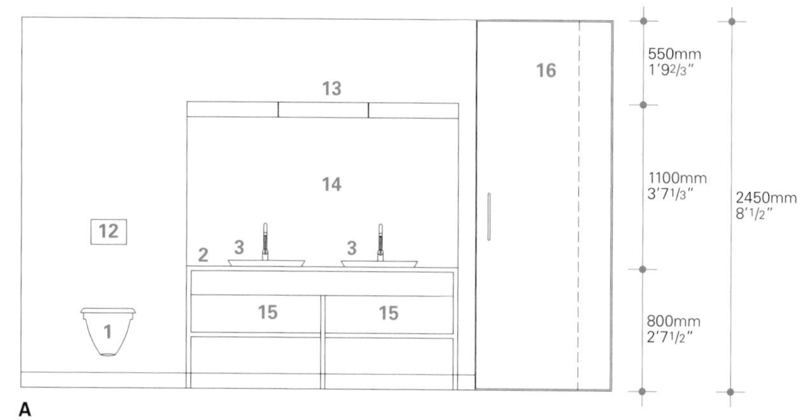

A

Materials
Countertop Texwood from Göteborgs Trä and Fanér
Joinery Texwood from Göteborgs Trä and Fanér
Floor Slate tiles
Walls Slate tiles
Lighting Fagerhult fluorescent lamp over basin and Erco low voltage armature in ceiling

Appliances and Fixtures
Basin Taps Mora Inxx from Mora Armatur
Basin Spout Mora Inxx from Mora Armatur
Basin Ifö Aqua from Ifö Sanitär
Shower Taps Mora Inxx from Mora Armatur
Shower Head Mora Inxx from Mora Armatur
Towel Rails INR Line from INR inredningsglas
WC Ifö Cera WC from Ifö Sanitär

Project Credits
Completion 2004
Structural Engineer F.B. Engineering
Mechanical Engineer N.V.K. V.V.S. Kontroll
Main Contractor Wickenberg Bygganalys
Lighting Consultant Schönbeck Elprojekt
Landscape Consultant NOD – Natur Orienterad Design

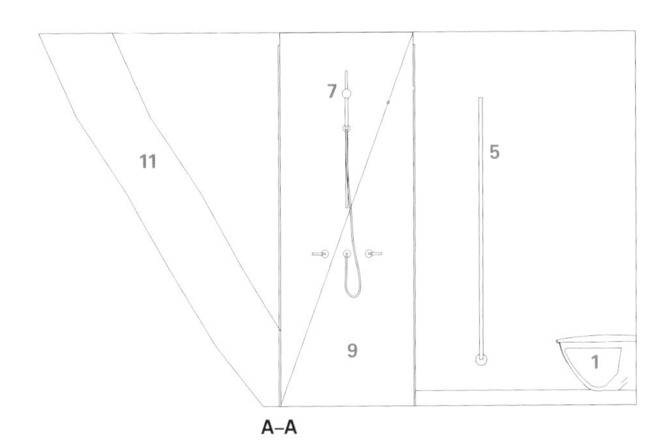

A–A

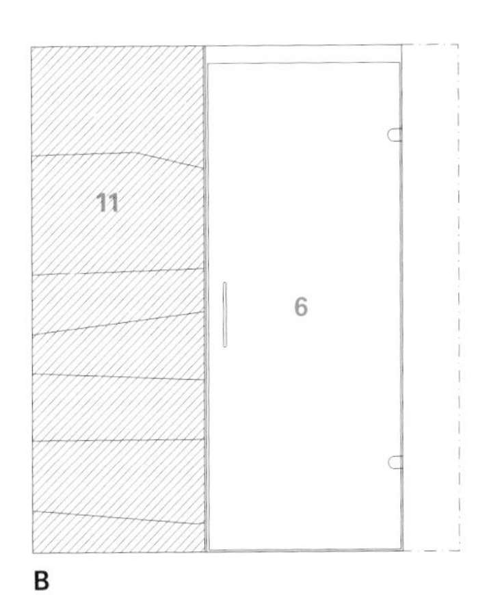

B

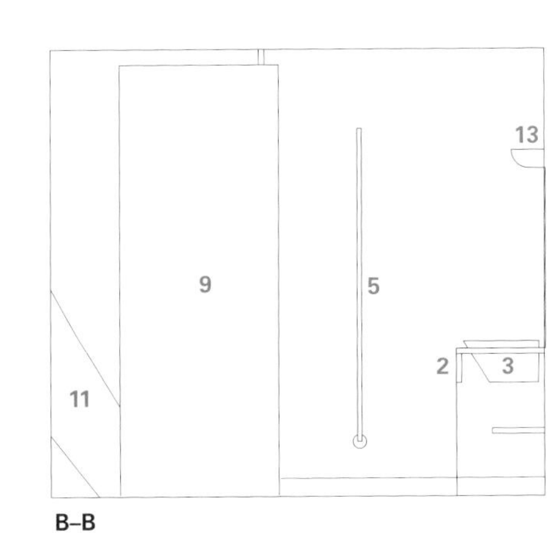

B–B

Kei'ichi Irie / Power Unit Studio

I–House Karuizawa, Nagano, Japan

This family house is situated on a steep wooded site and arranged over three levels to both negotiate the contours of the site and take advantage of expansive mountain views. The steel structure and solid masonry walls on the exterior are painted a dark grey to blend with the natural environment. In contrast, interior walls are painted white and floors are of pale polished stone to create bright, naturally lit living spaces. In addition, large expanses of glass facing the view feature on every level.

From the approach road at the top of the property, all that is visible is a stone-tiled bridge that leads directly to the garage pavilion and the dark steel of the deck roof to the upper floor. From the bridge, a flight of stairs leads to the entrance courtyard, which features an abstract sculpture.

The entrance, on the middle floor, accommodates the main social spaces including the kitchen, dining area, living area with suspended fireplace, and a cantilevered timber deck with panoramic views of the mountains.

The lower floor, accessed via an internal open-tread steel stair houses the private areas including the master bedroom with ensuite bathroom, a second bedroom, guest bedroom, family bathroom, a gym and a private terrace.

The large family bathroom is arranged as an open space, divided in two by a glass screen wall with connecting door. On one side of the screen are a vanity unit with raised glass countertop and glass basins, as well as a WC. Beyond the screen wall, a large bathtub with stone surround and a wet area shower have direct access to a terrace with spectacular views.

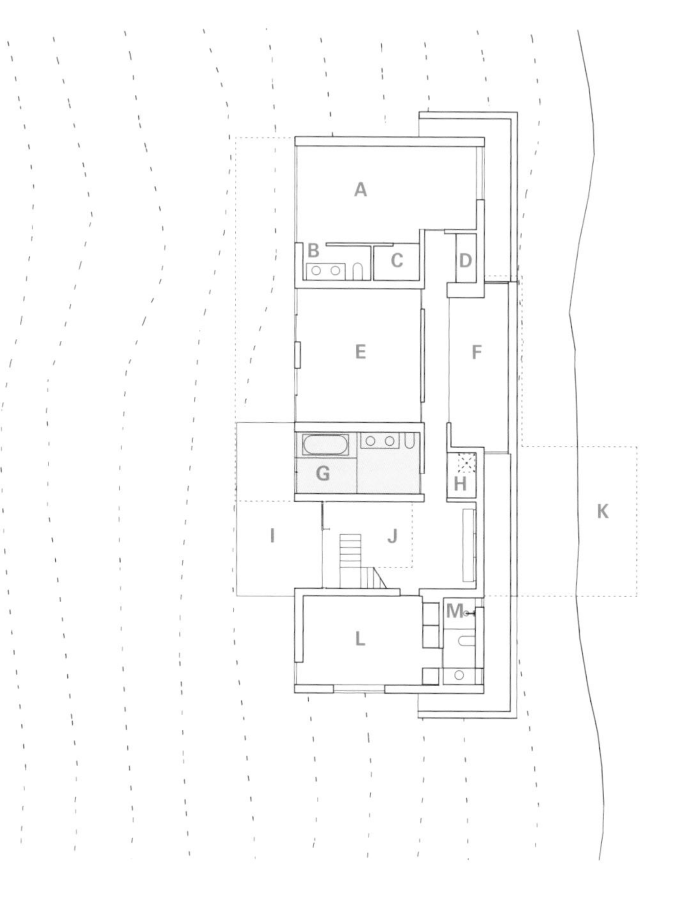

Opposite Left Above
The living areas on the middle level have access to a large timber-decked terrace.

Opposite Left Below
A double-height void houses a sculptural steel stair with a minimal stainless steel balustrade that connects the living spaces to the bedrooms and bathrooms below.

Floor Plan
A Master bedroom
B Ensuite bathroom
C Ensuite shower
D Closet
E Bedroom
F Gym
G Bathroom
H Laundry
I Terrace
J Hallway
K Line of roof canopy below
L Guest bedroom
M Ensuite bathroom

Above
The main bathroom, with access to its own terrace, is clad throughout in pale stone tiles. Accents of glass in the dividing screen, mirrors, basins and countertop lend the space a lightness of touch appropriate to a bathing retreat.

Stone

Kei'ichi Irie / Power Unit Studio
I–House
Karuizawa, Nagano, Japan

Bathroom Plan and Sections A–A, B–B, C–C and D–D
1:50

1 Stone bath surround
2 Bath spout
3 Shower fitting on flexible hose
4 White ceramic bathtub
5 Raised glass countertop on stainless steel legs
6 Glass basin
7 Basin spout and mixer tap
8 WC
9 Toilet-roll holder
10 Steel framed window
11 Steel framed glass door to balcony
12 Stainless steel ledge
13 Shower head
14 Glazed screen wall
15 Frameless glass door
16 Stainless steel towel rail
17 Door to hallway
18 Stone floor tiles
19 Mirror-clad doors to cupboards with adjustable shelves behind
20 Sprayed MDF cupboards
21 Stone wall tiles
22 Mirror panel to wall behind bath
23 Stone-clad recess in stone tiled wall

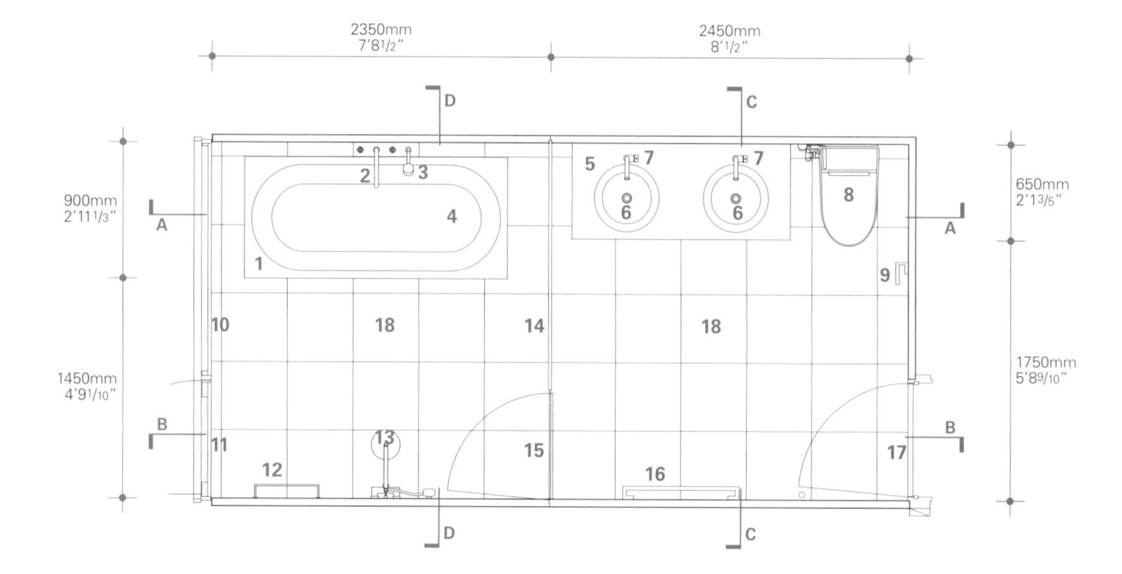

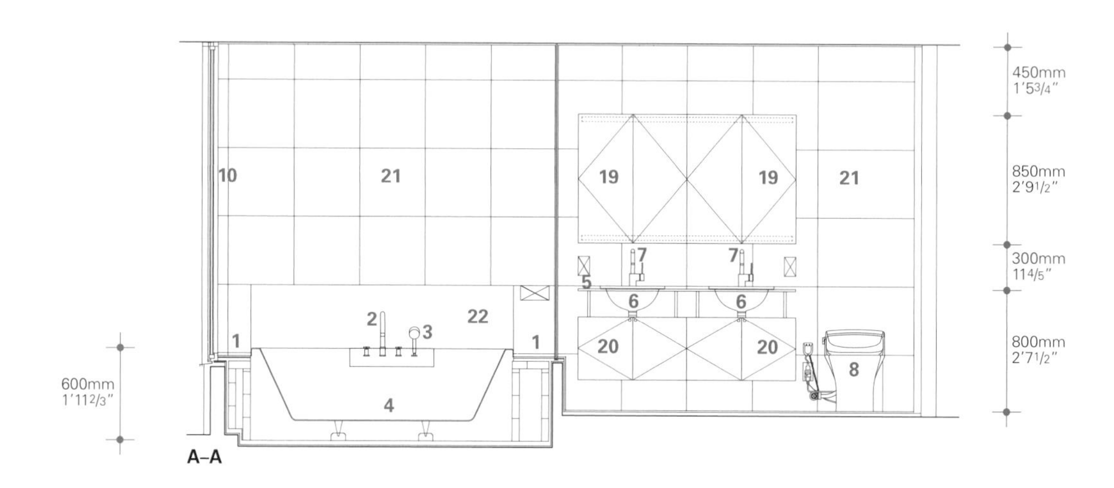

Materials
Countertop Toughened glass with stainless steel fixings
Joinery Sprayed MDF with stainless steel pull handles
Floor Stone tiles
Wall Tiles Stone tiles
Lighting Concealed fluorescent fittings above and below mirrored cupboards over vanity

Appliances and Fixtures
Basin Taps T-form
Basin Spout T-form
Basin Cera
Shower Taps T-form
Shower Head T-form
Bath Taps and Spout T-form
Bath T-form
Towel Rails T-form
WC INAX

Project Credits
Completion 2007
Project Architects Kei'ichi Irie
Structural Engineers City Plan
Main Contractor Sasazawa Construction

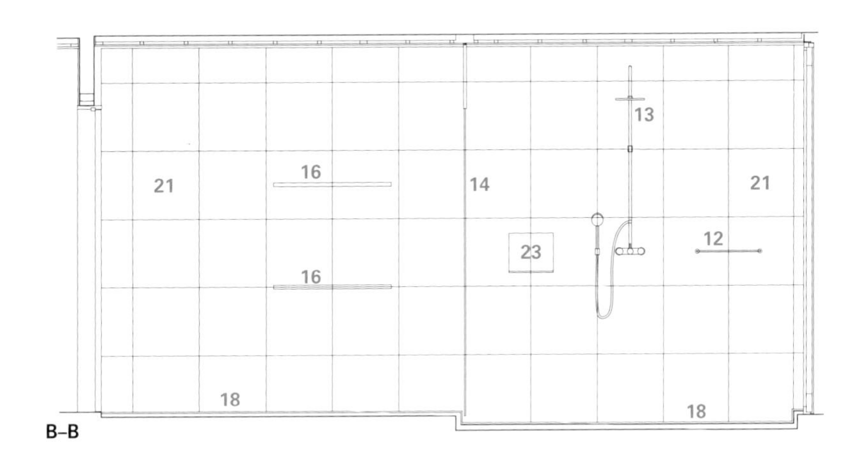

B–B

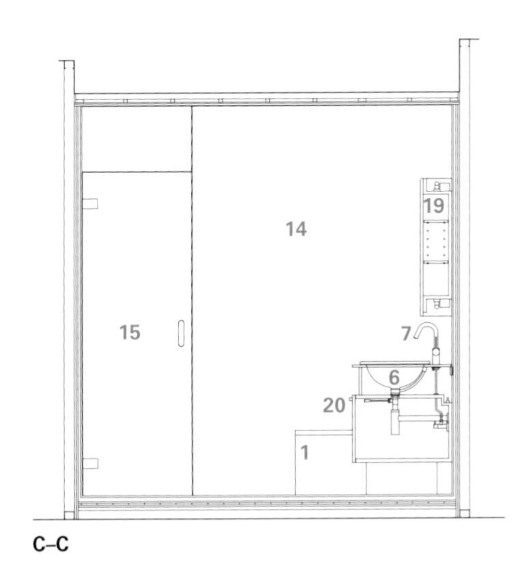

C–C

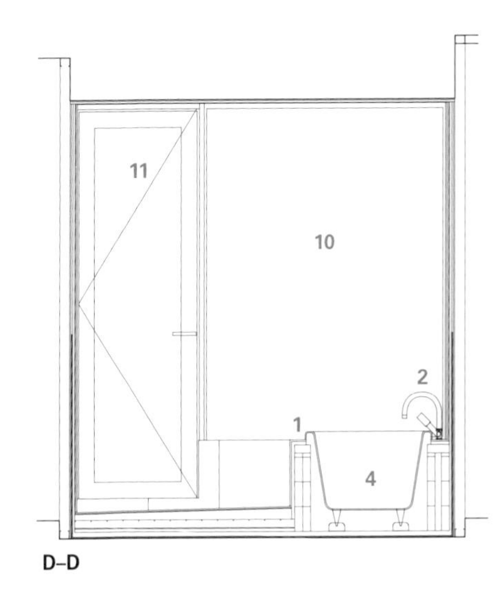

D–D

Coy + Yiontis Architects

Kew Residence
Melbourne, Victoria, Australia

This project involved the renovation of a large modern house built in the late 1960s which had been virtually untouched since that period. The approach was to strip back and clarify the existing spaces, combining some and dividing others to produce new spaces adapted to the needs of the present occupants.

The decision to use a minimal palette of materials and colours was made early in the design process and was as much a reaction to the frenzied palette of the original structure as an attempt to unify some of the newly created spaces and forge a link with the exterior. To this purpose, 90 x 90 centimetre (3 x 3 feet) slabs of Elba marble from Turkey were chosen to clad the floors of the main living spaces, the kitchen and the external paving around the pool.

The master bathroom is generously arranged to include a free-standing marble-clad bath and a walk-in double shower with skylight above. The shower forms the core of the dressing room which wraps around it to create a transition between the bedroom and bathroom. All of the surfaces are clad in the same Elba marble as elsewhere in the house. The floating vanity bench, like the kitchen counter, is fabricated from larger slabs of the same marble.

The detailing throughout the house is kept sparse, leaving the natural beauty of the stone to take centre stage, variety coming from the changing light. Windows and door frames are detailed with copper cladding, which will develop a patina with time. Recycled Blackbutt timber was reserved for key pieces of custom joinery and the new entry doors.

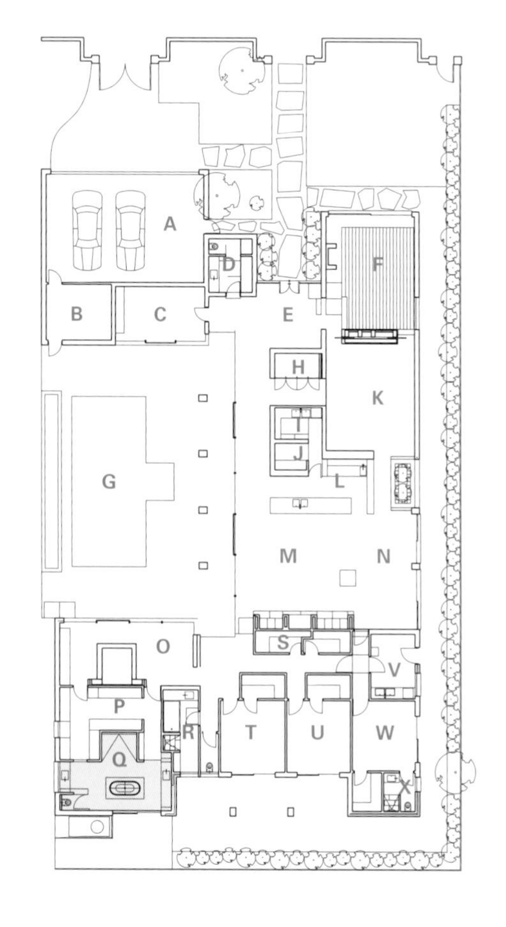

Opposite Left
The living spaces are arranged around a loggia and open up to the pool and landscaped courtyard. The marble flooring to both spaces seamlessly transitions from inside to out.

Floor Plan
A Garage
B Plant room
C Study
D Powder room
E Entrance hall
F Living room
G Pool and spa
H Storage
I Prep kitchen
J Pantry
K Entertainment room
L Kitchen
M Living area
N Dining area
O Master bedroom
P Dressing room
Q Master bathroom
R Bathroom
S Storage
T Bedroom
U Bedroom
V Laundry
W Bedroom
X Ensuite bathroom

Above Left
In the master bathroom, marble is used for the floor, walls and the surround to the free-standing bathtub.

Left
The bathroom includes a spacious double shower recess, a free-standing bath and a cantilevered marble vanity area with mirror backing above and below.

Stone

Coy + Yiontis Architects
Kew Residence
Melbourne, Victoria, Australia

Bathroom Plan and Sections A–A and B–B
1:50

1 Full-height storage cupboard with adjustable painted MDF shelves
2 Mirror-faced cupboard over vanity bench
3 Integrated marble sink
4 Marble countertop
5 Mixer taps to basin mounted to vertical face of vanity bench
6 Custom made shoe storage to dressing room
7 Shower taps
8 Wall-mounted shower head
9 Marble floor tiles
10 Marble bath surround
11 White ceramic bathtub
12 Floor-mounted bath spout
13 Bath taps mounted to outside face of marble bath surround
14 Full-height sliding glass door
15 Opening to dressing room
16 Stainless steel towel rail
17 WC
18 Mirror-clad wall above vanity countertop
19 Marble-clad boxed out zone below basin to conceal plumbing
20 Marble wall tiles
21 Marble floor tiles to shower recess laid to fall
22 Pivoting door to WC
23 Stainless steel toilet-roll holder
24 WC flush button

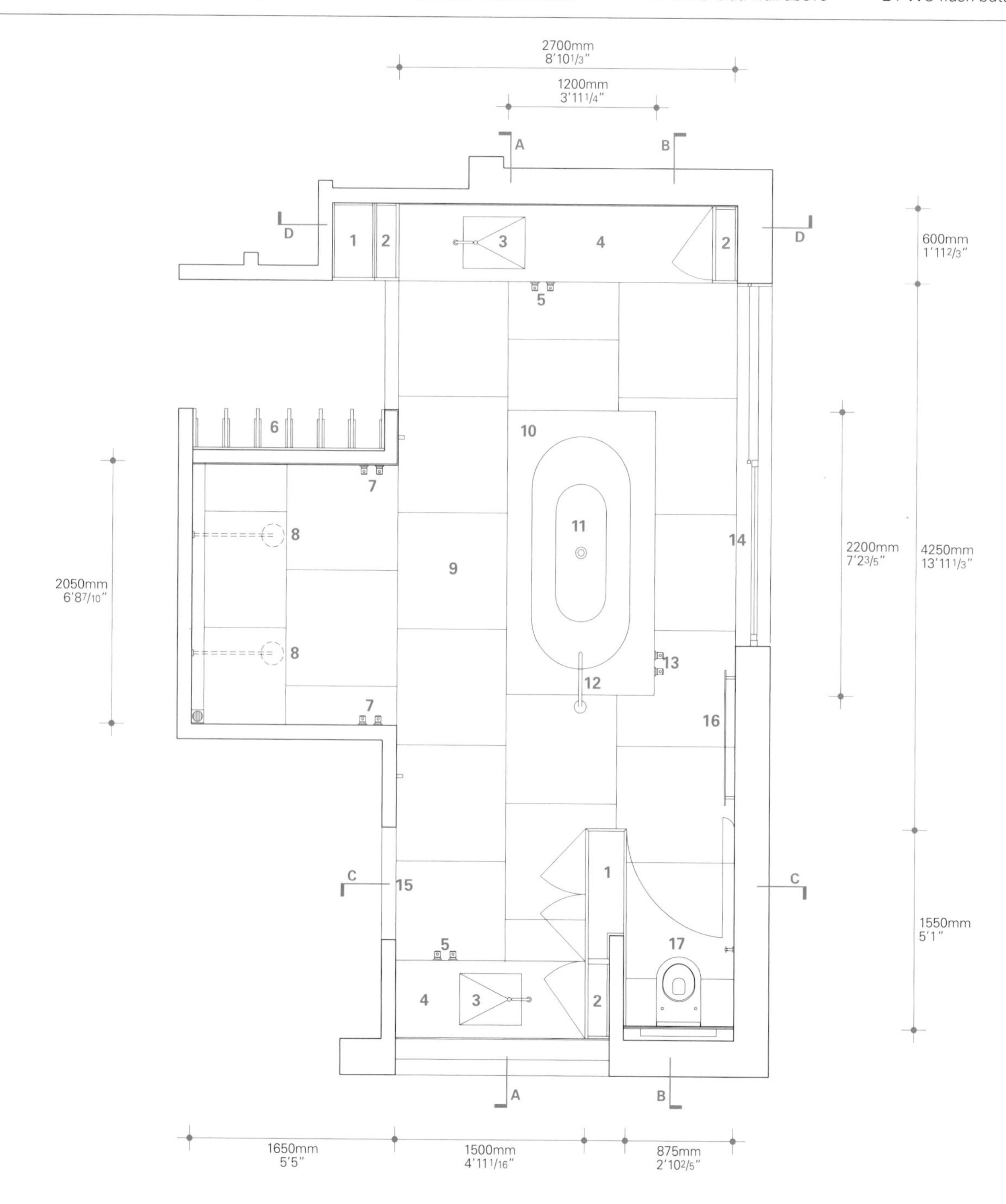

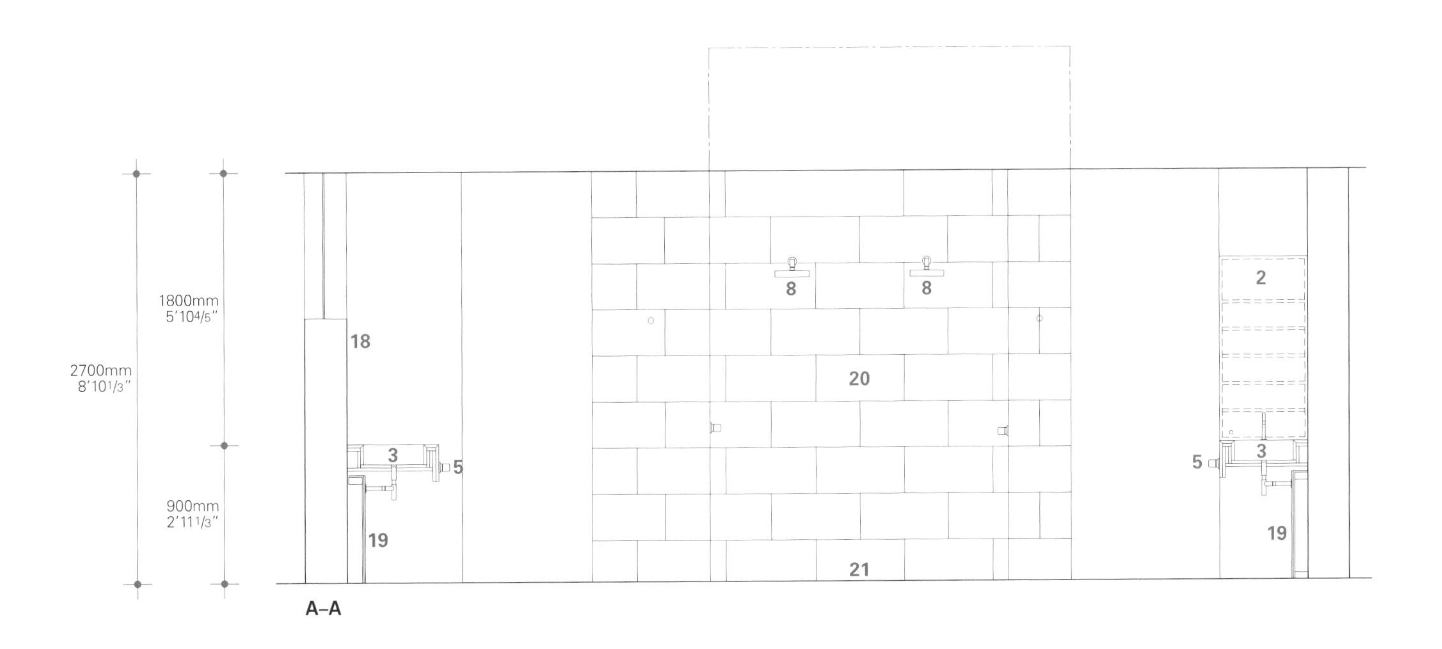
1800mm
5'10⁴/₅"
2700mm
8'10¹/₃"
900mm
2'11¹/₃"
2
8
8
18
20
3
5
5
3
19
19
21
A–A

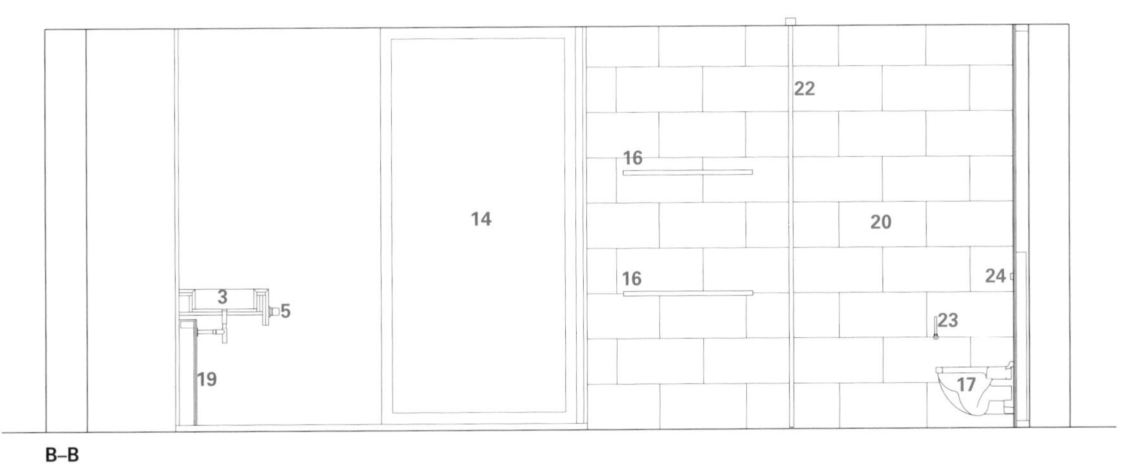
22
16
14
20
16
24
3
5
23
19
17
B–B

Stone

Coy + Yiontis Architects
Kew Residence
Melbourne, Victoria, Australia

Bathroom Sections C–C and D–D
1:50
1 Marble wall tiles to WC
2 WC flush button
3 Stainless steel toilet-roll holder
4 WC
5 Full-height storage cupboard
6 Marble face to vanity bench
7 Basin spout
8 Mirror-clad wall
9 Marble basin
10 Mixer taps to basin
11 Marble-clad boxed out zone below basin to conceal plumbing
12 Mirror-faced cupboard over vanity bench

Sectional Detail Through Countertop and Basin
1:10
1 Mixer taps to basin mounted to vertical face of vanity bench
2 Marble front panel to vanity bench
3 Marble countertop
4 Timber sub-structure to marble vanity bench
5 Basin spout
6 Marble basin
7 Basin drain
8 Stainless steel bottle trap
9 Marble panel to boxed out services zone below basin
10 Timber sub-structure to services zone to conceal plumbing

Opposite
In the bathroom, brushed stainless steel fixtures including the towel rails, shown here, complement the grey and white Elba Marble slabs that are used throughout the house.

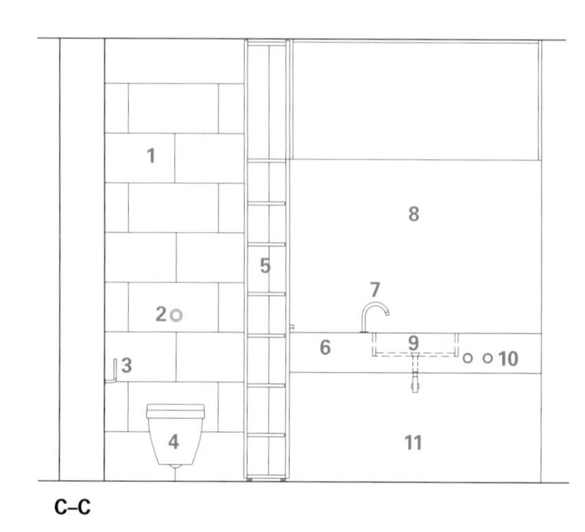

C–C

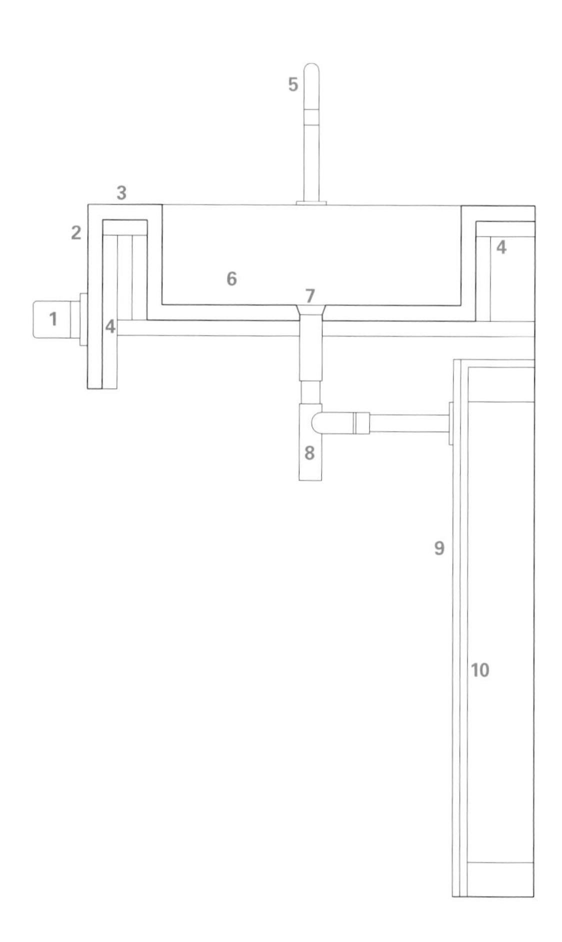

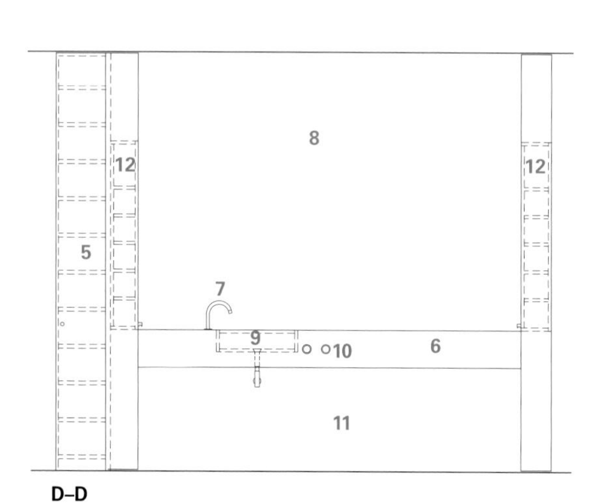

D–D

Materials
Countertop Elba Marble
Joinery MDF with two pack paint finish
Floor Elba Marble
Splashback Mirror
Wall Tiles Elba Marble
Lighting Megalit Rastaf

Appliances and Fixtures
Basin Taps Fantini Isola
Basin Spout Vola
Basin Custom made stone basin
Shower Taps Fantini Isola
Shower Head Dornbracht Tara
Bath Kaldewei with spa
WC Villeroy & Boch Subway

Project Credits
Completion 2007
Project Architects George Yiontis, Giorgio Marfella, Candice Bradley
Structural Engineers Ross Greer and Associates
Cost Consultants Geoffrey Moyle
Services Engineer Thomas Consulting Group

Tzannes Associates

Parsley Bay Residence Sydney, New South Wales, Australia

Located on Sydney's spectacular harbour front, the design for the Parsley Bay Residence evolved through an intensive collaboration between the architects and client.

The ensuite bathroom to the master bedroom suite is located on an upper level facing the harbour foreshore. It is positioned adjacent to the dressing areas and oriented to provide an axial view towards the water. The master bedroom and ensuite were provided with a wall of sliding glazed doors and screens that open onto a narrow balcony overlooking a dramatic double-height waterfront loggia. The sliding doors and screens can be closed or fully retracted to mediate the view, privacy, light and breezes.

Throughout the residence a restrained and controlled palette of materials and finishes assists a seamless flow between spaces. Sandblasted Pietra di Isernia limestone, the dominant floor finish throughout the residence, is continued into the ensuite on both the floors and walls.

A free-standing bath and open double shower area are located towards the balcony taking advantage of views, light and air. The WC is located behind a freestanding stone and stainless steel towel and linen storage area. The absence of doors or shower screens within the ensuite maximizes the sense of openness. A pair of wall-hung vanity basins sit below a long linear stone shelf with recessed lighting.

The selection of fittings and fixtures followed the general calm, minimalist approach to the overall design. The ensuite, as elsewhere, focuses on clean simple lines and geometries, quality of light, shadows, breezes and a complementary relationship with the site and the water beyond.

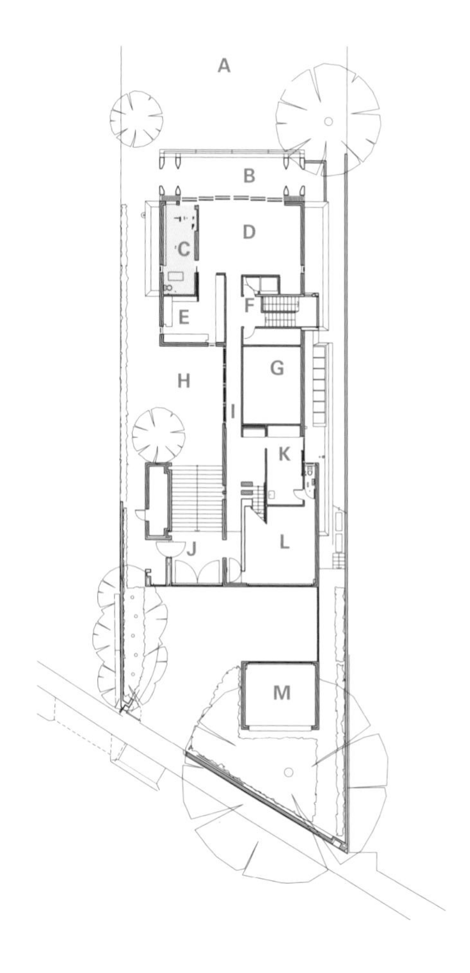

Opposite Left
The living spaces on the ground floor open up to the landscape, pool and harbour. On the first floor, a long run of sliding glass panels open the master bedroom (left) and ensuite bathroom (right) to the loggia and the views.

Floor Plan
A Garden
B Loggia
C Master bathroom
D Master bedroom
E Dressing room
F Stair and lift
G Void to ground floor below
H Courtyard below
I Bridge
J Entrance court
K Laundry
L Garage 1
M Garage 2

Above
View of the bath and shower area. Shower controls for the ceiling-mounted shower heads, as well as a hand held shower are placed in a stone-lined recess in the wall. Similarly, controls for the free-standing bath are located on the stone-clad vertical surface of the shelf to which the white ceramic basins are also attached. Above these, a long run of mirror-faced cabinets help to reflect light throughout the space.

Stone

Tzannes Associates
Parsley Bay Residence
Sydney, New South Wales, Australia

Bathroom Plan and Sections A–A, B–B, C–C and D–D
1:50

1 Shower taps
2 Stone recess
3 Hand held shower
4 Ceiling-mounted shower head
5 Stone floor laid to fall to waste
6 Floor-mounted bath spout
7 White ceramic bathtub
8 Heated towel rail
9 White ceramic wall-hung basin
10 Basin taps
11 Mirror-faced cabinets above stone shelf
12 Sliding door to bedroom and dressing room
13 Stone surround to glass shelves for linen storage
14 Stone floor to WC area laid to fall
15 WC
16 Concealed cistern to WC behind stone panel
17 Sliding window
18 Bath taps
19 Stone wall tiles
20 Stone shelf
21 Stone panel
22 Fixed mirror panel

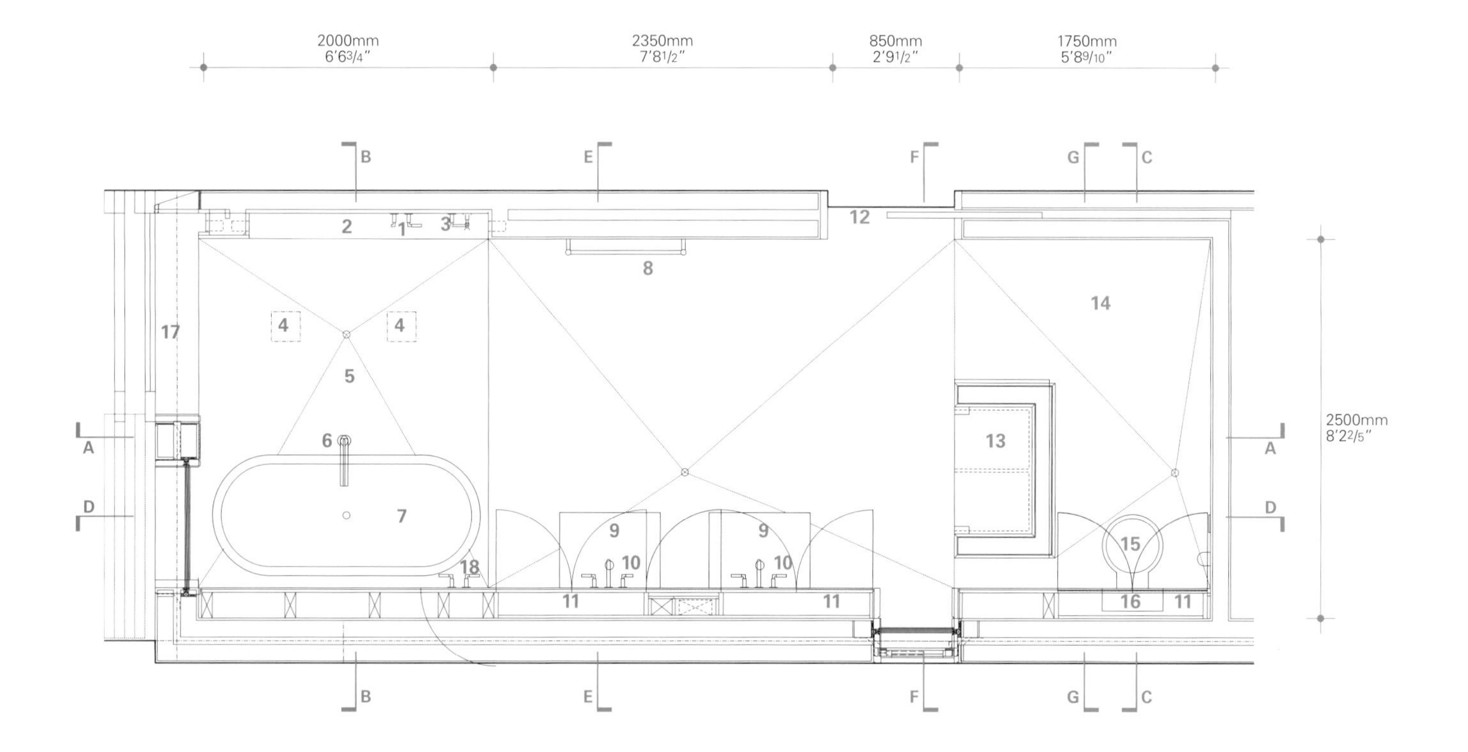

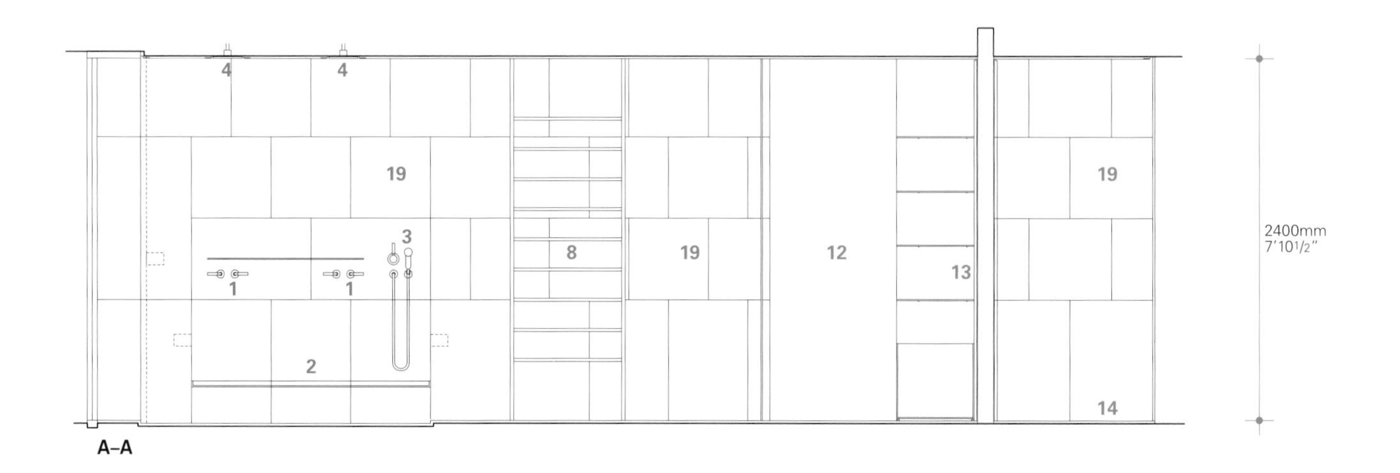

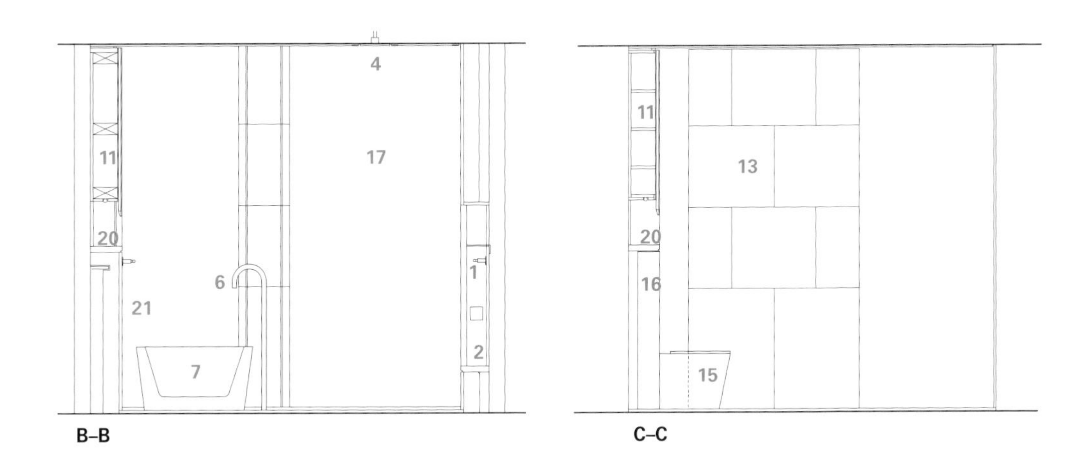
4
17
11
20
6
1
21
2
7
11
13
20
16
15

B–B

C–C

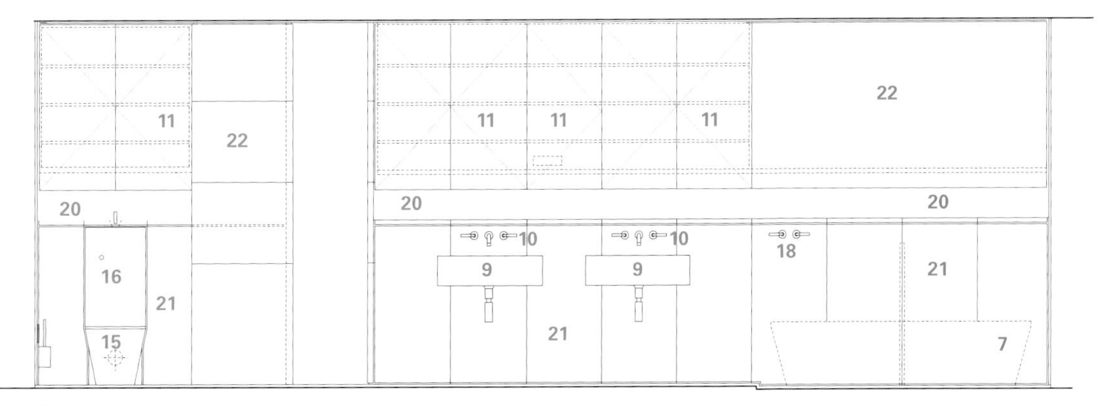
11
22
11
11
11
22
20
20
20
10
10
16
9
9
18
21
21
21
15
7

D–D

Stone

Tzannes Associates
Parsley Bay Residence
Sydney, New South Wales, Australia

Bathroom Sections E–E, F–F and G–G
1:50

1 Heated towel rail
2 Opening to WC enclosure
3 Stone surround to linen storage area
4 Glass shelves for linen storage
5 Laundry bins
6 Mirror-faced cabinets above stone shelf
7 Concealed lighting
8 Stone shelf
9 Wall-mounted basin spout
10 Wall-mounted white ceramic basin
11 Stone wall panel
12 Door to bedroom and dressing room
13 WC
14 Full-height window
15 Stone wall tiles

Opposite
View from the bathing area. The stone shelf with mirrored cabinets above continues along the entire length of the bathroom. The stone-clad linen storage area screens the WC from the main space.

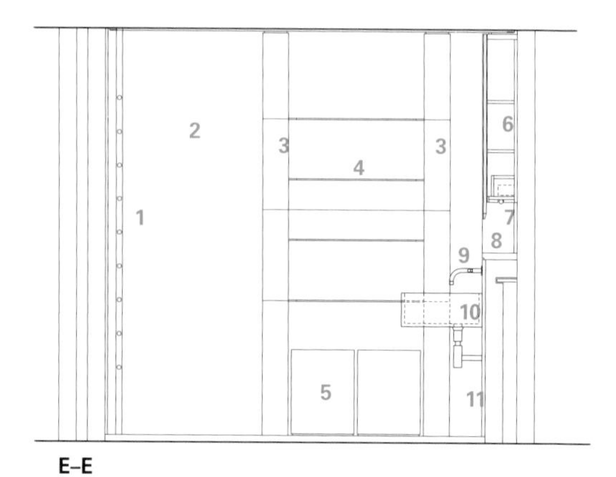

E–E

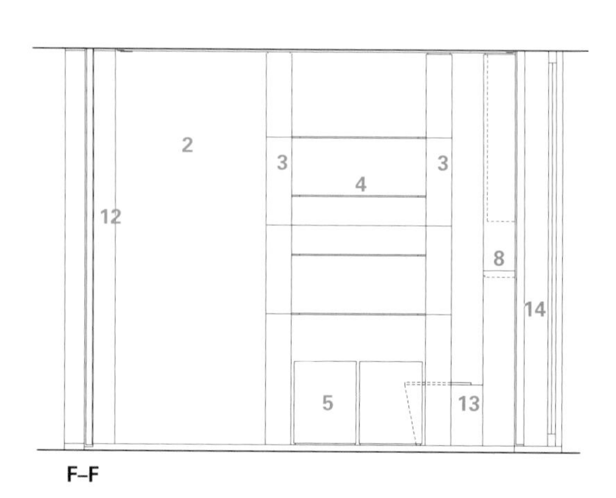

F–F

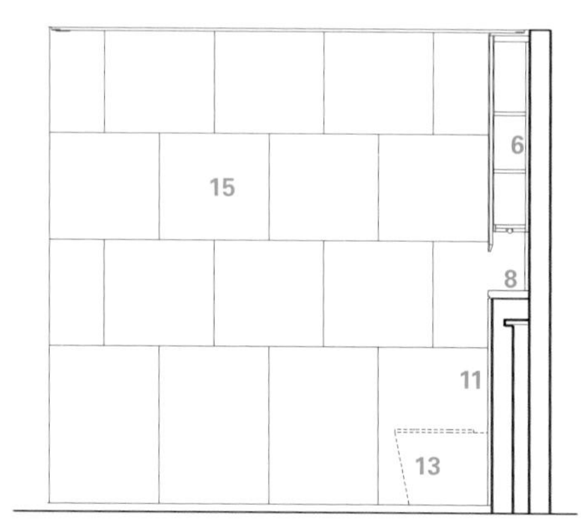

G–G

Materials
Countertop Sandblasted Pietra di Isernia stone
Floor Sandblasted Pietra di Isernia stone
Splashback Sandblasted Pietra di Isernia stone
Wall Tiles Sandblasted Pietra di Isernia stone
Lighting ZAL Fittings from Light 2

Appliances and Fixtures
Basin Taps Dornbracht Tara Classic
Basin Spout Brodware
Basins Villeroy & Boch Omnia-pro wall-mounted basins
Shower Taps Dornbracht Tara Classic
Shower Head Rogerseller Zen
Bath Taps Dornbracht Tara Classic
Bath Spout Omvivo Licciardi floor-to-bath spout
Bath Kaldewei Centreform
WC Duravit Starck 1

Project Credits
Completion 2006
Project Architects Alec Tzannes, Phillip Rossington, Bruce Chadlowe, Nadia Zhao, Emma Webster
Structural Engineers Sinclair Knight Merz
Hydraulic Consultant Whipps Wood Consulting
Landscape Consultant Sue Barnsley Design
Main Contractor Infinity Constructions
Lighting Consultant Light 2
Electrical Consultant Haron Robson
Maritime Consultant Taylor Lauder Bersten

Please affix postage
stamp here

Laurence King Publishing Ltd
c/o Chronicle Books
680 Second Street
San Francisco
CA 94107
USA

Timber Bathrooms

Serda Architects

Private Residence María de la Salut, Mallorca, Spain

This large country estate is located near the village of María de la Salut in the northeast of Mallorca. Almond trees are a striking feature of the hilly countryside and 200 old almond trees on the estate are framed by the preserved stone walls at the edges of the property. From the five bedrooms with ensuite bathrooms in the eastern wing of the house are views of the nearby village of Santa Margalida. The view from the roof terrace extends east to the Bay of Alcudia, and west to the Serra de Tramuntana mountain range.

Reflections of light, climatic regulation, privacy and – at the same time – access to the outdoors are just some of the criteria which justify the prominent positioning of the swimming pool in the centre of the villa. Surrounded by marble paving stones and a teak deck, the spacious pool opens up the courtyard to the landscape. In addition, two interior courtyards meet the requirements of combining a private atmosphere with Mallorcan hospitality.

The entrance hall separates the open courtyard in the south, which is used for communal gatherings, from the private quarters. With its meditative flair, the courtyard in the north acts as a haven of peace and quiet for the residents.

The master bathroom is a study in luxurious simplicity. The space is divided in two, with one side devoted to a large bathtub and vanity bench, and, behind two symmetrical openings in the vanity wall, a shower room and separate WC. Floors and walls of Mares stone are enriched with accents of timber in the vanity, door frames and louvred shutters. Throughout the villa, materials blend harmoniously into the surroundings through the use of traditional materials such as stone, red brick, timber and water.

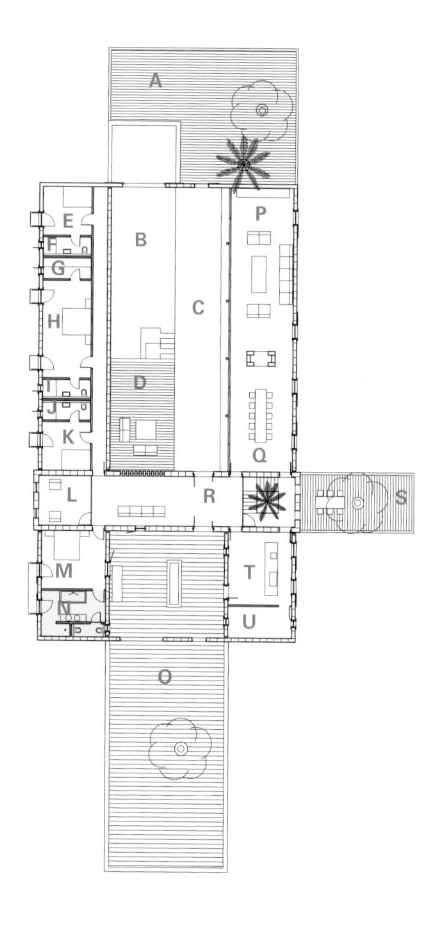

Opposite Left
At the centre of the social heart of the villa is a large pool which extends beyond the interior courtyard into the timber terrace with views out into the almond grove.

Floor Plan
A Timber terrace
B Pool
C Stone terrace
D Timber terrace
E Bedroom
F Ensuite bathroom
G Dressing room
H Bedroom
I Ensuite bathroom
J Ensuite bathroom
K Bedroom
L Study
M Master bedroom
N Master bathroom
O Timber terrace
P Living room
Q Dining room
R Entrance hall
S Timber terrace
T Kitchen
U Pantry

Top Left
View of the house and the courtyard pool from the almond grove.

Left
In the master bathroom, cool white finishes – limestone, marble and simple white ceramic fixtures – are contrasted with warm timber joinery. Each of the five bedrooms, as well as the master bathroom suite, feature private terraces with views over the typically Mediterranean landscape.

Timber

Serda Architects
Private Residence
María de la Salut, Mallorca, Spain

Bathroom Plan and Section A–A
1:50

1 Wall-mounted towel hooks
2 Timber-framed glazed door to terrace
3 Louvred timber shutter
4 Bath spout and mixer tap
5 White ceramic bathtub
6 Door to bedroom
7 Marble tiled floor
8 Towel rail
9 Solid timber countertop
10 White ceramic benchtop basin
11 Entrance to shower room
12 Shower room
13 Wall-hung WC with concealed cistern
14 Bidet
15 Timber door to WC
16 Ceiling-mounted pendant light
17 Mirror
18 Wall-mounted spout and mixer tap to basin
19 Mares stone wall tiles
20 Painted plasterboard wall

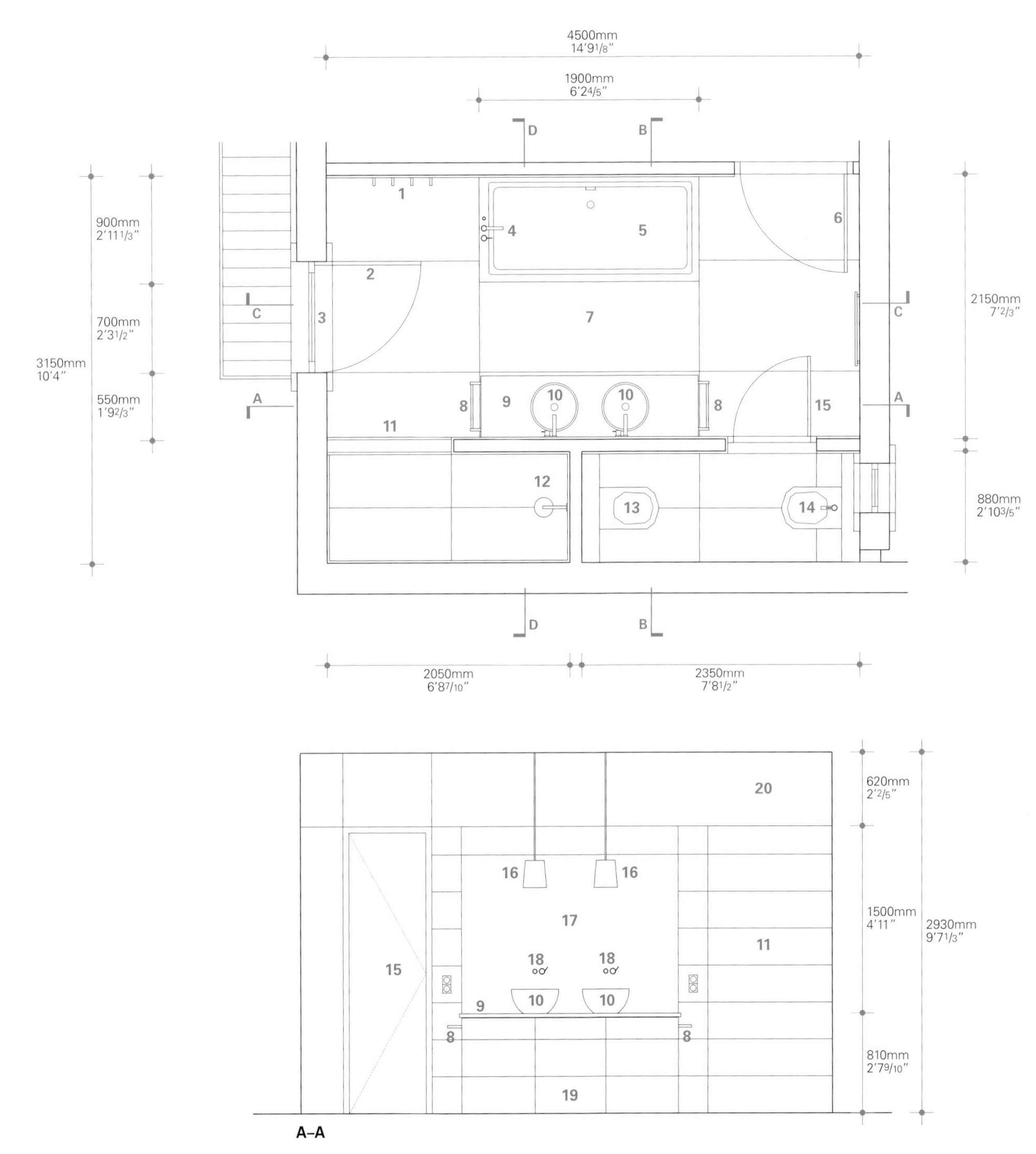

Sections B–B and C–C
1:50
1 White ceramic bathtub
2 Capri marble surround to bathtub
3 Heated towel rail
4 Ceiling-mounted pendant light
5 Wall-mounted spout and mixer tap to basin
6 White ceramic benchtop basin
7 Solid timber countertop
8 Glazed window with stone architrave
9 Mares stone wall tiles
10 Bidet
11 Wall-mounted towel hooks
12 Bath spout and mixer tap
13 Door to bedroom
14 Painted plasterboard wall

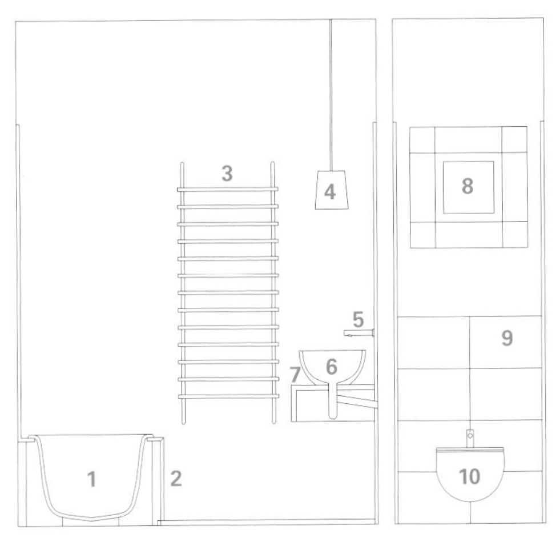

B–B

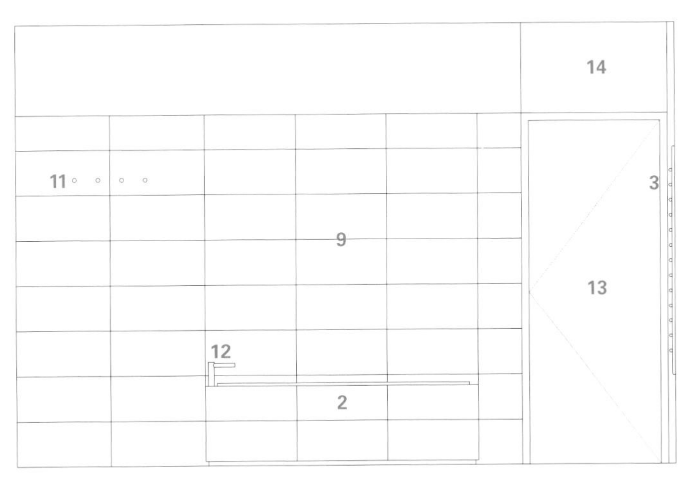

C–C

Timber

Serda Architects
Private Residence
María de la Salut, Mallorca, Spain

Section D–D
1:20

1 Painted plasterboard wall
2 Mares stone wall tiles to shower recess
3 Capri marble tiles to floor of shower laid to fall
4 Mares stone wall tiles
5 Ceiling-mounted pendant light
6 Mares stone architrave to terrace door
7 Timber-framed glazed door to terrace
8 Wall-mounted spout and mixer tap to basin
9 White ceramic benchtop basin
10 Solid timber countertop
11 Basin outlet pipe
12 Mixer tap to bath
13 Bath spout
14 Hand held shower fitting to bath
15 Mares stone cladding to bath surround
16 White ceramic bathtub
17 Wall-mounted towel hooks

Opposite
View of the bathing area for the master bathroom. The bathtub and vanity area enjoy views out over the almond grove.

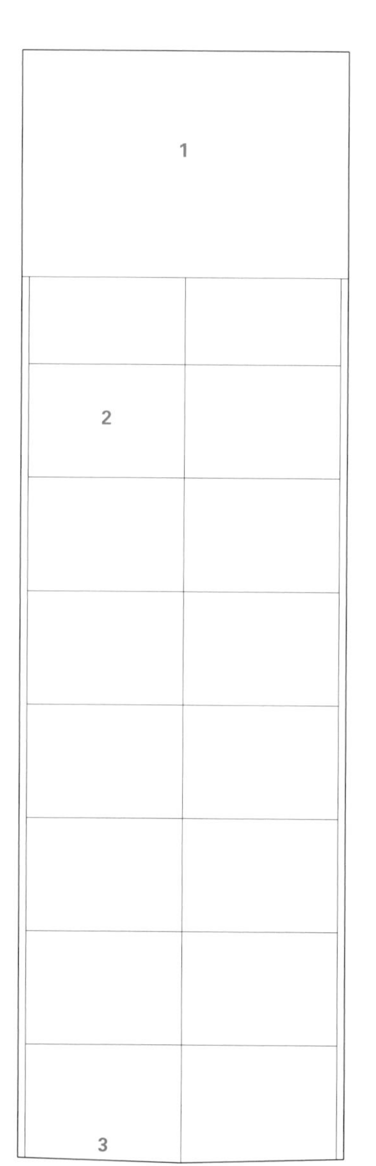

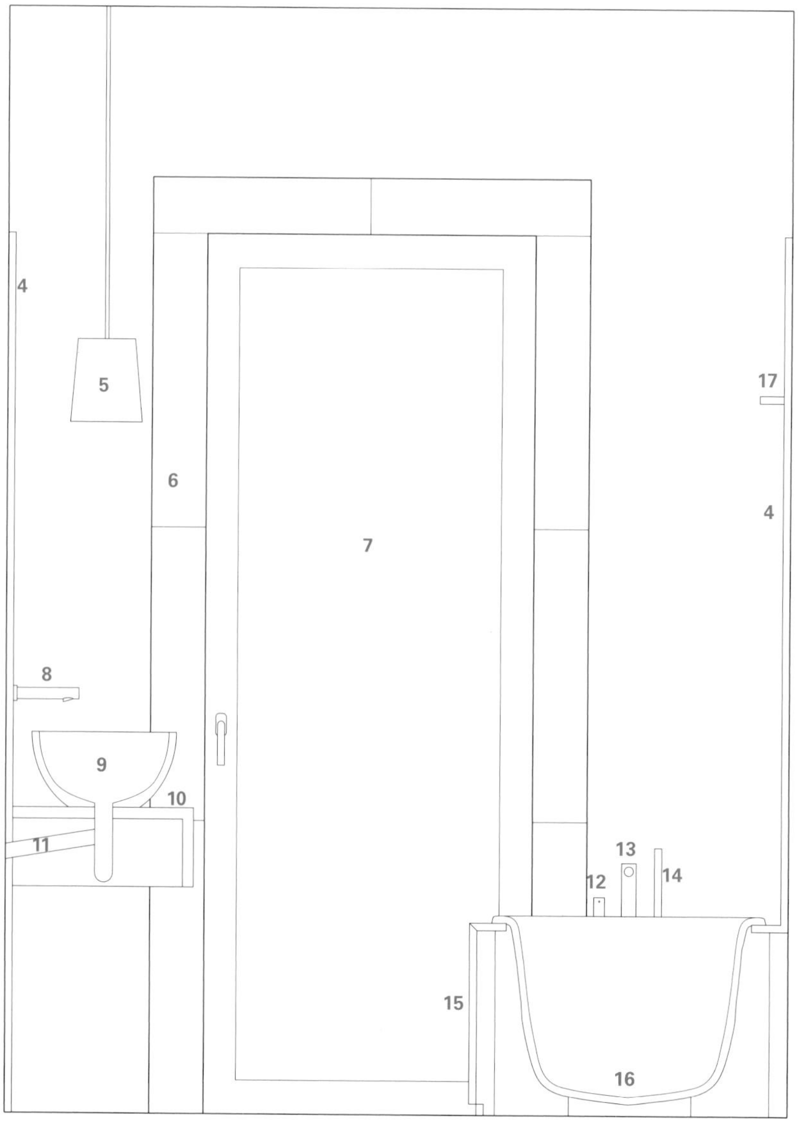

D–D

Materials
Countertop Solid teak
Joinery Solid teak
Floor Capri marble
Wall Tiles Mares stone
Lighting Vibia

Appliances and Fixtures
Basin Taps Roca
Basin Spout Roca
Basin Villeroy & Boch
Shower Taps Roca
Shower Head Roca
Bath Taps and Spout Roca
Bath Villeroy & Boch
WC Villeroy & Boch
Bidet Villeroy & Boch

Project Credits
Completion 2004
Client Alexander Eduard Serda
Project Architects Alexander Eduard Serda
Main Contractor Brues Baleares

Scape Architects

1 Perren Street London, England, UK

Commissioned as a private development for a British documentary film maker, 1 Perren Street is a significant new London town house in Kentish Town, North London. Originally an Organ Works, there is little that remains of its previous use in its new incarnation as a spacious five-bedroom house.

With minimal interventions to the façade, the project involved the remodelling of the interior to create a series of connected spaces and playful structural forms around a central stair. Guests arrive in a spacious entrance hall at ground level where private bedrooms are carved out of solid timber cladding.

A timber stair climbs towards the lighter, open-plan reception spaces of the upper floor, providing access to the social heart of the house. Visible from the kitchen and dining area, a six metre (20 foot) high translucent textured GRP (glass reinforced plastic) stair wall rises from the first floor to a frameless glass skylight two stories above, inviting guests upwards to the roof terrace.

On the top floor the stair wall rhymes with a sculptural bath in the master bedroom suite, which is cast in the same material. The bath is open to the bedroom area, and heralds two more private spaces situated behind it. One is a WC accessed via a sliding glass door, and the other is a larger space that houses the shower, basin and dressing area with larch-faced cupboard doors.

A restrained palette of warm natural materials is employed throughout: larch wood and phenolic-faced plywood and cork / rubber, with lighting fixtures embedded within the sculptural furniture components, including the bath, to further emphasize material warmth, movement and perspective depth.

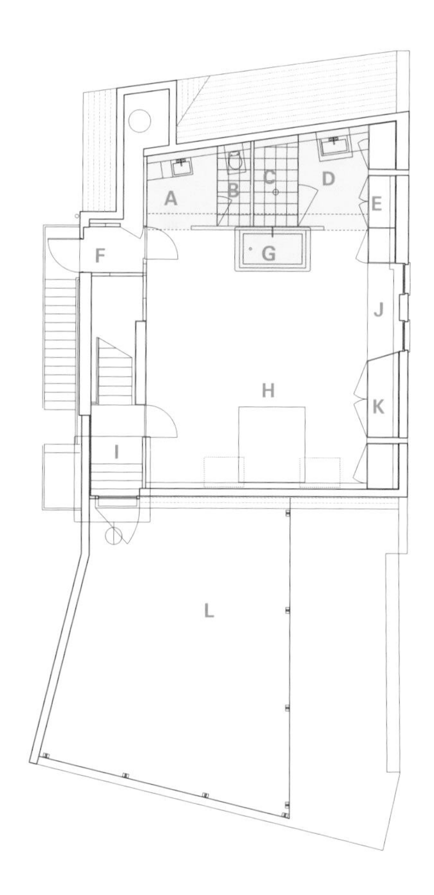

Opposite Left
A six metre (20 foot) high translucent textured glass-reinforced plastic stairwell rises from the first floor to a frameless glass skylight two stories above, inviting guests upwards to the master suite on the top floor.

Floor Plan
A Wash room
B WC
C Shower
D Wash room
E Storage cupboard
F Lobby
G Bathtub
H Bedroom
I Stair to roof terrace
J Window
K Storage cupboards
L Terrace

Left
The white ceramic rectangular wash basin sits on larch-clad joinery and is lit from above with a Velux window set into the slope of the roof structure. Beyond, a mirror-clad door leads to the shower enclosure.

Below
The glass-reinforced plastic bathtub is lit from within, and is a sculptural addition to the bedroom where it sits facing the bed.

Timber

Scape Architects
1 Perren Street
London, England, UK

Bathroom Plan, Elevation A and Section A–A
1:50

1 Larch-faced plywood benchtop
2 WC
3 Ceramic basin
4 Opal frost acrylic sliding door
5 Ceramic-tiled shower enclosure
6 Larch-faced plywood radiator cupboard under
7 Bathroom cupboard
8 Larch-faced plywood storage cupboards
9 Bespoke fibreglass bathtub with textured surround and integral lighting
10 White-painted plasterboard walls and ceiling
11 Roof light
12 Larch-faced plywood under-bench cupboards
13 Larch-faced plywood radiator cupboard
14 Opal frost acrylic door to shower enclosure

Opposite
Detailed view of the glass reinforced acrylic bathtub. The mould mimics rusticated stone, while the liquid nature of the material is revealed in tiny bubbles that are trapped in the acrylic as it dries.

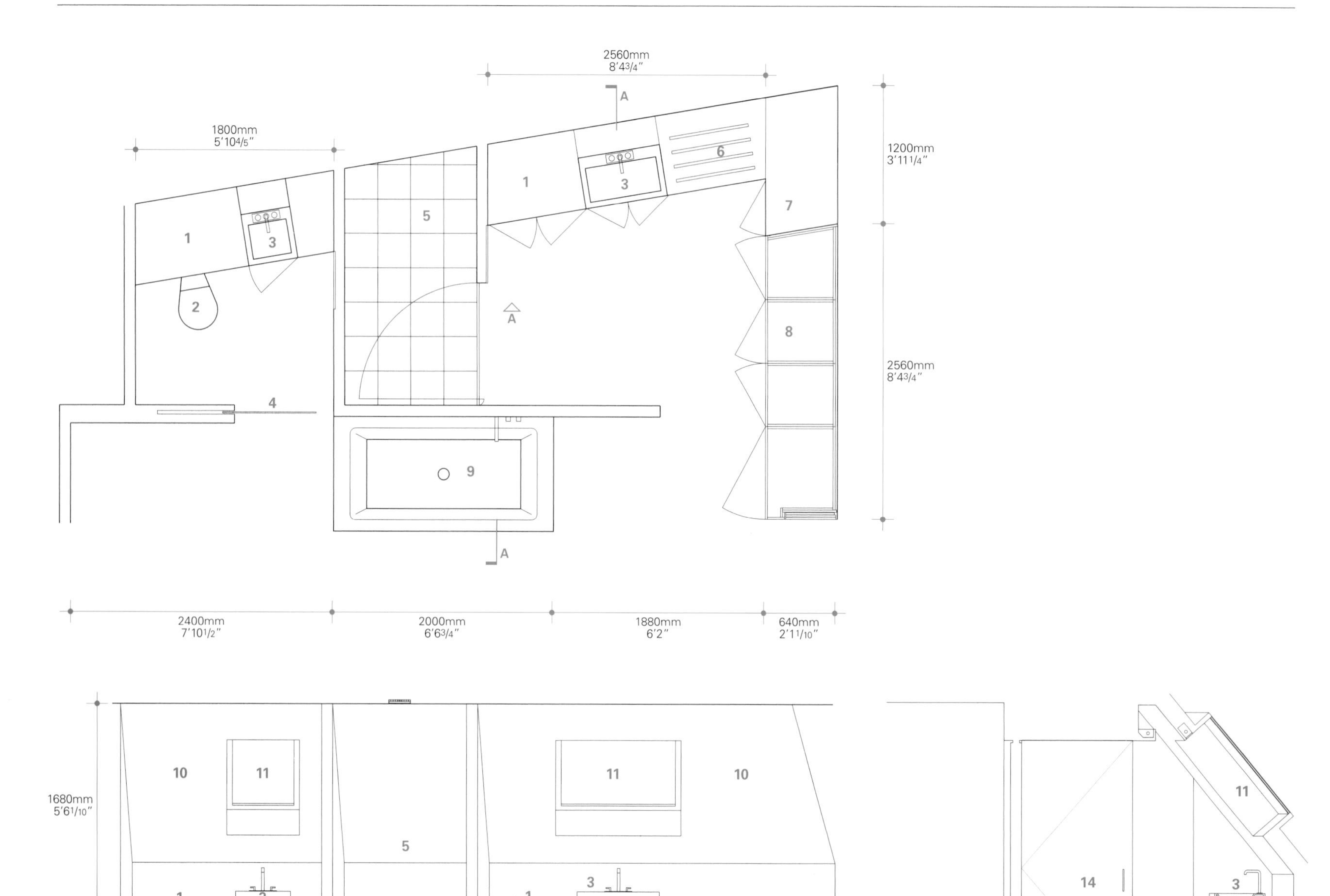

Materials
Benchtop Larch-faced plywood
Joinery Larch-faced plywood doors on melamine-faced birch plywood carcasses
Floor Larch-faced plywood

Fixtures
Taps and Spout Axor Hansgrohe three hole surface mounted mixer
Basin Aquaplus Solutions (APS-L87 Basin)
Bath and Jacuzzi Bespoke
WC Art / Design / Sculpture Tonic wall-mounted WC
Shower Head Bespoke
Lighting Bespoke

Project Credits
Completion 2006
Project Architects Chris Godfrey, Anya Wilson, Pieter Kleinmann, Tracy Mealiff, Ingrid Frydenbo-Bruvoll
Lighting Consultant Dan Heap Ltd
Main Contractor Turner Castle
Specialist Joinery Tin Tab
GRP Fabrications Design and Display Ltd

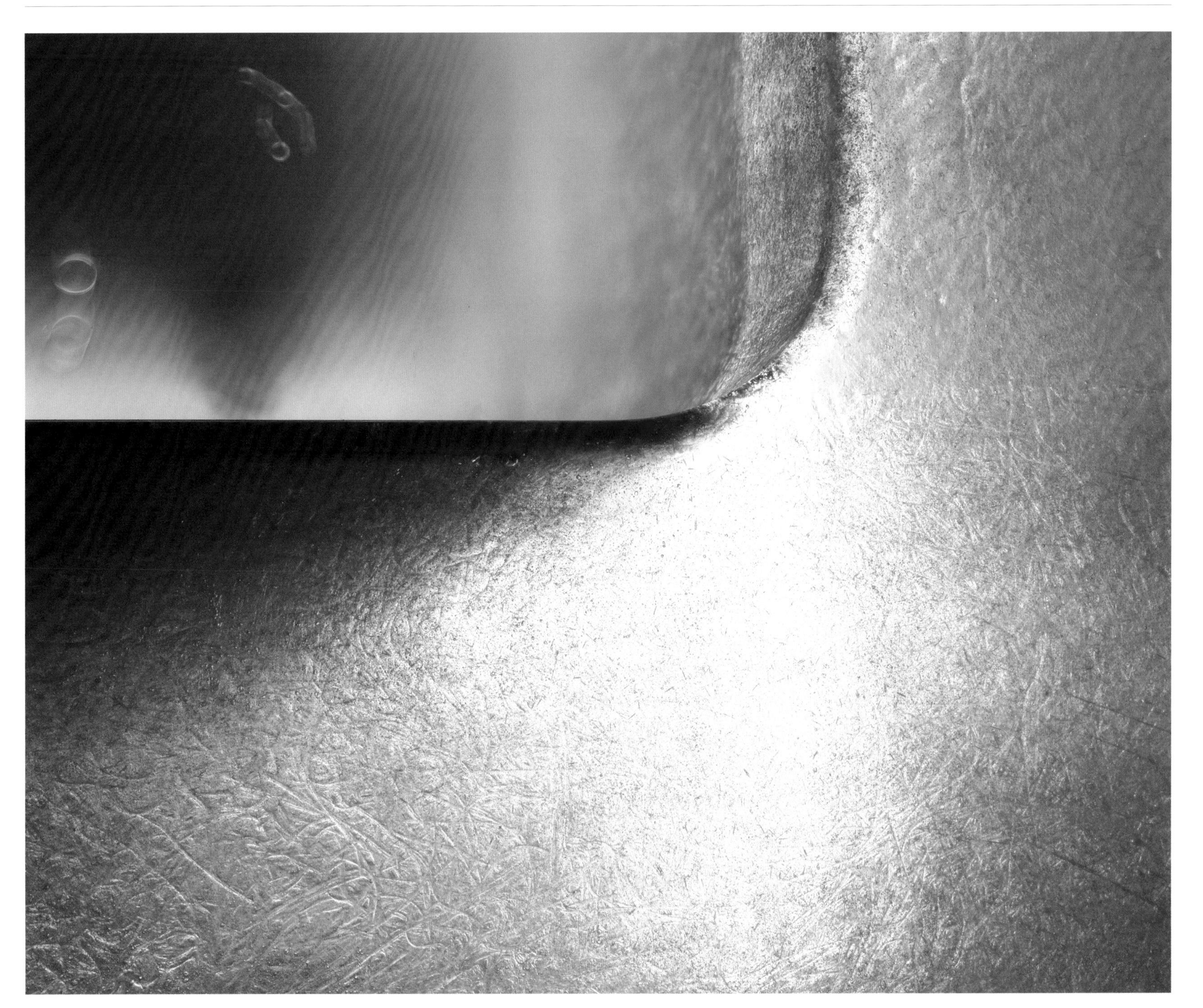

Mark English Architects Otani Residence Hayward, California, USA

The owner of this early 1970s tract home near San Francisco's East Bay area didn't deliberately aim to have an Asian-inspired master bathroom, although his Japanese heritage and training as an industrial designer may have influenced his preference for clean, straight lines and the natural colours and textures of wood and stone.

He decided to remodel his master suite as he was unhappy with its cluttered design and fussiness, characterized by dark-pine cabinets, wainscoting, and turned-wood accents. The architect, in response to this, set out to create a Zen-like bathing space.

All non-load-bearing walls were removed from the existing bathroom to create an uninhabited space, then additional space was borrowed from the adjoining bedroom for good measure. The extended bathroom also co-opted the attic above to give the bathroom a raked ceiling rising from its original 2.4 metre (8 foot) height at the sides to a 3.3 metre (11 foot) ridge line. The central ridge links a new dual vanity at one end and a soaking tub flanked by both open and enclosed shelving at the other.

Simplicity and logic also dictated the design of the vanity. Supported by steel brackets attached to the back of built-in bedroom storage, the limestone counter and maple drawers appear to float, without touching the floor or walls. Equally serene is the walk-in shower of shimmering glass block.

New joinery in the bedroom – a custom designed bed with many and varied storage spaces – complements the maple, limestone and stainless steel of the bathroom fittings.

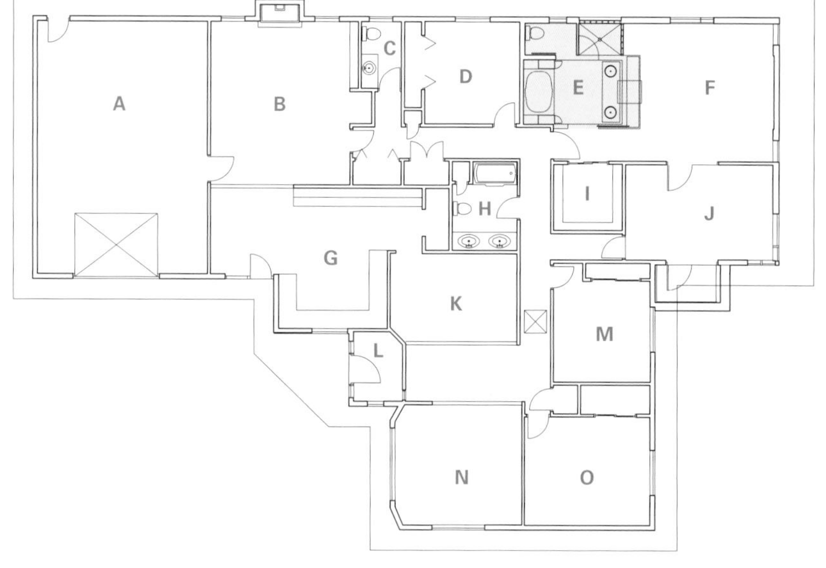

Opposite Left
The master bedroom features a new custom designed timber bed base with abundant storage at the foot and head.

Floor Plan
A Garage
B Living room
C WC
D Bedroom
E Master bathroom
F Master bedroom
G Kitchen
H Bathroom
I Dressing room
J Sun room
K Dining room
L Entrance
M Bedroom
N Family room
O Bedroom

Left
The double vanity area features a limestone counter with inset circular stainless steel basins. Underneath, maple veneer drawers provide ample storage, as do mirror-faced cupboards above.

Bottom Left
The bath area is designed to be a calm and relaxing enclave. Two sides of the enclosure are lined in maple cupboards and shelves.

Bottom Right
Adjacent to the vanity area, the shower is enclosed in glass blocks to create a bright, envigorating space, bathed in natural light.

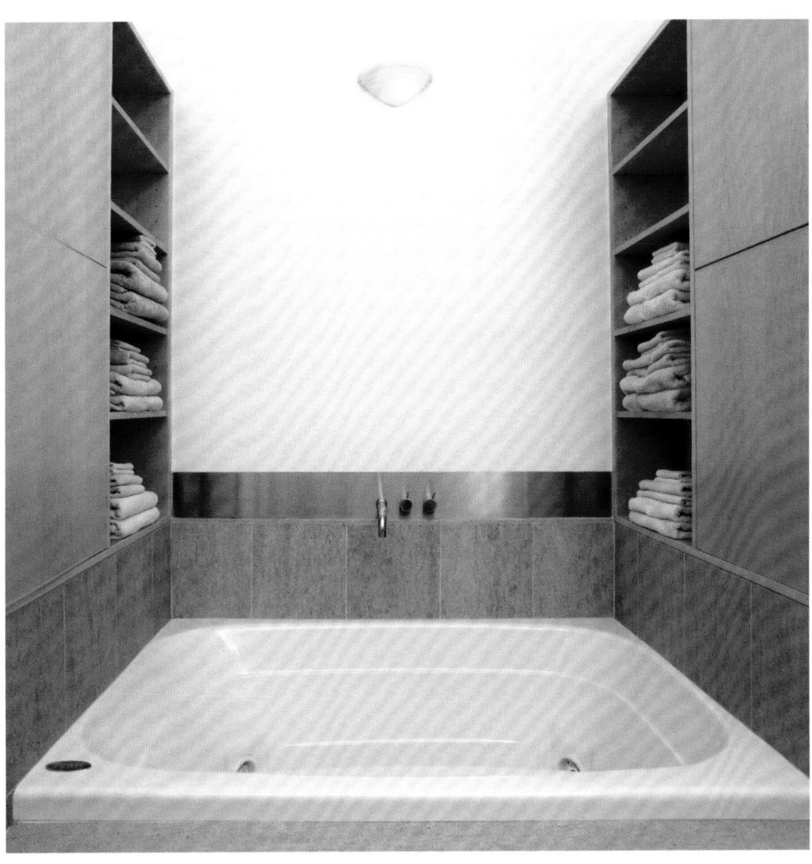

Timber

Mark English Architects
Otani Residence
Hayward, California, USA

Bathroom Plan, Sections A–A and B–B and Elevations A, B and C
1:50

1 WC
2 Glass block wall to shower enclosure
3 Shower
4 Maple veneer shelves
5 Maple veneer cupboards
6 Bathtub
7 Stainless steel basin
8 Limestone countertop
9 Mirror-faced cupboards
10 Limestone tiled floor
11 Limestone tiles to bath surround
12 Open shelving to WC
13 Maple veneer drawers under vanity bench
14 Painted plasterboard pitched ceiling
15 Limestone tiles to wall
16 Maple veneer shelves to bedroom
17 Maple veneer cupboards to bedroom

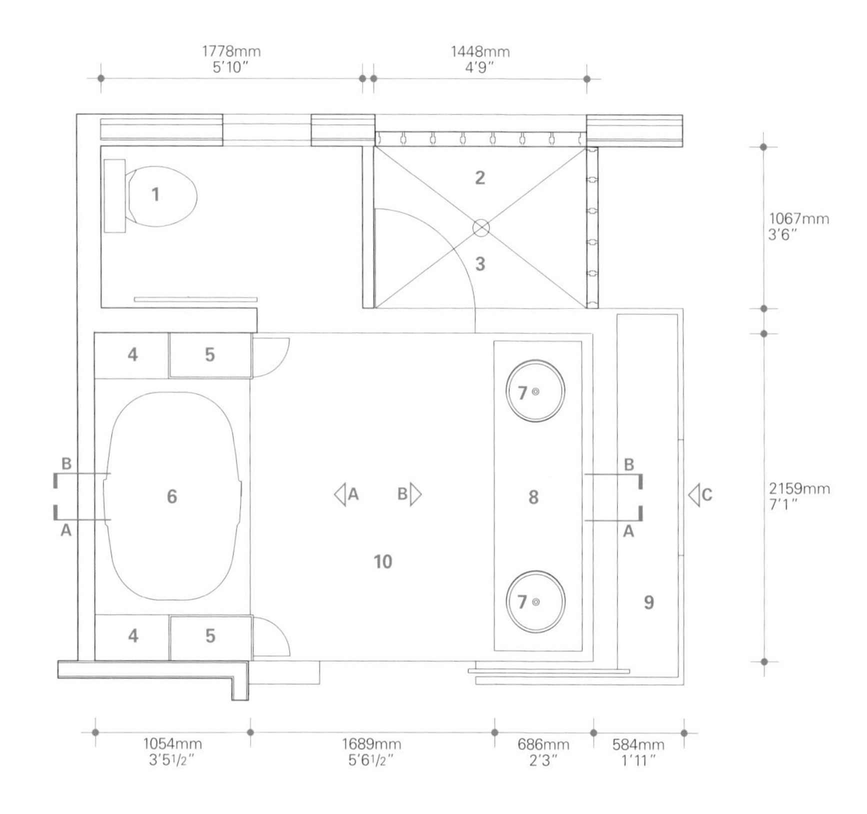

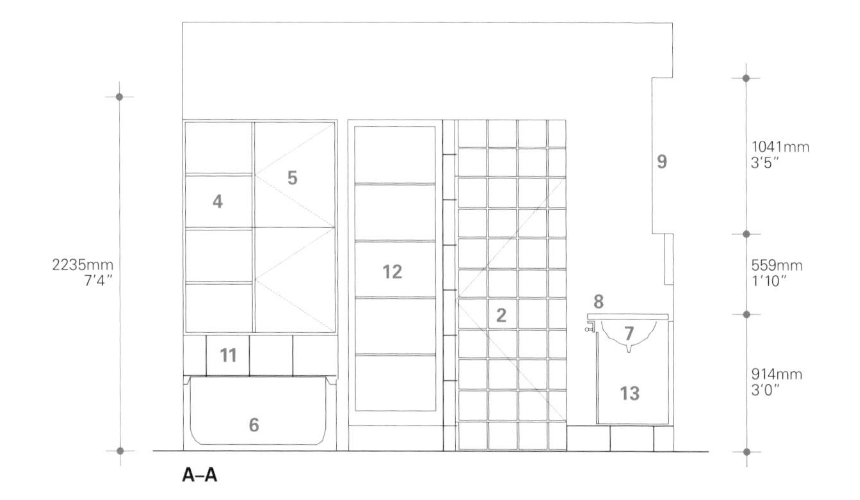

A–A

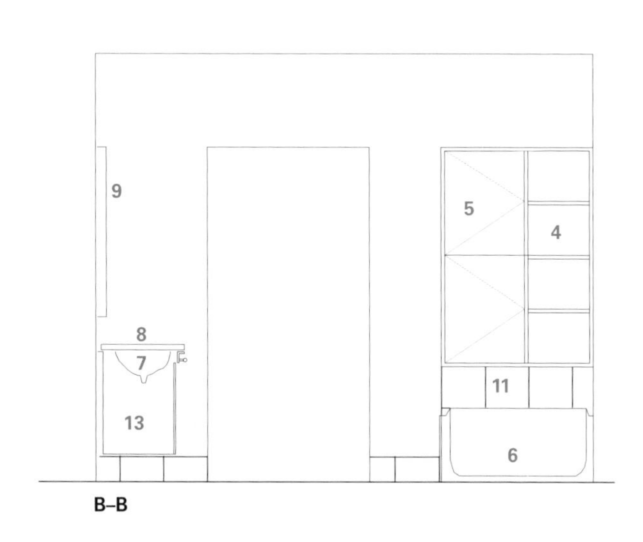

B–B

Materials
Benchtop Fontainebleau limestone on stainless steel frame
Joinery Quilted maple veneer
Floor Honed Fontainebleau limestone tiles
Glass Blocks Pittsburgh-Corning Vistabrik solid glass and Decora and Essex pattern regular series

Fixtures
Taps and Spout Kroin 111C
Basin Franke Rotondo stainless steel
Bath Jacuzzi Signa
WC Wall-mounted American Standard Afwall
Shower Head Grohe
Lighting Halo low-voltage

Project Credits
Completion 2003
Project Architects Mark English, Jeff Gard
Structural Engineer Mark English
Lighting Consultant Mark English

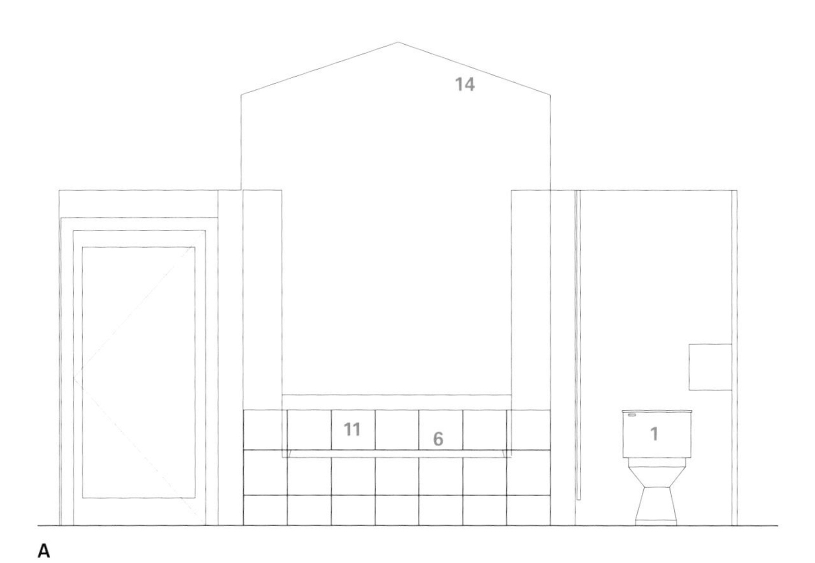

A

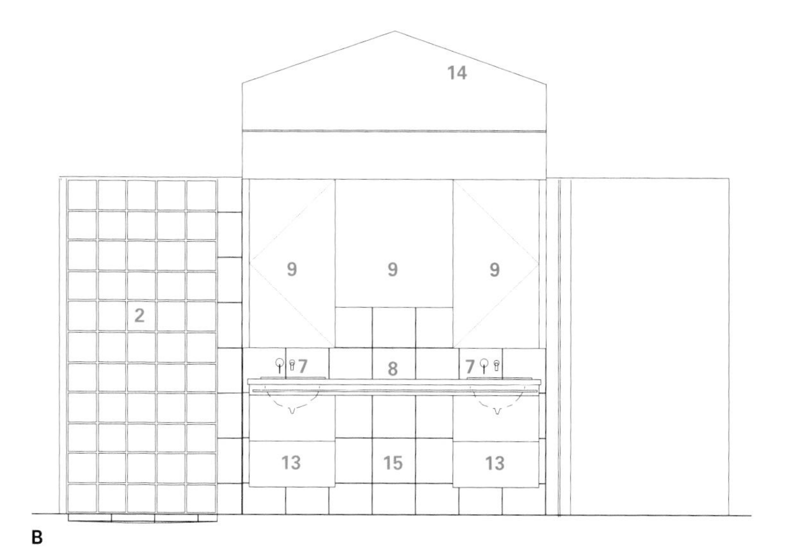

B

16
17
16
17
2
17

C

Stanic Harding

Hunters Hill Residence Sydney, New South Wales, Australia

This project involved the total remodelling of a dilapidated 1950s house on a waterfront property on Sydney harbour. The challenge was to create a light and airy house on this steep south-facing site while maintaining connections to the garden, the harbour and city views.

Three distinct pavilions were designed, linked by two courtyards allowing the house to gradually step down the site. The courtyards let sunlight enter the house via extensive glazing on the northern façades. The transparency and deep modulation of these façades offers protection from summer sunlight while permitting winter light to reach deeply into the house, while the courtyards provide access to level gardens and external living spaces. The waterfront terrace of the original house was maintained to offer a connection to the waterfront garden and the city, water and bridge views beyond.

The use of the low pitch skillion roof gives the house a subdued presentation to the harbour and neighbouring properties while the street frontage is deliberately restrained as a considered contemporary insertion offering limited visual access to the house.

The ensuite bathroom is an extension of the master bedroom, including the connection to the views. The space accommodates a large bath, shower, WC and double vanity. The simple palette of materials includes white wall tiling and dark large-scale ceramic floor tiles. A slatted timber step was introduced up to the bath, which also acts as a seat. The bath is clad in Italiana stone slabs which extend along the length of the vanity unit. The faces of the joinery within the vanity were finished to match to the colour of the wardrobes in the master bedroom.

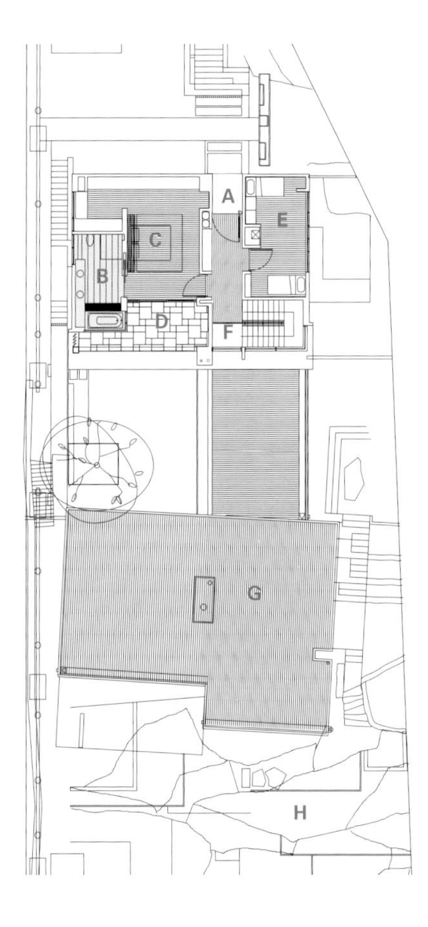

Opposite Left
View of the bedroom pavilion with the second bedroom (right) and the master bathroom (left). The bathtub projects out into a sheltered terrace which is directly accessible from the bedroom.

Floor Plan
A Main entrance
B Master bathroom
C Master bedroom
D Terrace
E Bedroom
F Stair down to lower level
G Roof to living pavilion
H Waterfront garden

Below Left
From two sides of the bathtub are panes of frameless glazing which look out over the roof of the living pavilion and to the harbour beyond. A panel of adjustable glass louvres provides ventilation and cooling.

Below Right
The minimal palette includes white painted walls, white roller blinds and a pale stone surround to the bathtub that continues into the countertop of the vanity unit. These are juxtaposed by the warmth of a reddish gold splashback of ceramic mosaic tiles, and by a deep timber step up to the bath that also acts as a seat.

Timber

Stanic Harding
Hunters Hill Residence
Sydney, New South Wales, Australia

Bathroom Plan and Section A–A
1:50
1 Italiana stone slabs to vanity countertop
2 Italiana stone slabs to bath surround
3 Clear glazed window
4 White ceramic bathtub
5 Louvred glazing
6 Timber bench and step up to bathtub
7 White ceramic basin
8 Basin spout and mixer tap
9 Magazine storage shelves
10 WC
11 Ceramic floor tiles
12 Sliding pocket door to bedroom
13 Heated towel rail
14 Shower head and controls
15 Fixed glass shower screen
16 Shower shelf
17 Fixed mirror panel
18 Mirror-clad cupboard doors with adjustable shelving behind
19 Ceramic mosaic tiled splashback
20 Spray polyurethane finish to MDF cupboard doors
21 White ceramic wall tiles
22 White painted plasterboard wall

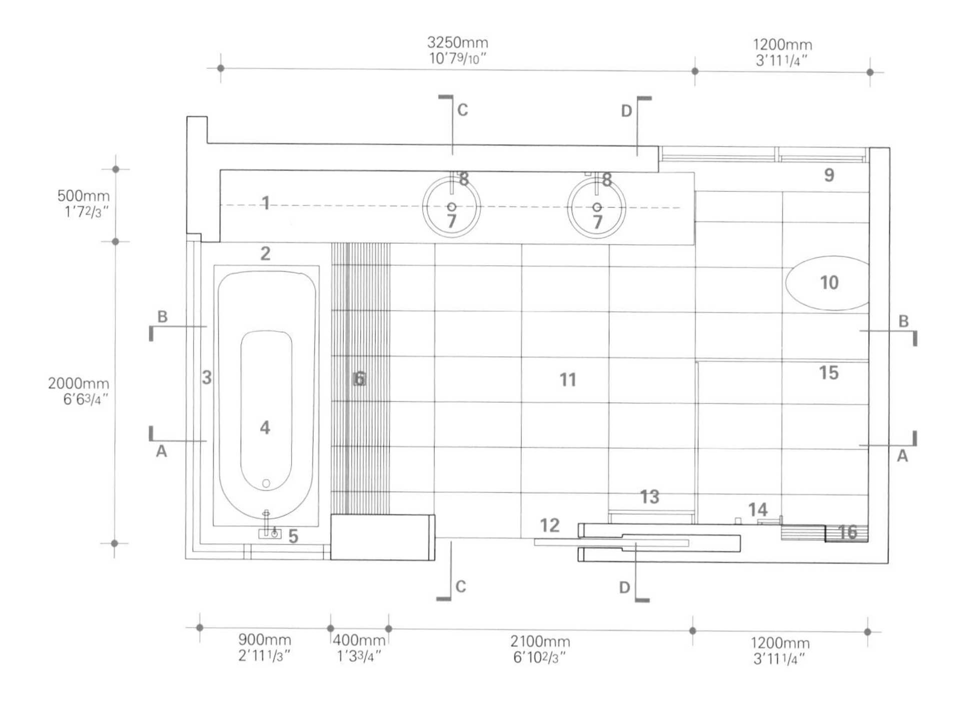

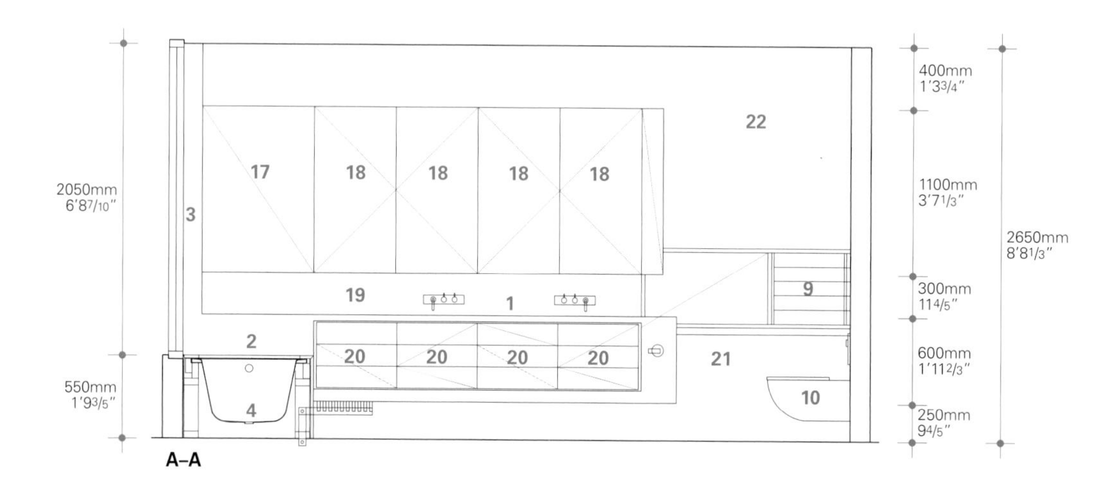

Sections B–B and C–C
1:50
1 Shower shelf
2 Shower head
3 Shower control valve
4 Heated towel rail
5 White ceramic wall tiles
6 Sliding pocket door to bedroom
7 Louvred glazing
8 Clear glazed window
9 Timber bench and step
10 White ceramic bathtub
11 Italiana stone slabs to bath surround
12 Concealed fluorescent light fittings
13 Mirror-clad cupboard doors with adjustable shelving behind
14 Basin spout and mixer tap
15 White ceramic basin
16 Spray polyurethane finish to MDF cupboard doors

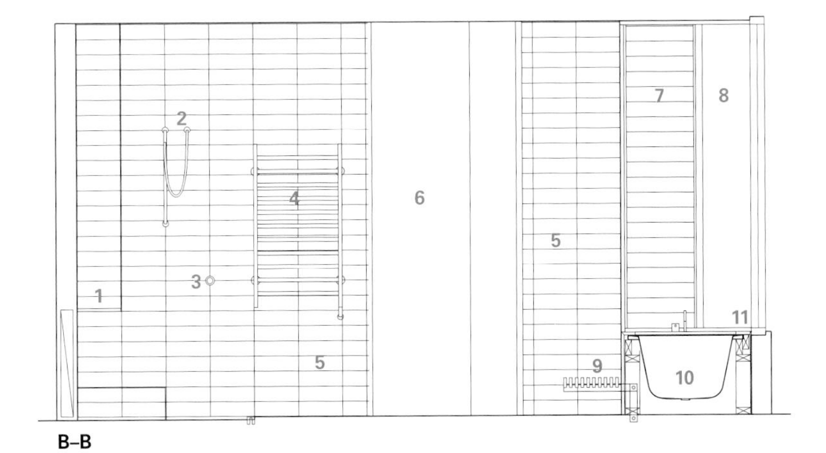

B–B

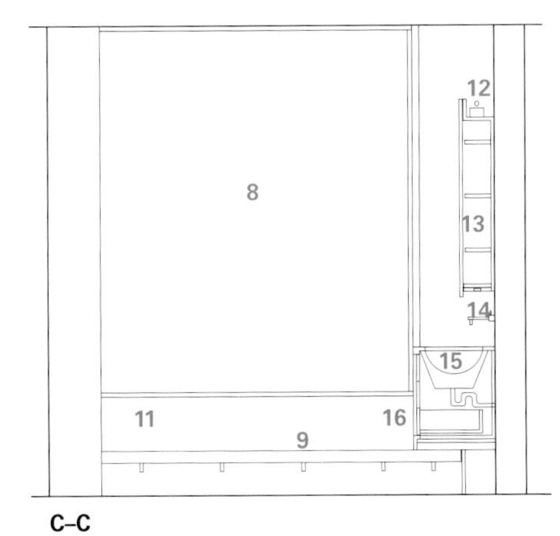

C–C

Stanic Harding
Hunters Hill Residence
Sydney, New South Wales, Australia

Section D–D
1:20
1 Window
2 Magazine storage shelves
3 WC flush panel
4 WC
5 White ceramic wall tiles
6 Fixed glass shower screen
7 Shower shelf
8 Ceramic floor tiles laid to fall in shower

Opposite
The predominantly white finishes are relieved by a selection of contrasting colours and textures including the variegated mosaic splashback and sprayed drawers to the vanity unit with integrated handles.

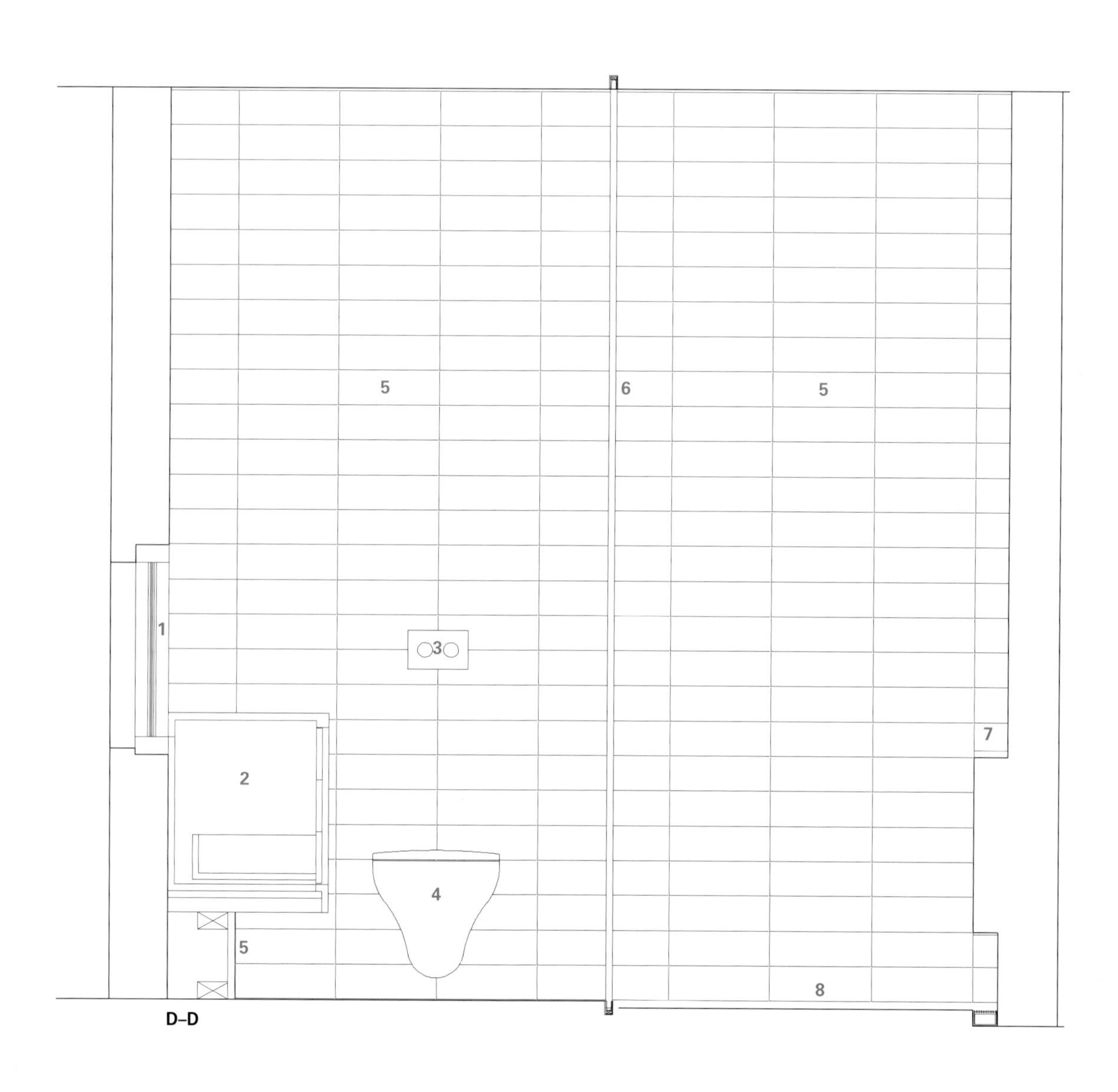

Materials
Countertop Italiana stone slabs with Cristal White – Q finish
Joinery MDF with polyurethane finish in Champagne Bronze 70 per cent gloss
Floor 600 x 300 mm (2 x 1 foot) Savannah Naturale ceramic tiles from Bisanna
Splashback 20 x 20 mm (3/4 x 3/4 inch) ceramic mosaic Dahlia tiles from Bisanna
Wall Tiles 600 x 100 mm (2 foot x 4 inch) Arabian Matt White from Onsite
Lighting Modular downlights

Appliances and Fixtures
Basin Taps Vola
Basin Spout Vola
Basin Caroma Concorde 400 underslung basins
Shower Taps Vola
Shower Head Vola
Bath Taps and Spout Vola
Bath Kaldewei Classic 1800
WC Duravit Columba
Timber Step Blackbutt decking timbers set on edge

Project Credits
Completion 2006
Project Architects Andy Harding, Michael Alder, Harriet Spring, Bianca Pohio
Structural Engineers Partridge Partners
Cost Consultants Q.S. Plus
Main Contractor Prime Form
Landscape Architect Jane Irwin Landscape Architecture
Joiner Mark Watson Design
Electrician West + West
Stone Mason Sharwood Stone

Barton Myers Associates

Rogers Residence
Los Angeles, California, USA

This elegant house is comprised of a group of three buildings positioned around a central courtyard. The three buildings form an ensemble that frames and encloses the intimate central courtyard and lap pool. The courtyard's location, facing southeast, takes full advantage of sunlight and encompasses a sun filled area for the lap-pool, a covered and semi-protected patio for year-round outdoor dining and covered porches for lounging and entertaining.

The main building is an exposed structural steel frame, with a metal deck ceiling and concrete floors. The structures are open loft spaces, enclosed by glazed aluminium sectional doors, which can be opened and closed to varying degrees. North-facing clerestory windows provide the exterior elevation with constant, even light. Galvanized rolling shutters above every glazed opening create a secondary envelope that provides additional security, insulation and sun control.

The main focal point of the residence's public areas is the kitchen, which is designed for entertaining. An intimate seating area in front of the fireplace provides the perfect spot for enjoying the morning coffee and newspapers.

The master bathroom is divided into 'his' and 'her' sections. The 'his' side features a marble counter with above-counter mounted sink and under-counter drawers and cabinets. Closets by Poliform accommodate clothing storage.

'Her' side contains the large bathtub and the water-closet enclosure. A large shared shower connects both sides of the master bathroom. A generous north-facing skylight provides an abundance of daylight. As in the rest of the house, heating and cooling is supplied through unobtrusive under-cabinet stainless steel grilles.

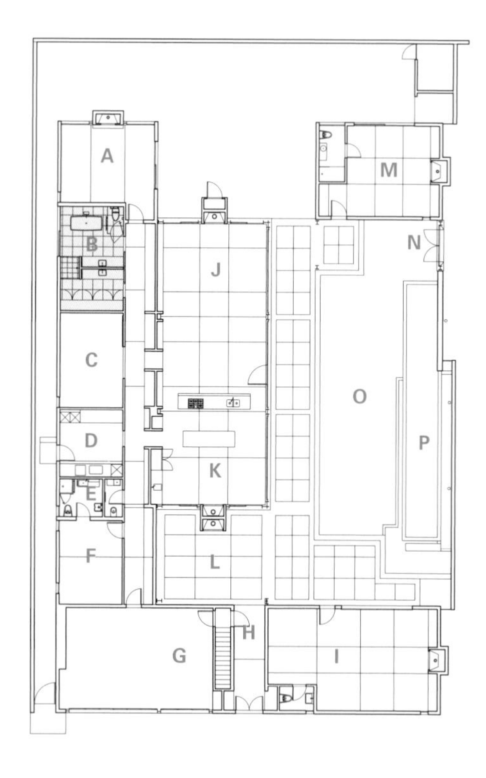

Opposite Left
View of the main living space from the courtyard. A covered area of polished concrete mediates between the structured formality of the house and the informality of the garden where drought-resistant native plants, gravel and boulders create a striking relaxation space.

Floor Plan
A Master bedroom
B Bathroom
C Media room
D Butlers pantry
E Bathroom
F Bedroom
G Garage
H Secondary entrance
I Games room
J Living and dining room
K Kitchen
L Outdoor dining area
M Guest house
N Main entrance
O Landscaped courtyard
P Lap pool

Left
View of the main living spaces from the garden. Secondary spaces such as bedrooms and bathrooms are located beyond the expansive library wall along the perimeter of the house.

Bottom Left
View of the master bathroom from 'her' side, where a large bathtub (bottom left) takes pride of place. The shower enclosure (right) is accessible from both 'his' and 'her' sides of the bathroom. Stone-clad dividing walls contrast with warm timber for the joinery and perimeter walls.

Timber

Barton Myers Associates
Rogers Residence
Los Angeles, California, USA

Bathroom Plan, Section A–A, Elevations A and B
1:50

1 Storage cupboards
2 Walk-through shower
3 Towel rail
4 Line of skylight over
5 White ceramic basin on marble countertop
6 Sliding glass doors to hallway
7 Sliding glass doors to exterior
8 Ceramic bathtub
9 Free-standing column bath taps and spout
10 Towel rail to bath area
11 WC
12 Ceramic floor tiles
13 Shower head
14 Track-mounted light fixture
15 Skylight over vanity bench
16 Ceramic tile-clad dividing wall between vanity bench and shower area
17 Mirror
18 Wall-mounted basin spout
19 Under-counter drawers
20 Under-counter cupboards
21 Stainless steel grille

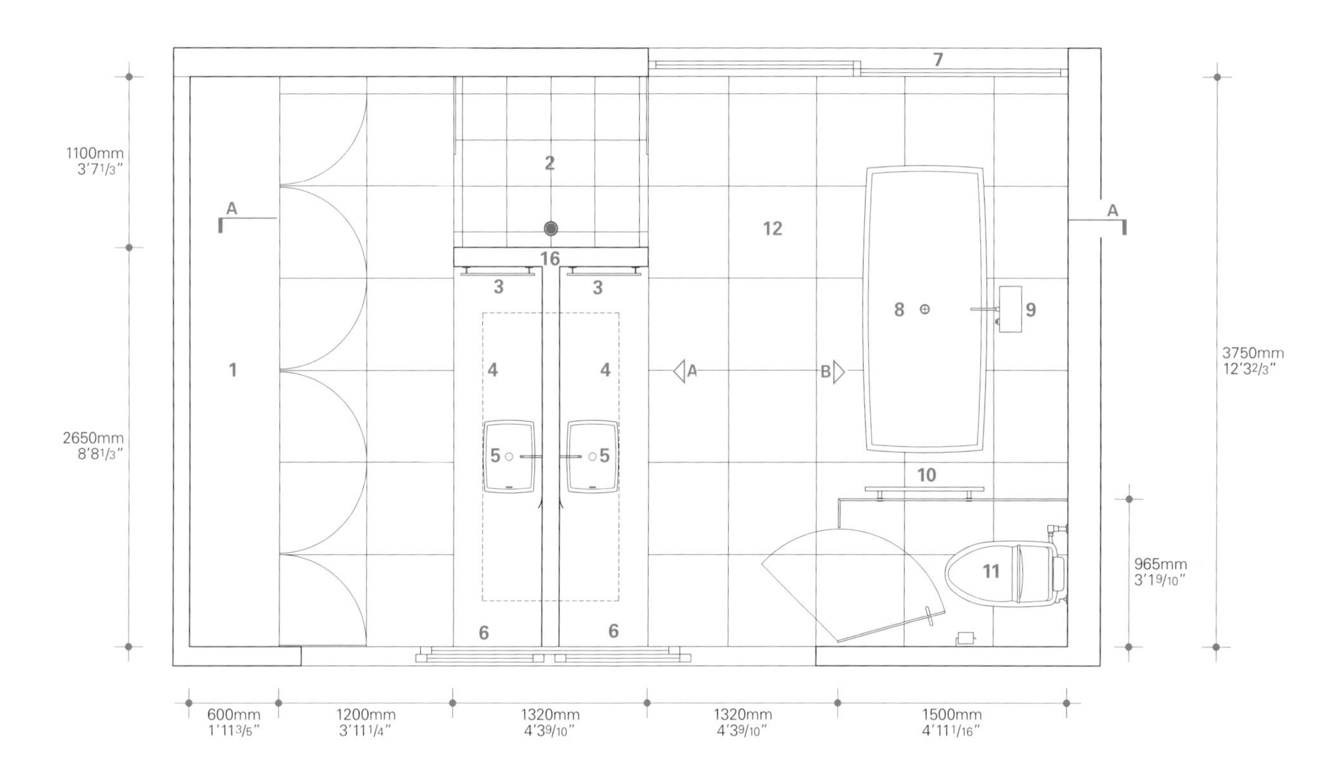

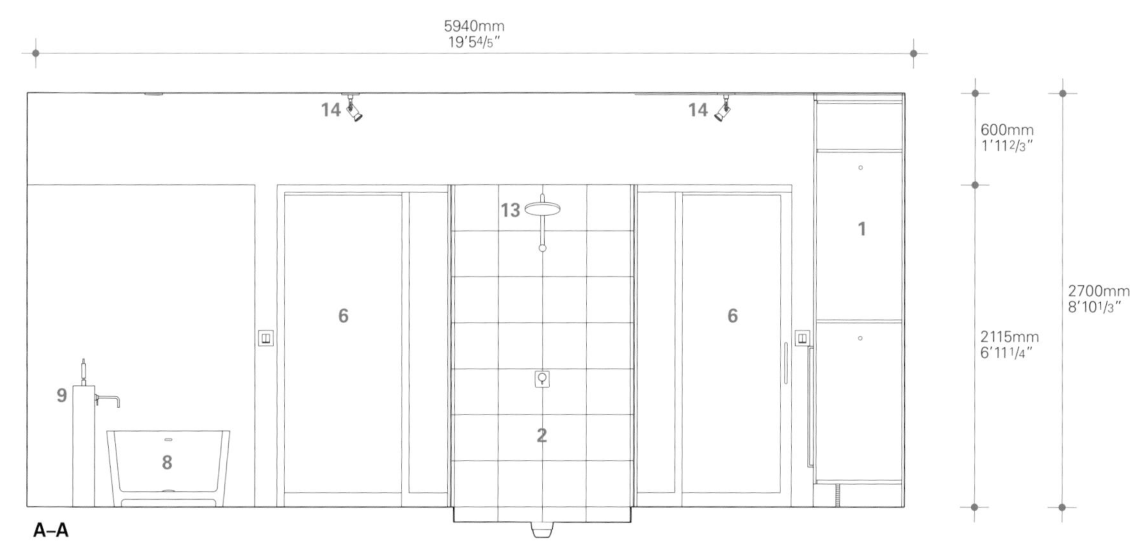

Materials
Countertop Carrara marble
Joinery Poliform USA
Floor Royal Mosa ceramic tiles
Tiles Royal Mosa ceramic tiles
Lighting Boffi and Aucco lighting fixtures

Appliances and Fixtures
Basin Gobi wash-basin from Boffi, designed by Marcel Wanders
Shower Taps Boffi minimal thermostatic built-in shower tap with wall plate designed by Giulio Gianturco
Shower Head Boffi shower head designed by Giulio Gianturco
Bath Taps and Spout Floor-mounted KWC mechanical system designed by Giulio Gianturco with stainless steel satinized finish
Bath Monoblock Gobi bathtub from Boffi
WC Toto Neorest 600

Project Credits
Completion 2006
Project Architects Barton Myers, Thomas Schneider, Ed Levin, Jorge Narino
Structural Engineers Norman J. Epstein
Services Engineers The Sullivan Partnership
Landscape Architect Landscapes Designed
Lighting Consultant Horton Lees Brogden
General Contractor Mark Caputo
Cost Consultant C.P. O'Halloran & Associates

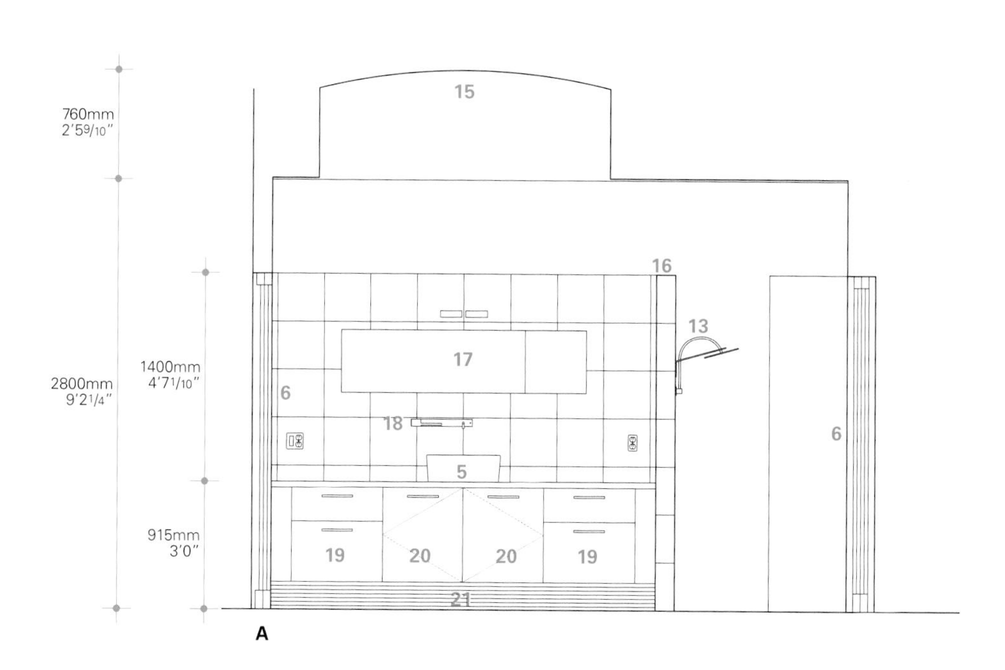

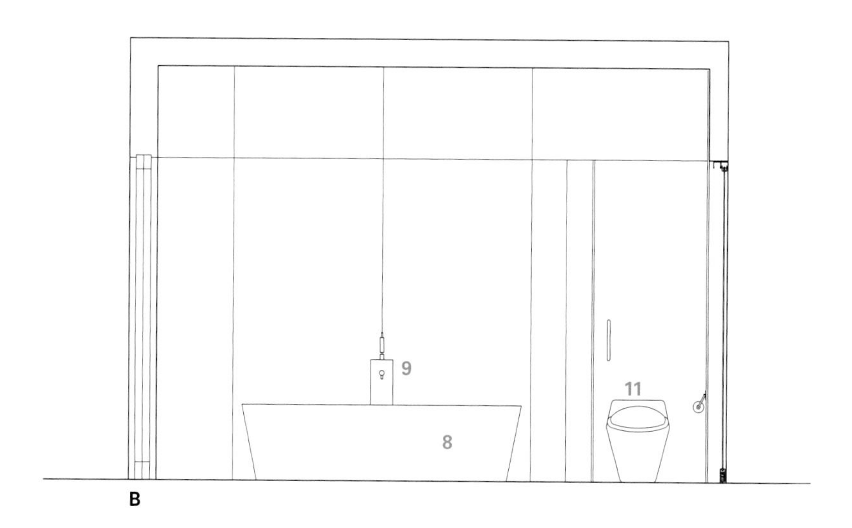

Waro Kishi + K. Associates Architects

Musashino Hills House Tokyo, Japan

This house, designed for a writer, is located on a hillside overlooking Tamagawa River to the south. The site is situated off the street and surrounded by a wooded environment. The writer works at home, and therefore required a house that provided a distinct separation between the private sleeping and work places, and the living spaces.

The house is situated on a steeply sloping site which suggested a three-storey building that would naturally allow for the separation of elements of the programme that the client wished for. The structure is arranged as a double-deck concrete structure with a box made of steel and glass placed on top. Only the top floor can be seen from the approach which is located on the highest level of the site, and it is here that the large open-plan living spaces, including the kitchen and dining areas, float in their glass box over the suburban landscape.

One level down is the private floor with the master bedroom, bathroom and a large terrace. The bathroom occupies a long slender space, accessed directly from the bedroom. At one end are a vanity and WC, with the other devoted to a wet room containing showering space and a sunken bath accessed via a rise of timber steps and with a picture window with views of the landscape.

The lowest floor houses a large guest room with its own entrance as well as the writer's office. The house is arranged so that as one steps down from the top floor that opens itself toward the urban landscape, the view gradually closes in and transforms into an outlook over the trees and greenery in the immediate vicinity.

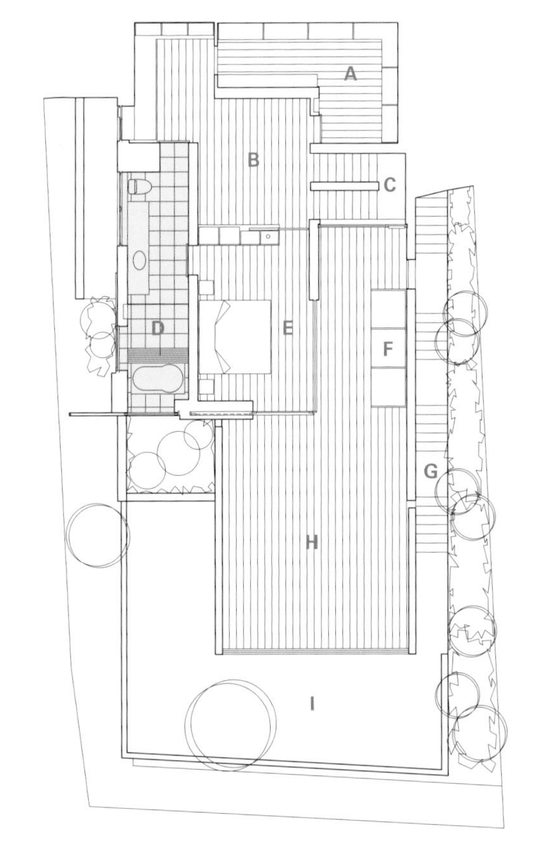

Opposite Left
View of the house from the street, where the entrance gives direct access to the living spaces. Here, the concrete frame acts as a privacy screen, stepping down the site and creating walls, some with punctured openings, to the terraces that feature on every level.

Floor Plan
A Terrace
B Sitting room
C Stair from upper and lower floors
D Master bathroom
E Master bedroom
F Skylight to lower level
G Garden stair
H Terrace
I Garden terrace below

Left
View of the master bathroom from the bedroom. Timber joinery provides warmth and texture in the otherwise polished stone interior. A full-height wall of glass separates the showering and bathing area at the end of the space.

Above
The bathroom (lower left) features a large picture window with views over the wooded site. The adjoining bedroom (lower right) enjoys direct access to a large terrace. Above, the living spaces cantilever over the terrace in a steel-framed glass box.

Timber

Waro Kishi + K. Associates Architects
Musashino Hills House
Tokyo, Japan

Bathroom Plan and Section A–A
1:50

1 Stone tile-clad services duct with hand held shower fitting over bath
2 Clear-glazed openable picture window
3 Stone tile-clad bath surround
4 White ceramic sunken bathtub
5 Timber stairs up to bath level
6 Clear-glazed openable picture window
7 Floor drain for ceiling-mounted shower over
8 Frameless full-height glass screen wall with door
9 Timber cabinet with cupboards under and polished stone countertop
10 Timber cabinet with drawers under and polished stone countertop
11 White under-mounted ceramic basin in polished stone countertop with cupboards under
12 Timber cabinet with integrated washing machine under and polished stone countertop
13 WC / bidet
14 Polished stone floor tiles
15 Door to bedroom
16 Wall-mounted mirror
17 Polished stone wall tiles

Opposite
View of the sunken bathtub. A short flight of timber steps leads up to a polished stone surround. A picture window provides calming views of the leafy landscape.

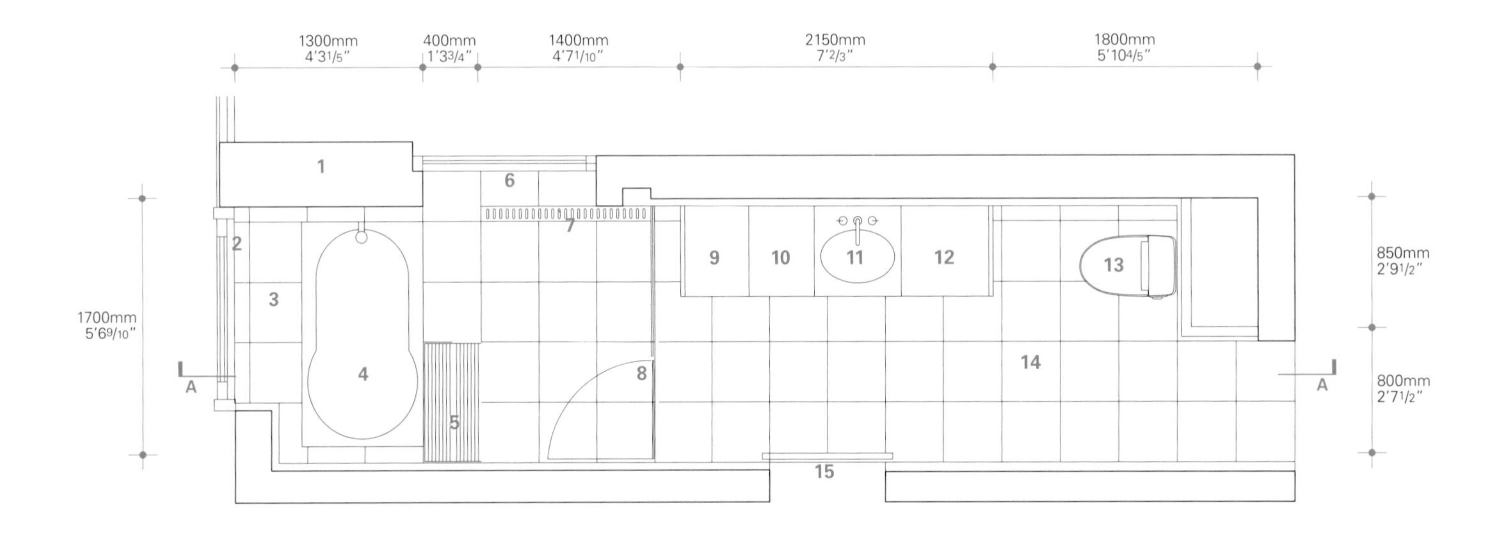

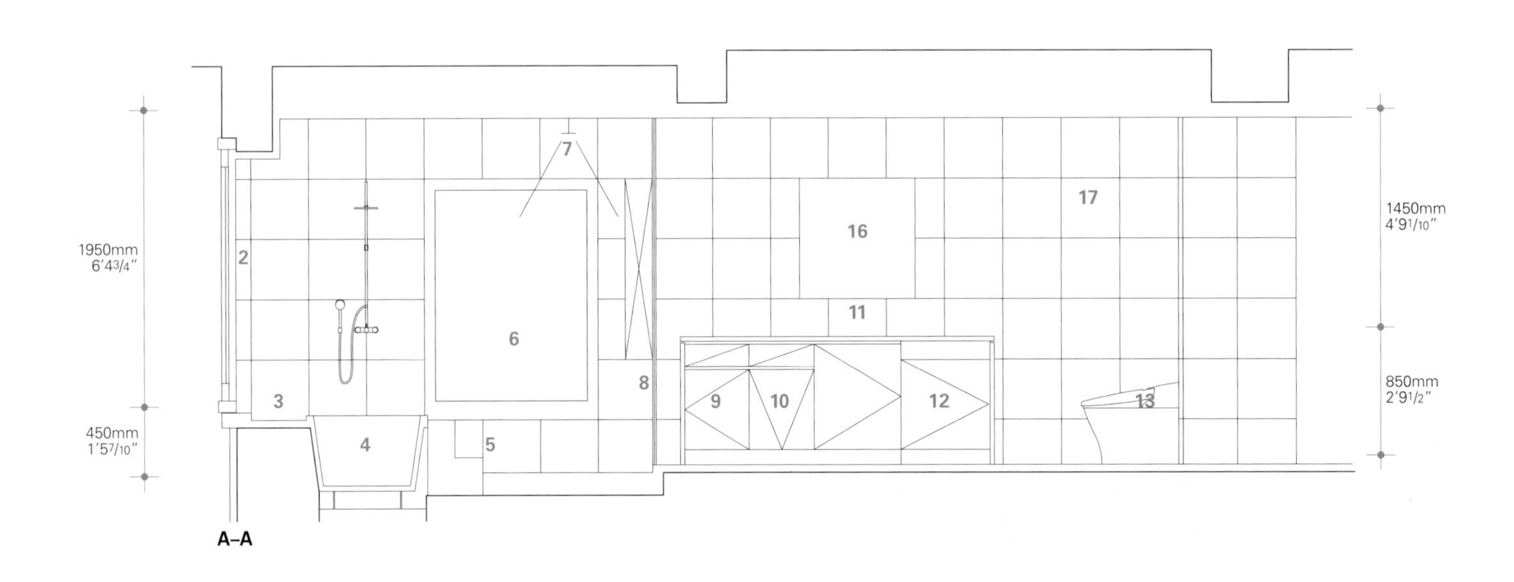

Materials
Countertop Marble
Floor Marble
Wall Tiles Marble
Lighting Ceiling-mounted spot lights

Appliances and Fixtures
Basin Taps Vola
Basin Spout Vola
Basin INAX
Shower Taps INAX
Shower Head Grohe
Bath Taps and Spout Toto
Bath Jaxson
Heated Towel Rail PS
WC / Bidet INAX

Project Credits
Completion 2005
Project Architects Waro Kishi, Miki Murakawa
Structural Engineer Urban Design Institute
Main Contractor Mori Kenetsu-Kogyo

Seth Stein Architects

Golob House
North Caicos, Turks and Caicos Islands, British West Indies

This luxurious holiday home is located on a deserted beach on North Caicos Island. Each of the three bedrooms, and the main living accommodation, are expressed as individual structures connected by a raised timber walkway. The indigenous dwarf tropical dry forest provides natural screening between the individual pavilions.

The plan, whilst adhering to the constraints of the local authorities regarding the distance of buildings from the beach, nevertheless follows a rational grid dictated by the various forms of enclosure as set out in the brief.

Various aspects of shelter are provided through a range of enclosure options – mesh screens to maintain air movement, and louvres within sliding or fixed panels to manipulate natural light, ventilation and storm protection. The elimination of glazing as an enclosing element, in conjunction with the shaded perimeter, maximizes openness while eliminating solar gain. The façade system, which consists of a timber frame module, acts as a filter to the natural environment by adjusting manually to daylight, storm or insect conditions.

In the bedroom pavilions, the rear elevation can be opened up completely to unite the shower with the natural vegetation which itself becomes an enclosing element.
The bedroom pavilions are arranged with the sleeping area at the centre, gradually opening up towards the beach with a screened sitting area and an open verandah.

On the other side of the bedroom, the bathroom occupies one structural bay and includes a semi-enclosed WC and bidet area, cupboards to house the hot water tank and wardrobes and a niche for hanging rails and hooks. The main space features a shower with a curved corrugated steel screen that opens up to the landscape, and a custom made cantilevered concrete bench with a sculptural stone basin.

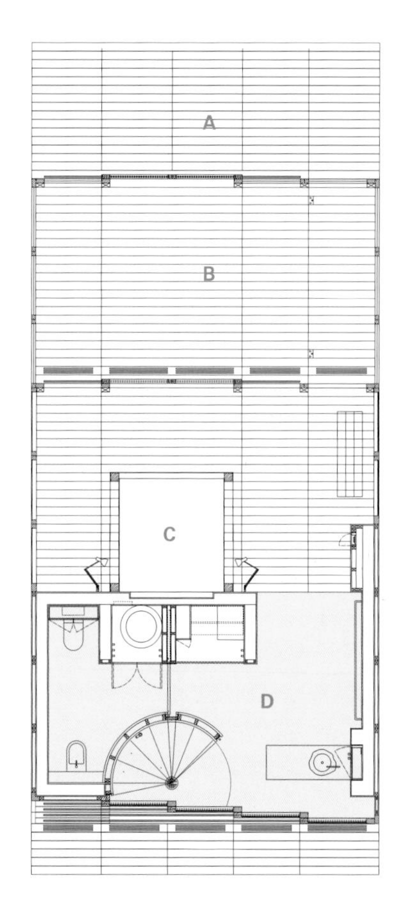

Opposite Left
View of the bedroom pavilions. The open verandahs face the beach and are protected by an overhang on the curved roof which culminates in a louvred *brise soleil*. The bedroom area is enclosed by timber louvres that are highly adjustable in order to respond to changing environmental conditions.

Floor Plan
A Open verandah
B Semi-enclosed terrace
C Bedroom
D Bathroom

Below
In the bathroom, the open shower and sculptural vanity bench take centre stage. The galvanized corrugated screen to the shower is attached to a structural timber frame with the shower set mounted at the centre, and making minimal contact with the screen. The basin, sculpted from stone to resemble a natural boulder, echoes the apparent rusticity of the shower screen while contrasting with the otherwise refined aesthetic evident in the finishes and fixtures.

Timber

Seth Stein Architects
Golob House
North Caicos, Turks and Caicos Islands, British West Indies

Bathroom Plan and Sections A–A and B–B 1:50

1 White-painted alcove with hooks and hanging rails
2 Cupboard with shelving and razor socket to interior and mirror to inside face of doors
3 Carved stone basin
4 Cantilevered concrete bench
5 Sliding panelled doors on recessed floor and ceiling tracks
6 Wardrobe alcove with hanging rail, adjustable shelves and drawers with unbleached calico curtain
7 Spray finish cupboard doors with circular finger-pulls to hot water cupboard
8 Concealed cistern to WC with cupboards above
9 WC
10 Bidet with mirrored panel to wall behind
11 Corrugated cladding to shower enclosure
12 Stainless steel shower set
13 Shower drain
14 Polished concrete floor to shower area
15 Timber decking
16 Basin spout
17 Cupboard above WC
18 Cupboard containing air-conditioning unit

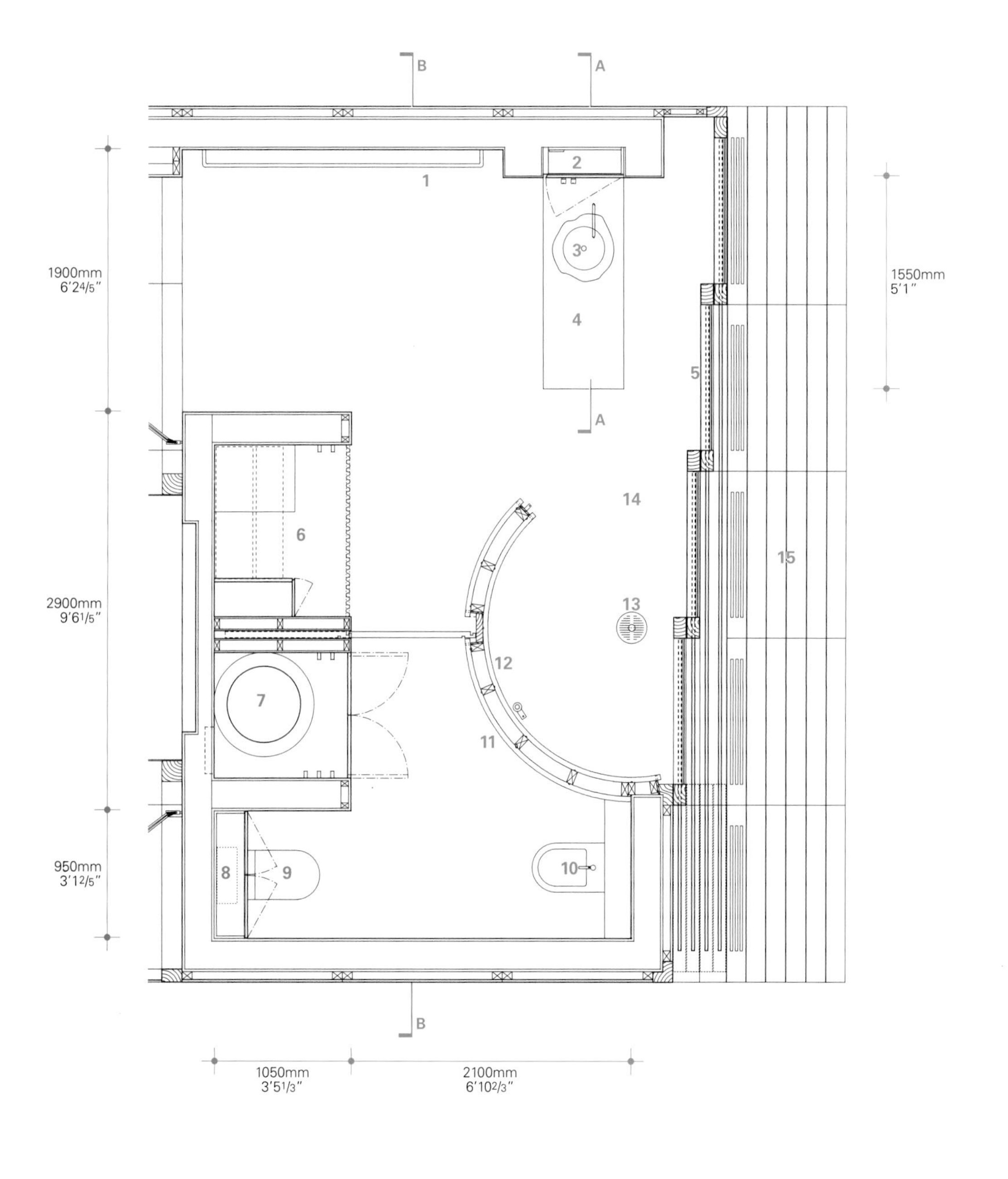

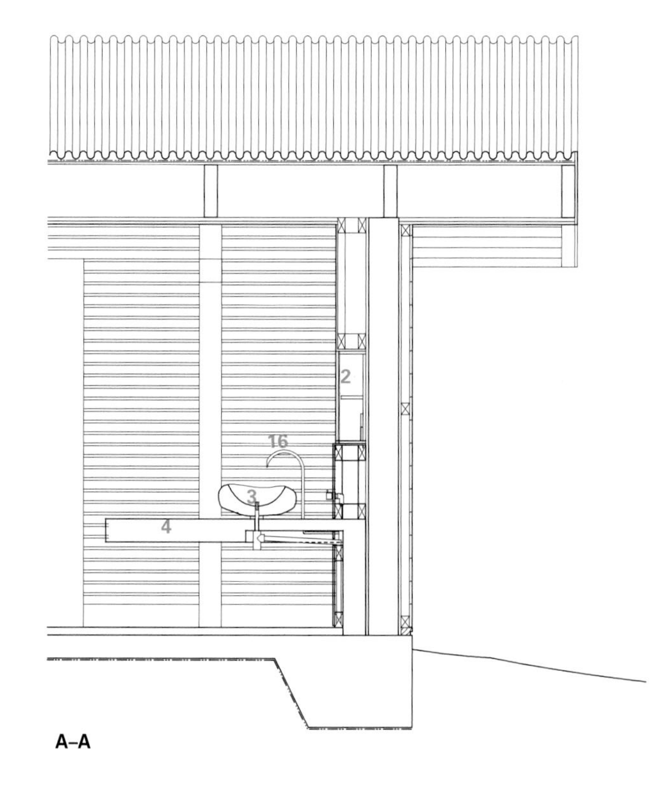

A–A

Materials
Countertop Polished concrete
Joinery Sprayed MDF
Floor Polished concrete
Shower Enclosure Galvanized corrugated sheet metal on timber frame
Lighting Recessed downlights

Appliances and Fixtures
Basin Taps Vola
Basin Spout Custom fabricated by specialists
Basin Custom made carved stone
Shower Taps Axor Starck shower column by Hansgrohe
Shower Head Axor Starck shower column by Hansgrohe
WC Villeroy & Boch
Bidet Villeroy & Boch

Project Credits
Completion 2007
Project Architects Seth Stein, Andrew Abdulezer, Richard Vint
Structural Engineers Atelier One Engineers
Executive Architect Rolf Rothermel, RBS Architects

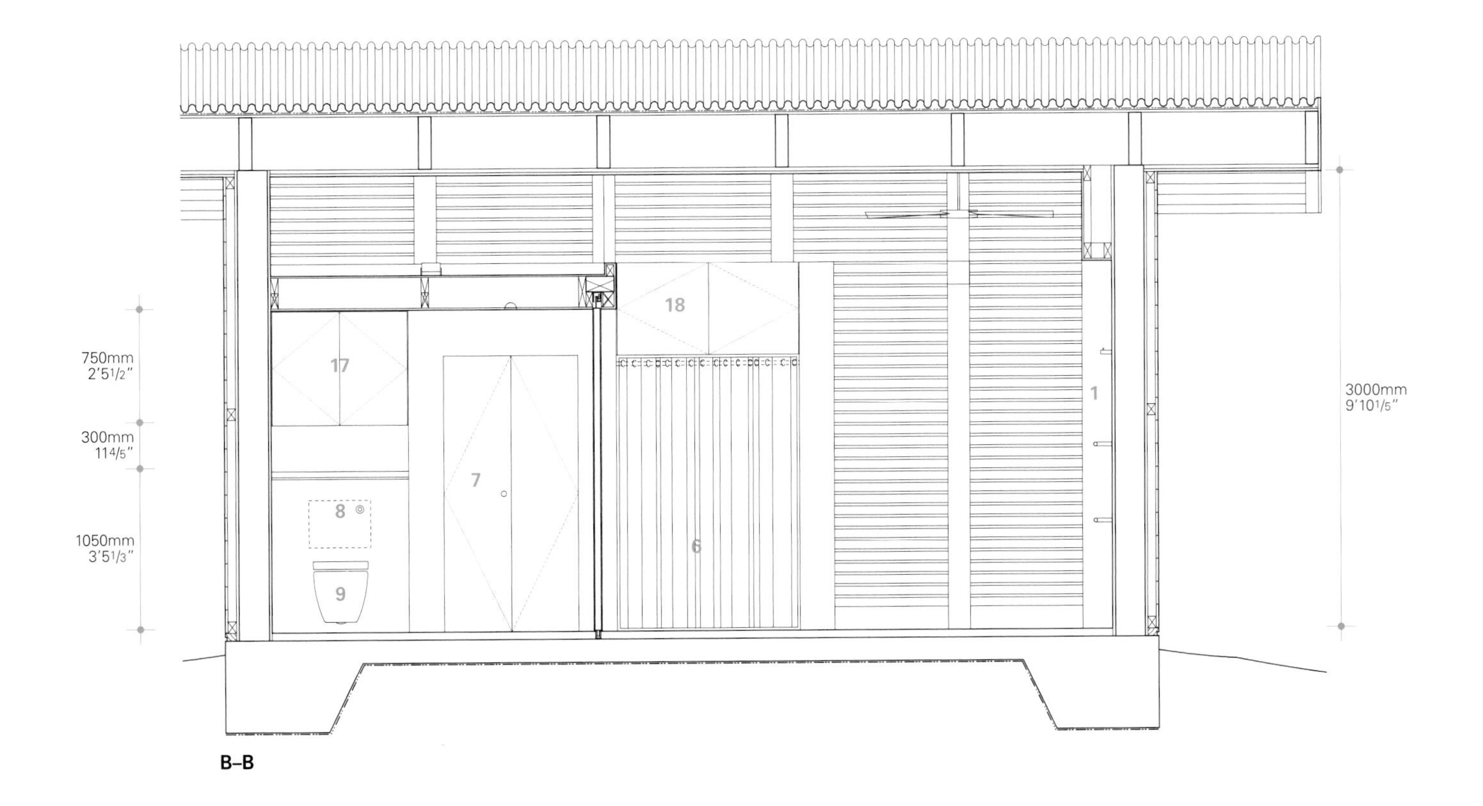

B–B

Ezzo

Outeiro House
Porto, Portugal

At the beginning of the renovation of this nineteenth-century house, the main façade and the timber beams were the only original elements remaining. It was decided that all of the existing structural elements would be maintained, however a new interior would be slotted into the existing structure.

The interior is arranged with the entrance on the ground floor, the bedroom on the first floor, and the bathroom and laundry located on a half floor in between. The second floor accommodates the living room, kitchen and dining room, with the office and terrace on the top floor. The purpose of this distribution was to support the connection between the social areas and the landscape.

Each of these new spaces has a distinct character, identified through varying outlooks, textures and colours. On the ground floor, a coarse sand plaster complements the brown painted exterior. By contrast, the brilliant white stairwell travels up into the house, revealing two pink panels along the way that conceal the guest bathroom and the storeroom. The first floor was found to have large blocks of yellow granite which was maintained, giving this floor a golden glow.

On the two upper floors, the walls are smooth and white. The kitchen, which acts as a central element, brings together the living and dining rooms, which are designed as areas for socializing. The outdoor terrace echoes elements of the interior with brown timber and pink flowering plants.

The main bathroom is a continuation of the interior spaces, and uses the same finishes – white-painted plaster walls and timber floor. The countertops have been fabricated from thick planks of cantilevered timber, on which is placed a white basin. The combination bathtub and shower are covered in red mosaic tiles to highlight the fact that this is the most significant zone in the bathroom.

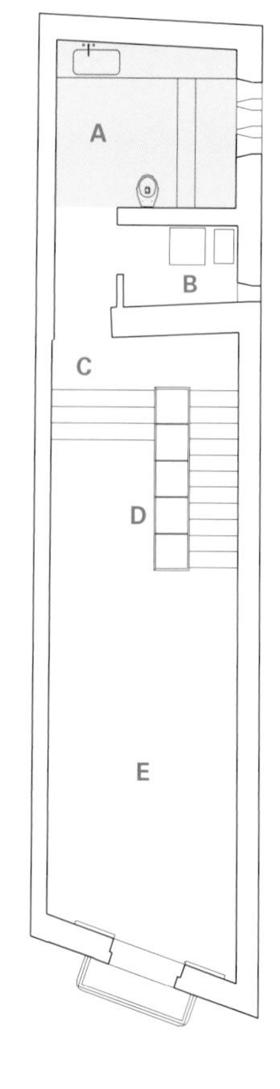

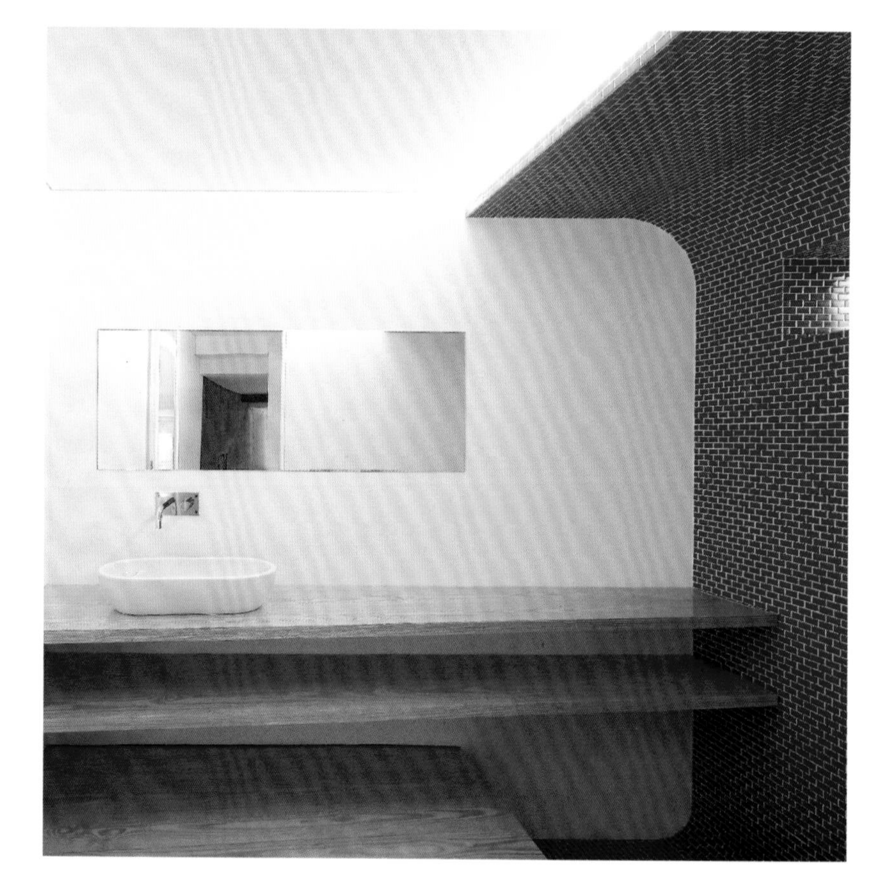

Opposite Left
The earliest records relating to the construction of the house in Outeiro Street date back to the early nineteenth century. Constructed using granite masonry and timber structure, the building has undergone several modifications and tenures over the past 200 years. With the preservation of the handsome exterior and the thorough re-working of the interior, this latest occupation and renovation brings the house right into the twenty-first century.

Floor Plan
A Bathroom
B Laundry
C Half landing
D Dressing area
E Bedroom

Opposite Right
The majority of the bathroom employs the same simple, clean materials and finishes as the majority of the house. White-painted walls, white sanitary fixtures and pine flooring and countertops lend an understated elegance that contrasts dramatically with the curved shell of the red mosaic-tiled bath and shower.

Left
The tiled bath and shower wall curves at the bottom, where an intermediate step takes bathers from the timber floor into the shower, and at the top where the horizontal element is dropped below the line of the plasterboard ceiling to create a concealed lighting slot.

Timber

Ezzo
Outeiro House
Porto, Portugal

Bathroom Plan and Sections A–A, B–B and C–C 1:50

1 Window
2 Tiled bath and shower
3 Step down to bath floor
4 Timber countertop
5 White ceramic basin
6 Pine floor boards
7 WC
8 Timber-framed polycarbonate door to bathroom
9 Timber-framed polycarbonate door to laundry
10 Laundry
11 Wall-mounted basin taps and spout
12 Line of dropped ceiling to tiled shower wall
13 White-painted dropped plasterboard ceiling
14 White-painted plasterboard wall
15 Wall-mounted hand held shower set
16 WC flush to concealed WC cistern
17 Wall-mounted mirror

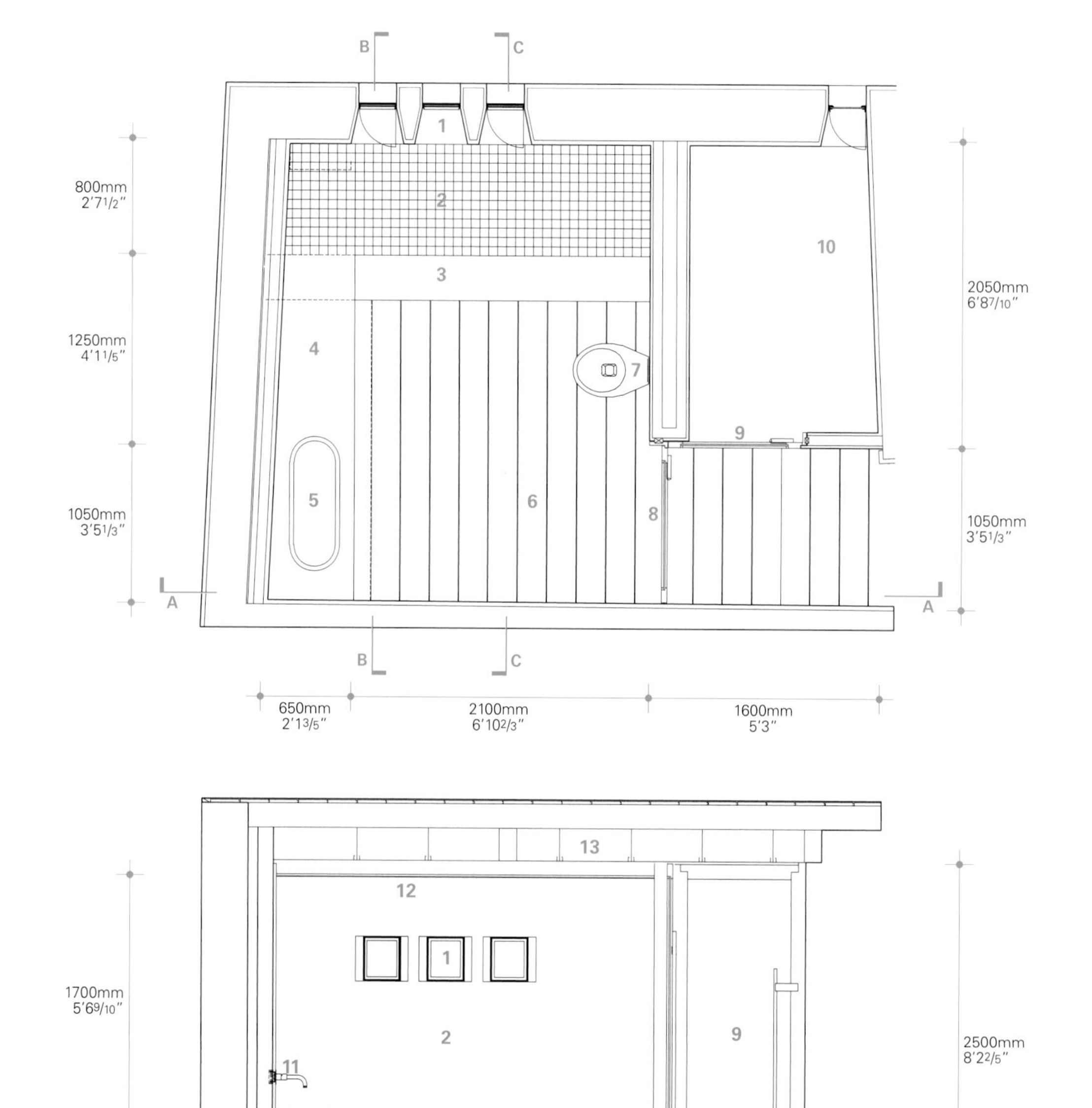

A–A

Materials
Countertop and Joinery American pine
Floor American pine
Wall Tiles Red glass tiles from Bisazza
Lighting Fluorescent light fittings

Appliances and Fixtures
Basin Taps Stainless steel taps from Bruma
Basin Spout Stainless steel taps from Bruma
Basin Catalano
Shower Taps and Spout Stainless steel tap and spout from Bruma
Shower Head Stainless steel shower head from Bruma
Bath Taps and Spout Stainless steel tap and spout from Bruma
Bath Interior finished in red glass tiles from Bisazza
WC Catalano

Project Credits
Completion 2007
Client Marta Mello Sampayo
Project Architects César Machado Moreira
Structural Engineer Oval
Services Engineer Oval

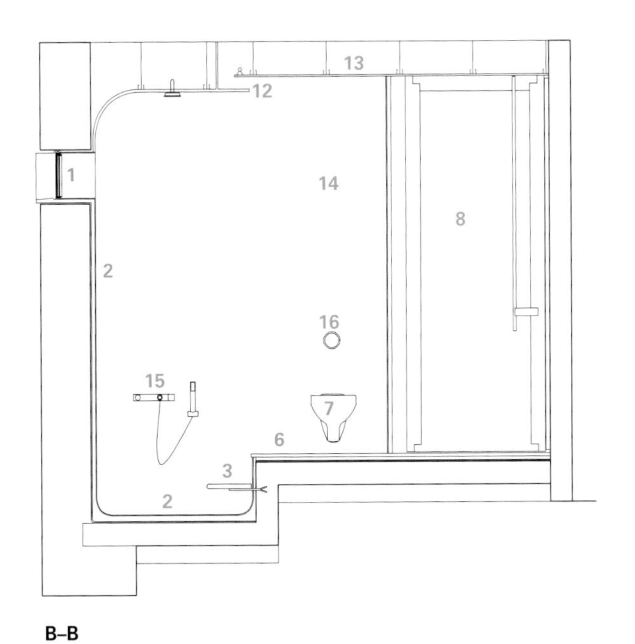

B–B

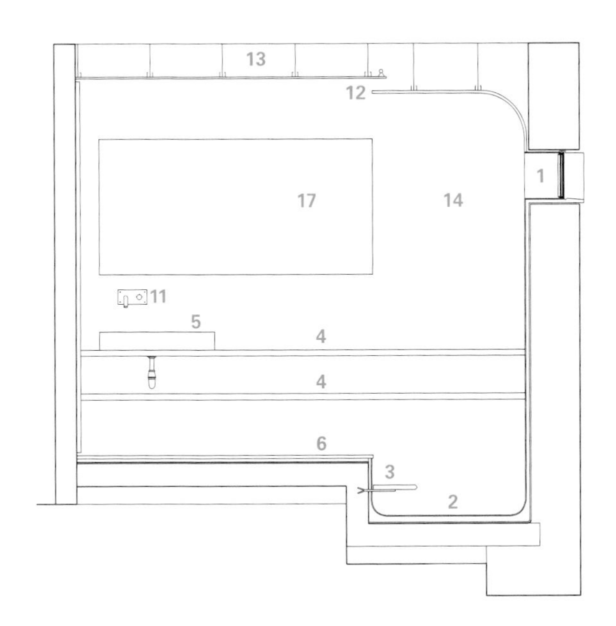

C–C

José António Lopes da Costa Architect / Tiago Meireles Architect

Ovar House
Ovar, Portugal

This luxurious family home is located just inland from the northern stretches of Portugal's Atlantic Ocean coastline. The house is situated in the centre of its large triangular suburban plot, making the most of existing and new landscape elements to screen it from its neighbours.

The building, a long rectangular prism, takes advantage of the natural slope of the site so that to the front of the house both storeys rise out of the ground and overlook the pool terrace, whereas at the rear, where the site is higher, only the upper level and a strip of ribbon windows below are exposed, giving the house a lower profile. A moat-like reflecting pool surrounds the house, giving it the appearance of floating in a shallow lake.

On the ground floor are all of the living spaces including the kitchen, dining and living spaces, as well as recreation facilities including a play room, billiards room and an indoor swimming pool that occupies a slender rectangular volume arranged perpendicular to the main house.

The upper level is accessed via a central staircase where a corridor leads to four bedrooms, all with dressing rooms and ensuite bathrooms. To one end of the space, a gallery overlooks the kitchen and dining room below, while at the other, a dramatic terrace over the pool, accessed from the master bedroom, enjoys views across the landscape.

The master bathroom consists of a large, white-tiled open space housing the double vanity bench and a free-standing bathtub, with a separate raised area to house the WC and shower. These two more private spaces are divided by a wall of polished Negro Marquina black marble. The pure white walls, floor, ceiling and fixtures are relieved by accents of dark timber joinery and lit by a recessed skylight in the ceiling above the bathtub.

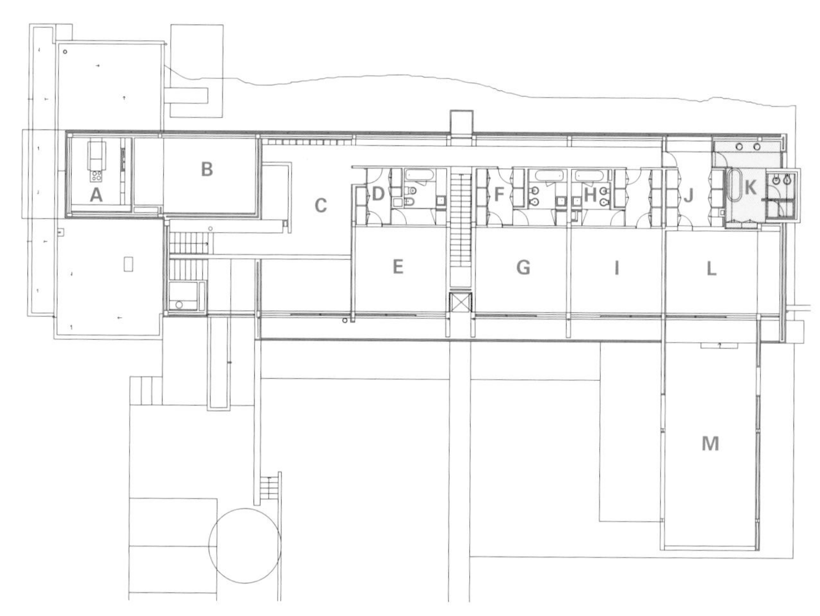

Opposite Left
The landscaped grounds include various games courts supported by a separate outbuilding. The master bedroom suite (top right) has direct access to the large terrace over the swimming pool, with its cutaway timber-clad balustrade walls.

Floor Plan
- A Kitchen below
- B Dining room below
- C Open gallery
- D Ensuite bathroom and dressing room
- E Bedroom
- F Ensuite bathroom and dressing room
- G Bedroom
- H Ensuite bathroom and dressing room
- I Bedroom
- J Master suite dressing room
- K Master bathroom
- L Master bedroom
- M Terrace

Above
The master bathroom features a polished black wall that cantilevers out over the floor, which separates the WC (left) from the shower enclosure (right). The large double-ended bathtub is lit from above by a slot of glazing in the ceiling.

Timber

José António Lopes da Costa Architect / Tiago Meireles Architect
Ovar House
Ovar, Portugal

Bathroom Plan and Sections A–A, B–B, C–C and D–D
1:50

1 Wardrobes to dressing room
2 Timber countertop
3 Counter-mounted white ceramic basin
4 Wall-mounted basin taps and spout
5 Timber floor
6 Window
7 Double-ended white ceramic bathtub
8 Timber sideboard
9 WC
10 Bidet
11 Line of skylight over
12 Black granite wall
13 Gloss white tiled floor
14 Glass screen to shower enclosure
15 Shower enclosure
16 Wall-mounted light fitting over mirror
17 Wall-mounted mirror
18 Timber cupboard fronts
19 Gloss white tiled wall
20 Timber drawer fronts
21 Door to dressing room

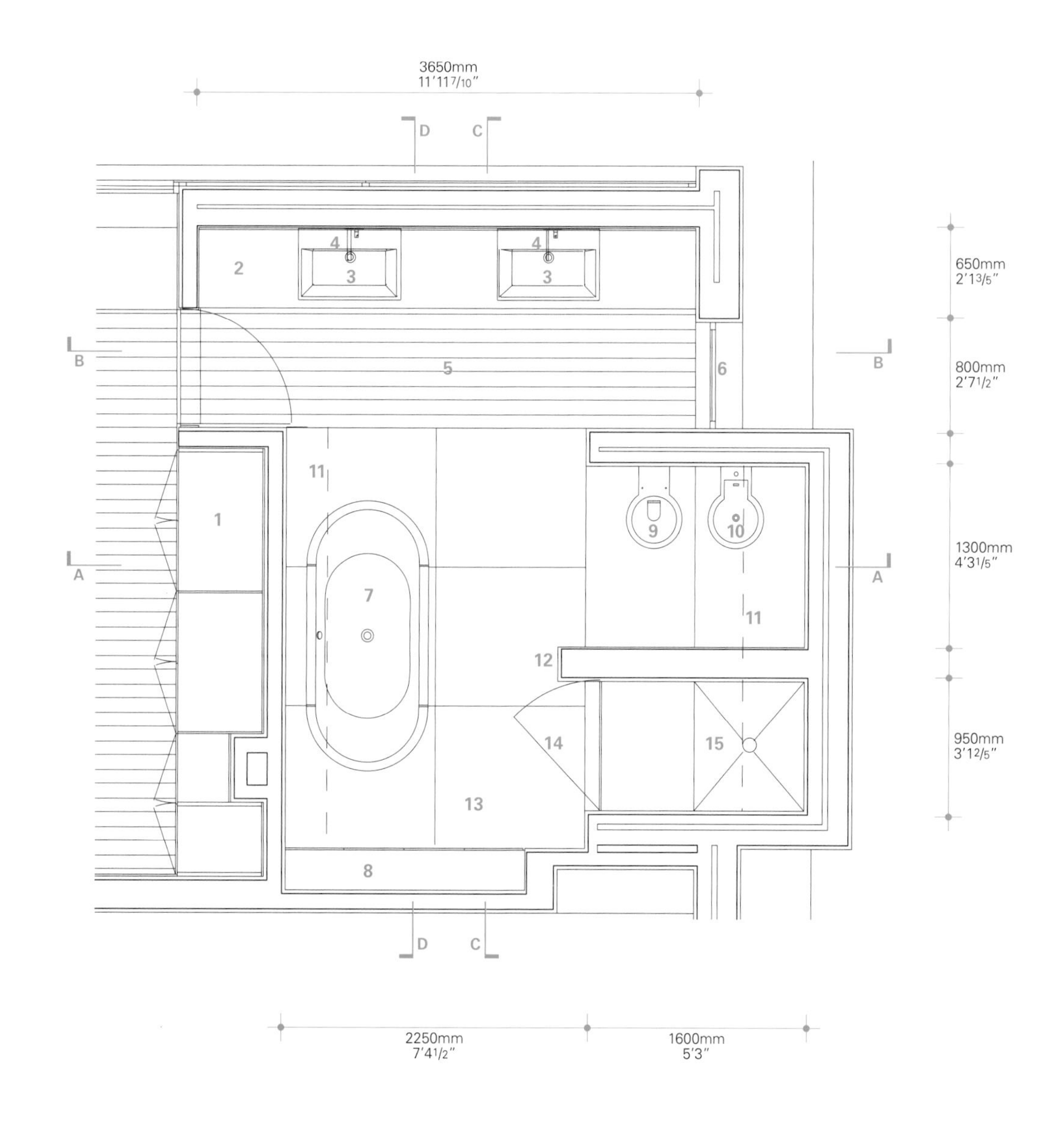

Materials
Countertop White silica agglomerate
Joinery Wenge timber
Floor Afzelia timber and white silica agglomerate
Splashback Glass
Wall Tiles White silica agglomerate and Negro Marquina black marble
Lighting Nimbus

Appliances and Fixtures
Basin Taps Vola
Basin Spout Vola
Basin Catalano
Shower Taps Fantini
Shower Head Fantini
Bath Taps and Spout Vola
Bath Duravit Starck
WC Duravit Starck 1

Project Credits
Completion 2005
Project Architects José António Lopes da Costa, Tiago Meireles with collaborators Rui Ventura and Filipe Ribeiro
Structural Engineer Alípio Guedes
Services Engineer Henrique Duarte
Lighting Engineer Artur Santos
Main Contractor Construtora do Loureiro

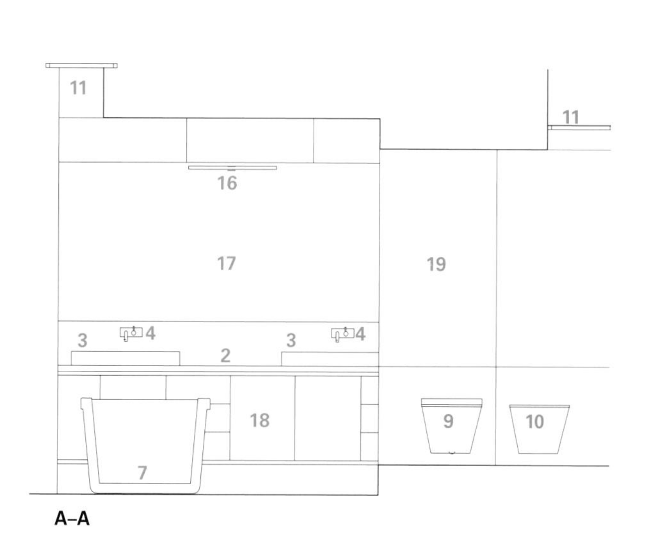

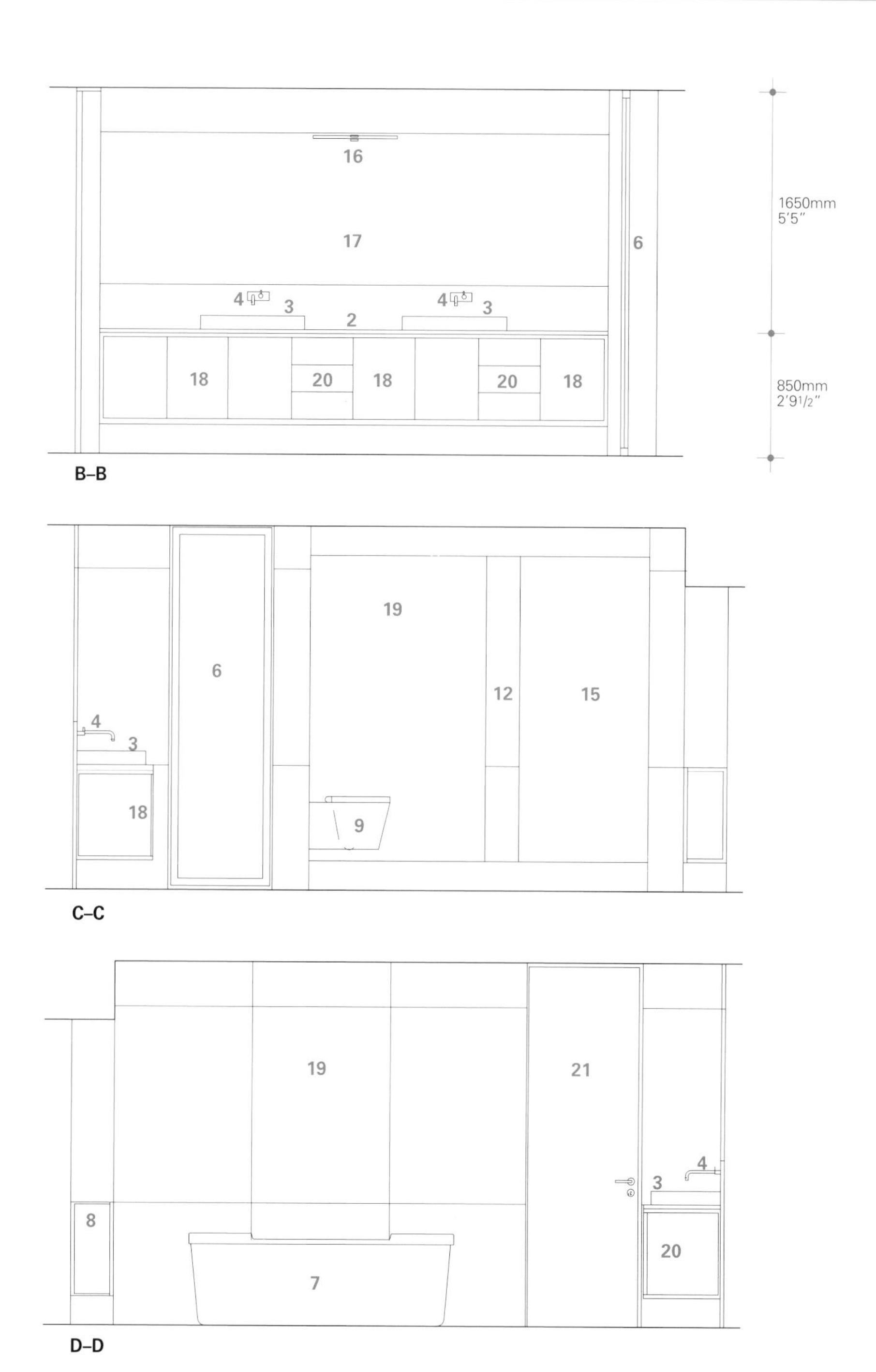

Glass Bathrooms

Kubota Architect Atelier

I–House Hatsukaichi City, Hiroshima Prefecture, Japan

I–House stands on the shore opposite Miyajima Island in Hiroshima. The site, located on a curving road, benefits from panoramic ocean views. When the tide is high, the difference in level between the sea and the land is about four metres (13 feet), accounting for the magical feeling that the site is floating on the sea.

The owners, a couple, very much wanted to enjoy a living environment that would celebrate the proximity to the ocean and, as a result, the focus of the design was to create opportunities for all of the spaces within the house to relate in as direct a manner as possible to the water.

Inspired by the image of a sheet of paper rocking in the waves, the architect, Katsufumi Kubota, decided to express the structure of the house as a bent sheet of concrete. This elemental slab – essentially an upside-down L-shape cranked at an angle – opens up towards the sea to embrace the view and closes towards the road to protect the privacy of the inhabitants. The bent slab, painted white, is supported and stabilized by a steel structure and raised on exposed concrete blade walls.

Elsewhere, glass features extensively throughout the house, both as a foil to the monolithic concrete structure, and to allow maximum exposure to the views.

The guest bathroom is located on the ground floor and features a full-height, full-width glazed door that opens directly onto the waterfront. One wall of the space features an unpainted expanse of one of the concrete structural walls. Minimal white fixtures and fittings, including a large double-ended bath, allow the view and the moods of the ocean to take centre stage.

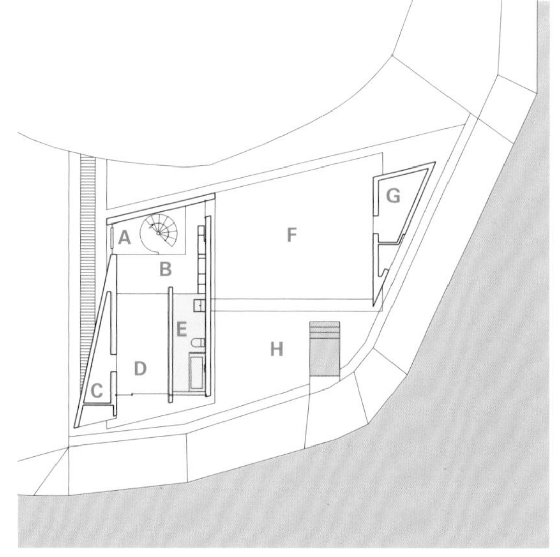

Opposite Left
View of the house from the street. The opening in the concrete carapace is a carport, protected from ocean spray by a glass wall. To the left a concrete triangular prism houses a storage space, while to the right are the domestic spaces arranged over two levels. The living, dining and master bedroom spaces are on the first floor and guest quarters and double-height entrance gallery are on the ground floor.

Floor Plan
- A Circular stair to first floor
- B Entrance hall
- C Storage
- D Guest room
- E Guest bathroom
- F Carport
- G Store
- H Courtyard

Top Left
The living room, viewed here from a terrace that spans two-thirds of the width of the house, features three walls of full-height glazing. A slender profile steel roof with overhangs protects the glazing from the sun.

Bottom Left
An elegant spiral steel staircase rises from the entrance hall on the ground floor to the living room above. An unpainted concrete blade wall protects the space from neighbouring houses, while expanses of glass open it up to the views.

Above
A wet area in the guest bathroom on the ground floor features a large bathtub and shower area, both of which take advantage of views of the water via the massive glazed end wall.

Glass

Kubota Architect Atelier
I-House
Hatsukaichi City, Hiroshima Prefecture, Japan

Bathroom Plan and Sections A–A, B–B, C–C, D–D and E–E
1:50

1 Storage cupboards to entrance hall
2 Basin spout and taps
3 White ceramic wall-hung basin
4 Chrome-plated hand-towel rail
5 Laundry cabinet with integrated washing machine
6 Chrome-plated toilet-roll holder
7 WC
8 Large white latex floor tiles
9 Concrete bath surround with urethane paint finish
10 White acrylic resin double-ended bathtub
11 White ceramic floor tiles to wet area
12 Chrome-plated towel rail
13 Hand held shower fitting with flexible hose and wall-mounted shower head
14 Full-height glazed window
15 Wall-mounted mirror panel with integrated lighting above basin
16 Cupboard with adjustable shelving above washing machine
17 Exposed concrete wall
18 Door to entrance hall
19 Ventilation duct above glazed opening
20 Paint finish on waterproof substrate

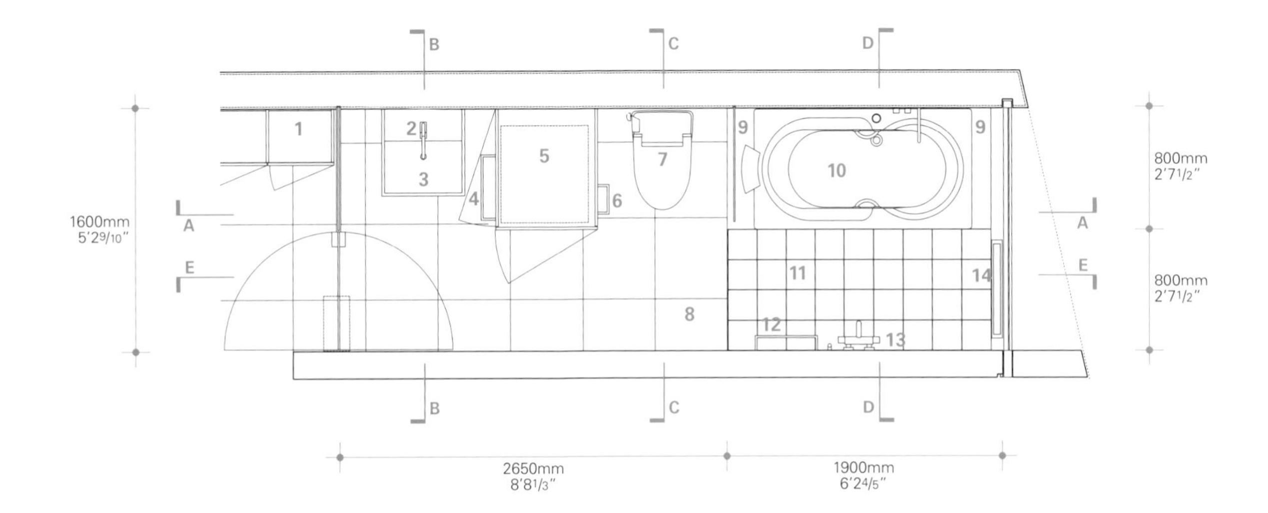

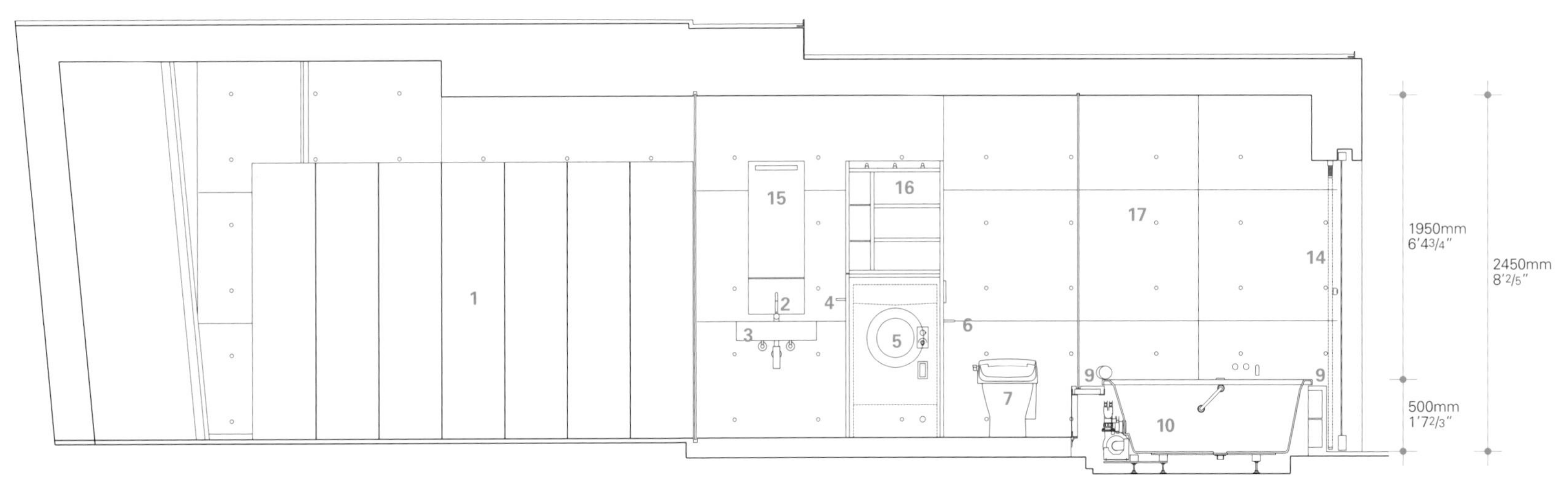

A–A

Materials
Joinery Bespoke cabinetry from Kozen Mokko, Hiroshima
Floor Nichiman Astroface (R)SOFT Plane rubber tiles to main area and Danto ceramic tiles to wet area
Lighting Panasonic fluorescent light concealed above laundry cabinet

Appliances and Fixtures
Basin Taps and Spout Vola KV1CDR
Basin Cosmic ceramic basin
Shower Taps Axor Hansgrohe
Shower Bar and Head Axor Starck
Bath Taps and Spout Vola 620
Bath Jaxson 'Giardino' with jets
WC INAX 'Satis' with sheet warmer and electro-bidet

Project Credits
Completion 2004
Project Architects Katsufumi Kubota, Kazuya Toizaki, Yuko Mishima
Structural Engineers SAK-Takeo Sakuka
Main Contractor Nomura Architecture Construction

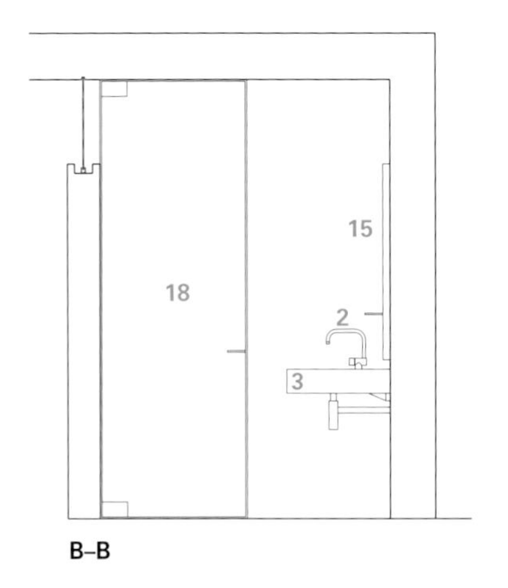

B–B

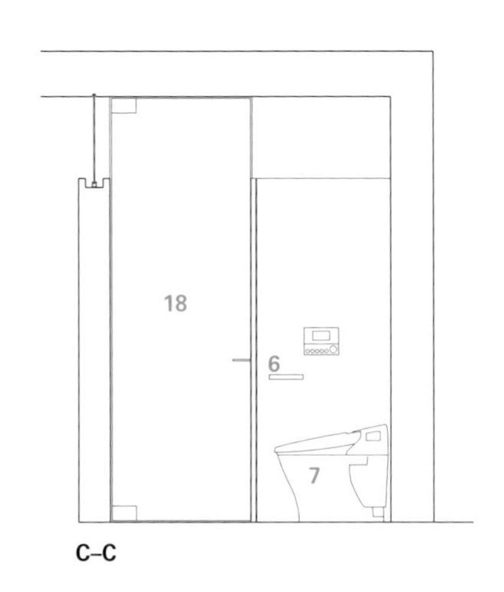

C–C

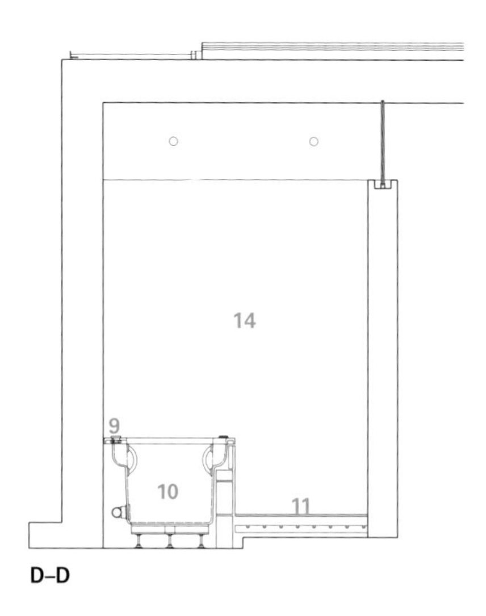

D–D

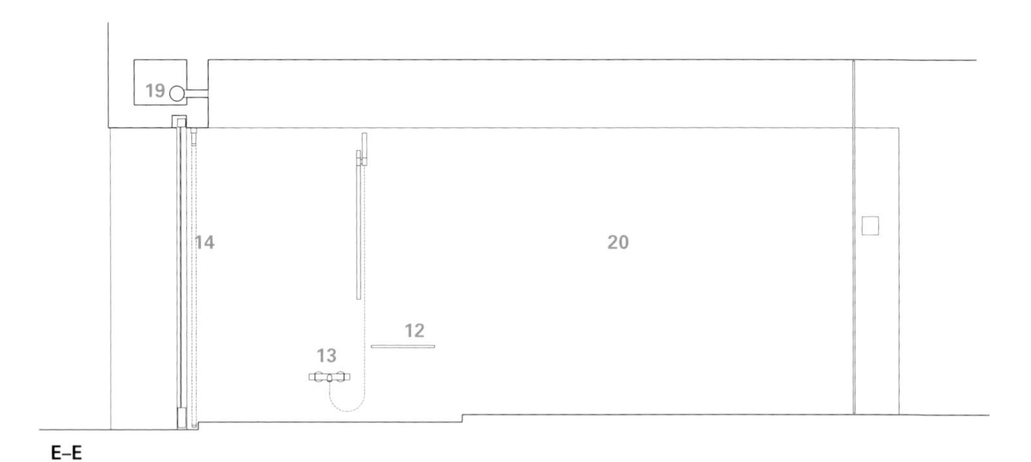

E–E

Crepain Binst Architecture (Luc Binst)

Lofthouse
Humbeek, Belgium

This private house is a sculptural synthesis of the client's personal creativity and an interpretation of the flexibility of a loft space. The design avoids a room-based approach, in which the enjoyment of the house invariably results in a fragmented setting. Instead, everything is organized as one large space, in which everything interrelates.

The house is constructed entirely from concrete, supported on fins of solid sheet steel, with a substantial cantilevered element. The two split-level floors allow the integration of the programme into the volume and create the required visual relationships. From the living space one is in contact with the carport, and from the carport with the office, the entrance hall and the living space. The composition of these relationships enables one to achieve a considerable degree of visual control over the organization of the house.

For example, the office worktop, 13.5 metres (44 feet) in length, resembles a concrete catwalk anchored in the wall like a suspended plinth. The monumental black access stairs to the living space provide an advance announcement of the shift in scale, which is especially evident in the living space. The marble kitchen island, with its integrated light panel, becomes a multifunctional object in the space. On the same axis lies the larger-than-average shower, looking out over the entire living space, which is given a central place in the dwelling.

Together with the entrance staircase, the black storage and dressing closet with basin and private WC forms the home's backbone. The bath is sunk into the floor above the ground-floor toilet. The bottom of the bath can be reached via an access hatch in the toilet ceiling for maintenance. The shower is a custom designed room with a lateral drainage strip along the black shower wall. From the shower, there is an uninterrupted view of the living space, kitchen and projection wall.

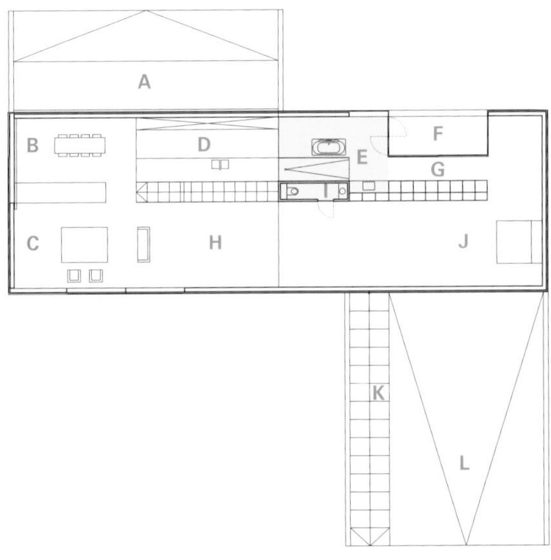

Opposite Left
The 200 millimetre (7⁴/5 inch) thick structural concrete skin of the façade is, unusually, coated in black cement which is attached to the frame using a ventilated cavity system. The two pictograms on the front of the house symbolize the humanity of architecture in the form of two filters over the sliding windows. These touches also represent an allusion to the abstraction of this project.

Floor Plan
A Terrace
B Dining area
C Living area
D Kitchen
E Bathroom
F Terrace
G Dressing area
H Living area
I WC
J Bedroom
K Stair from garage below
L Ramp from garage below

Above
Planes of glass, black Corian and mirrors give the bathroom a dazzling reflective quality. Located behind the kitchen, in a central position on the main living level, the bathroom is given a central place in the hierarchy of the programme.

Glass

Crepain Binst Architecture (Luc Binst)
Lofthouse
Humbeek, Belgium

Bathroom Plan and Sections A–A, B–B, C–C and D–D
1:50

1 Sunken bathtub
2 White ceramic bath surround
3 Poured epoxy floor
4 Pivoting door to terrace
5 Ramped floor to shower recess
6 Black Corian ledge over WC cistern
7 WC
8 Black Corian countertop
9 White ceramic basin to WC
10 Custom made black Corian basin
11 Black Corian countertop to bathroom vanity
12 Full-height cupboards to dressing room
13 Full-height glazing to terrace
14 Full-height cupboards
15 Adjustable shelves to over-counter cupboards
16 Mirror
17 High-level cupboards
18 Wall-mounted basin taps
19 Shower head
20 Shower valve
21 Concealed overhead lighting
22 Wall-mounted power outlet
23 Adjustable shelves to full-height cupboards
24 Drawers to full-height cupboards

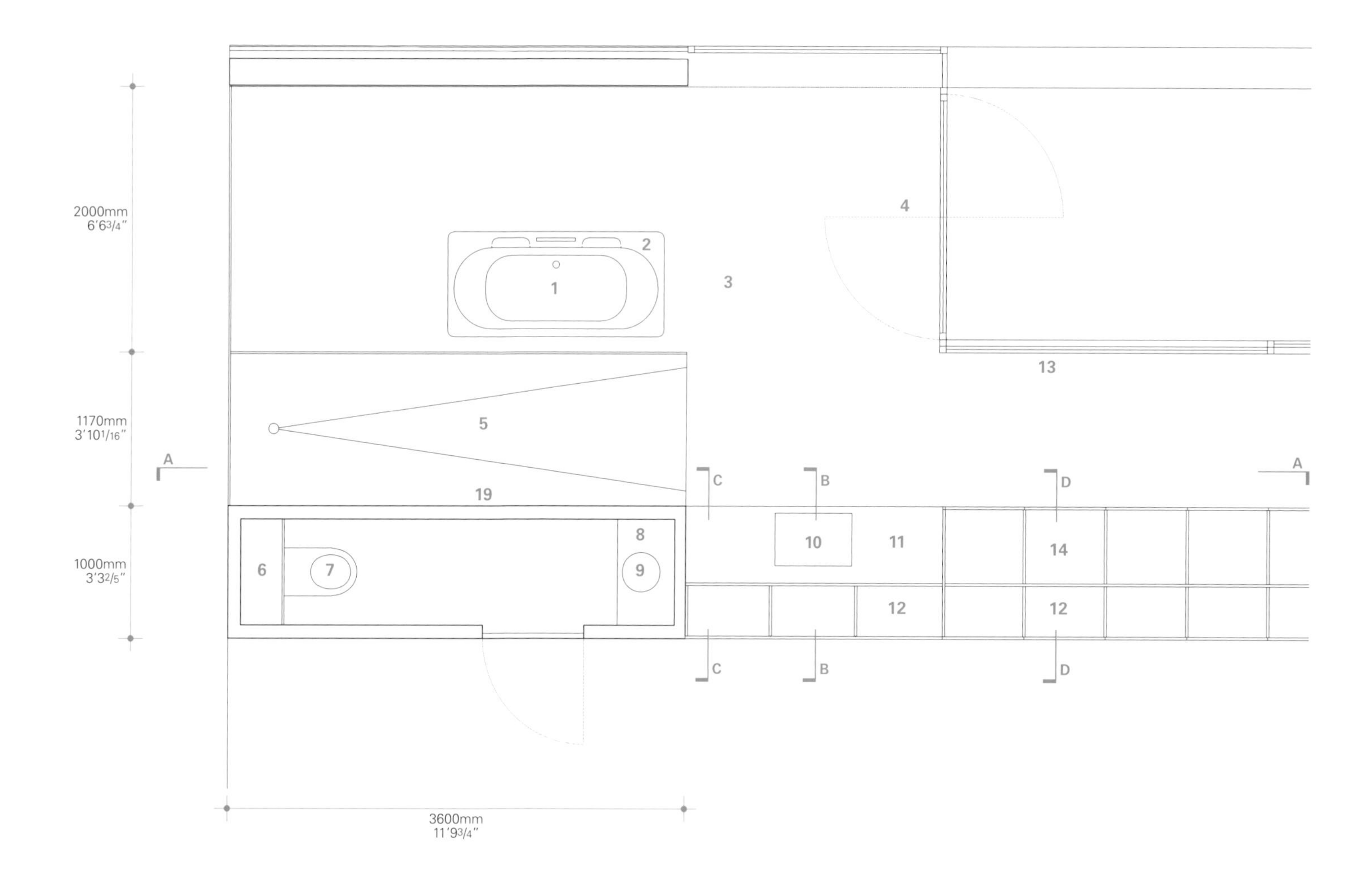

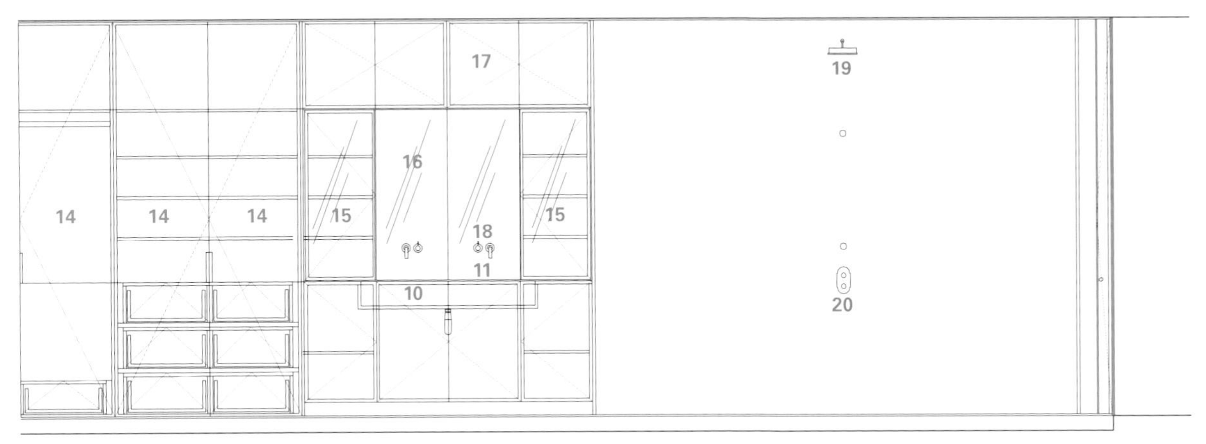
17
19
16
14
14
14
15
18
15
11
10
20
A–A

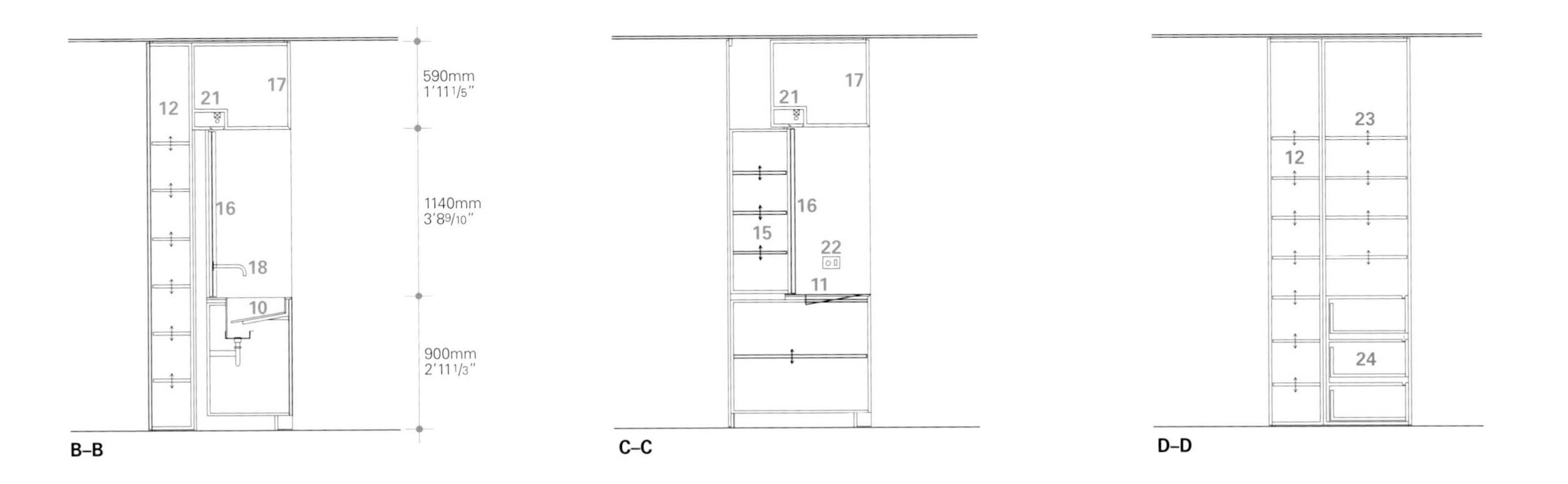
12
21
17
16
18
10
590mm
1'11 1/5"
1140mm
3'8 9/10"
900mm
2'11 1/3"
21
17
16
15
22
11
23
12
24
B–B

C–C

D–D

Glass

Crepain Binst Architecture (Luc Binst)
Lofthouse
Humbeek, Belgium

Detail Section Through Hand Basin
1:5

1 Fixed mirror
2 Wall-mounted basin tap
3 Stone-clad countertop
4 Timber substrate to counter structure
5 Stone back panel to basin
6 Stainless steel bottom to basin
7 Concealed basin drain
8 Black Corian panel to basin
9 Waterproof timber substrate to basin structure
10 Black Corian edge to basin with mitred joint to stone front panel
11 Fixed black Corian panel to basin front

Opposite Left
In a complete departure from the usual ideas about privacy and seclusion, the glass-enclosed shower looks out over the kitchen and living room beyond.

Opposite Right
The bath is dropped into a raised floor of seamless poured synthetic resin, and is connected to a terrace via a large glazed pivot door.

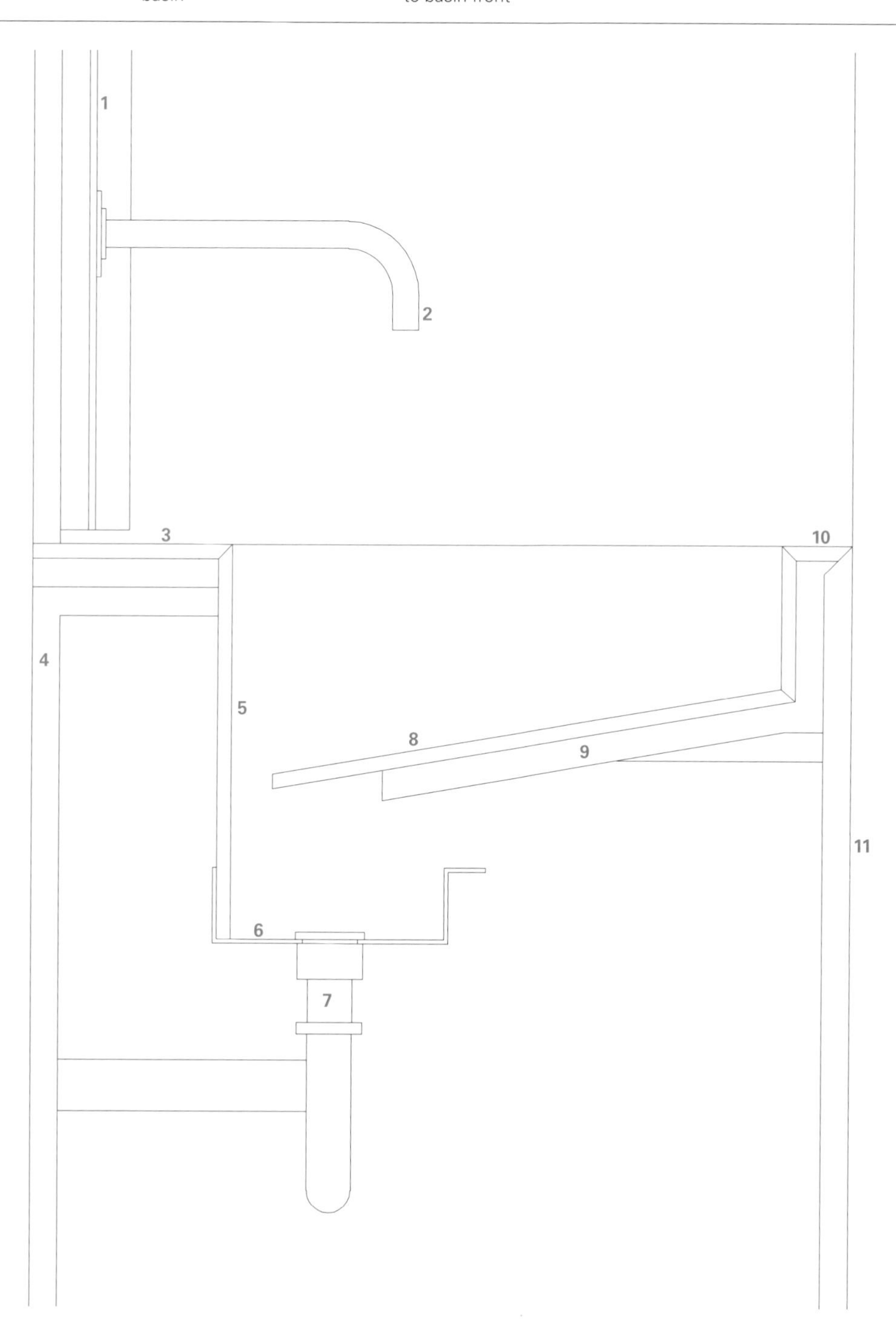

Materials
Countertop Black Corian
Joinery Seamless glued MDF
Floor Poured epoxy floor
Lighting Integrated spotlights by Modular

Appliances and Fixtures
Basin Taps Vola
Basin Spout Vola
Basin Vola
Shower Taps Dornbracht
Shower Head Radiance
Bath Taps and Spout Dornbracht

Project Credits
Completion 2004
Client Luc Binst
Interior Designer Luc Binst, Tom de Meester
Structural Engineers Bas bvba
Main Contractor Janssens bvba
Quantity Surveyor Luc Binst

Craig Steere Architects

Shenton Park Lake Residence Perth, Western Australia, Australia

The brief for this two-storey dwelling described an easy to maintain house that maximizes the outlook to the park and lake whilst maintaining privacy from the street as well as providing inviting spaces for entertaining.

An offset footprint and open planning with limited internal walls and support structure helped to access the views, whilst creating an intimate rear entertaining court that also relates directly to the swimming pool. The plan allows views through the house towards the lake, which is reinforced through the use of a dual purpose two-storey high anchor wall on the front façade, protecting the interior from the harsh western sun.

The front deck is designed to seemingly float whilst drawing attention away from the basement garage, store and wine cellar. To the rear of the house, an aqua blue pool provides a burst of colour in a framed landscape. A sense of calm is created by warm white internal walls that accentuate the sculptural lines of walls, ceilings and cabinetwork, whilst offering an appropriate back drop for the owner's art collection.

The master bathroom has a his-and-hers basin mounted on a quartz resin stone benchtop on white lacquered cabinets with concealed finger grips. The cabinet is hung from a glass mosaic-tiled plinth wall which offers a shelf for accessories and cosmetics. Above is a recessed mirror cabinet offering further storage.

Polished heated concrete floors combine with glazed ceramic tiles and the glass mosaic vanity wall to form a simple palette and easy-clean surfaces. Polished chrome accessories, including towel rails, hand-towel rails, toilet brush and paper holder unite with chrome soap dispensers and taps to add a touch of polish and contrast to the white space.

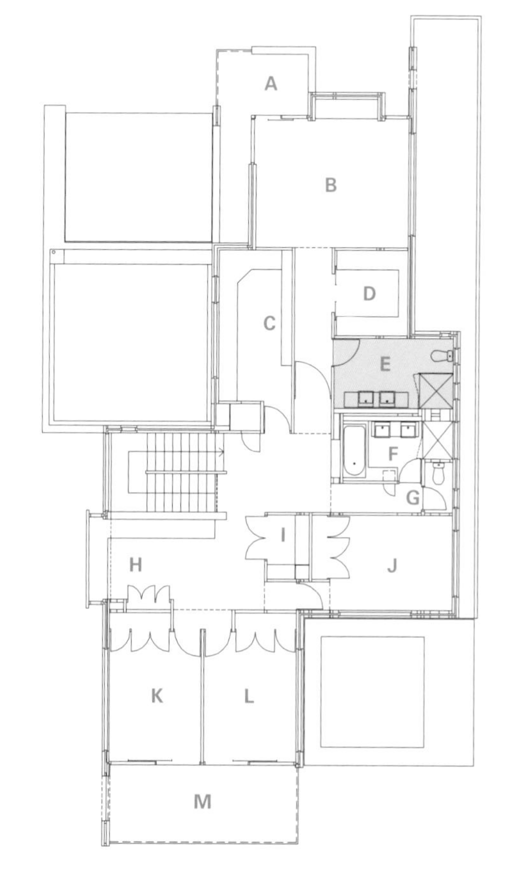

Opposite Left
From the street, the house has a sculptural presence, with both horizontal and vertical layered elements that combine to create a harmonious architectural composition. A two-storey-high blade wall (left), wraps over the house, helping to protect the interior from the harsh western sun.

Floor Plan
A Terrace
B Master bedroom
C Office
D Dressing room
E Master bathroom
F Bathroom
G WC
H Study
I Linen cupboard
J Bedroom
K Bedroom
L Bedroom
M Terrace

Left
The bathroom is designed as a calm, simple, white space with accents of glass (including mirrored cabinets and the glass shower screen), texture (the mosaic tiled splashback and polished concrete floor) and polished chrome accessories.

Glass

Craig Steere Architects
Shenton Park Lake Residence
Perth, Western Australia, Australia

Bathroom Plan and Sections A–A, B–B and C–C 1:50

1 WC
2 Polished chrome toilet brush
3 Shower with frameless glass enclosure
4 Shower head with flexible hose connection
5 Tiled shower shelf
6 Polished chrome toilet-roll holder
7 Polished chrome towel rail
8 Polished chrome hand-towel rail
9 Quartz resin stone countertop
10 White ceramic basin
11 Polished chrome basin spout and taps
12 Mirror-faced cabinets above vanity bench with adjustable shelving
13 Polished concrete floor with under-floor heating
14 Power outlet
15 White mosaic tiled ledge and splashback
16 White sprayed drawers below counter
17 White sprayed cupboard doors below counter
18 White mosaic wall tiles
19 Clear glazed shower door
20 Window
21 White ceramic wall tiles

Opposite
Detail view of the basins, which are mounted onto a composite stone worktop over cabinetry containing drawers and cupboards. The simple tiled splashback incorporates a shelf for products and cosmetics with concealed recessed lighting in the cabinet above.

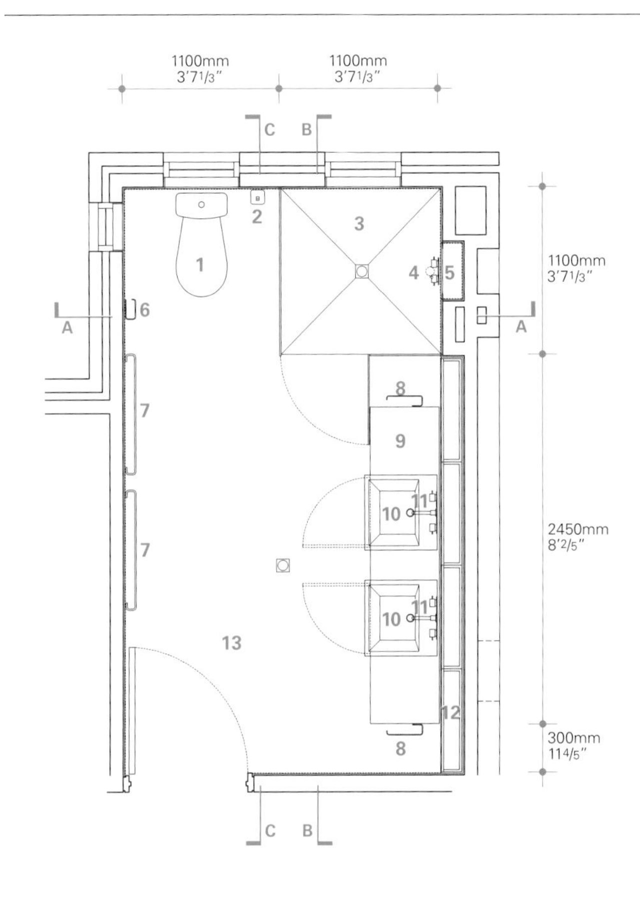

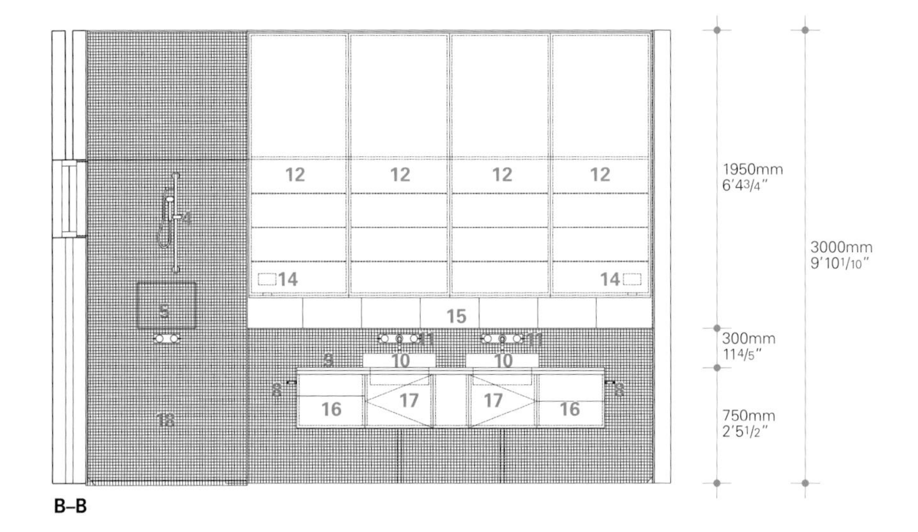

B–B

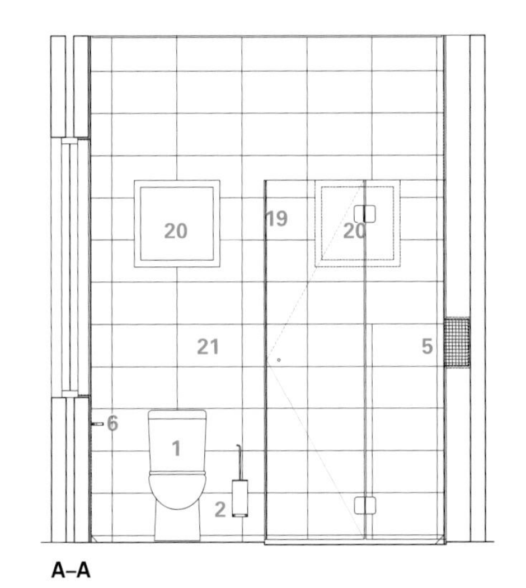

A–A

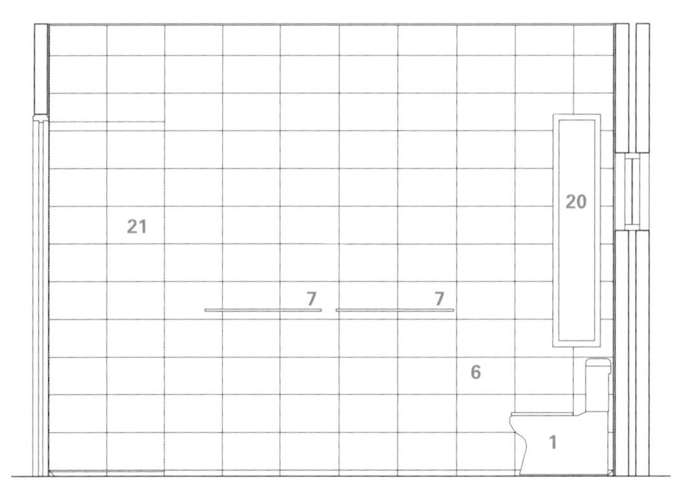

C–C

Materials
Countertop Quartz resin stone
Joinery White lacquered MDF
Floor Polished concrete with underfloor heating and mosaic tiles
Splashback White mosaic tiles
Wall Tiles White ceramic tiles
Lighting Recessed square 12 volt halogen downlights in ceiling and recessed fluorescent lights in cabinet

Appliances and Fixtures
Basin Taps and Spout Rogerseller Logic Tap and Spout assembly with backplate
Basin Rogerseller Zero Washbasin 50
Shower Taps Rogerseller Logic Wall Top assembly with backplate
Shower Head Rogerseller Waterslide with removable spout
WC Villeroy & Boch Omnia Pro Back to Wall White

Project Credits
Completion 2005
Project Architects Craig Steere, Travers Elliott, Sid Thoo
Structural Engineers C.B. Cornforth
Cabinetwork Austwest Cabinets
Stone Benchtops Forezzi
Lighting Consultants Light Four

EDH Endoh Design House

Natural Strips II
Tokyo, Japan

This three-storey house in the centre of Tokyo was designed for a retired couple. The clients wanted a house that would reflect their new lifestyle while at the same time responding to the inevitably small site in Tokyo.

The ground floor accommodates a small shop with its own dressing room, the first floor is the main living and dining space with kitchen, and the top floor houses the bedroom and bathroom. The structural system makes itself present in the plan – two curved walls of 16 millimetre (2/3 inch) thick bent plate steel support the concrete floor slabs and enclose the dressing room on the ground floor, create a sculptural feature in the living room and a container for the bathroom upstairs.

The frame is wrapped in a glass curtain wall which, because it is insufficient to insulate the house, is lined with hollow-core clear polycarbonate moveable screens which the inhabitants can close off or open up as they wish according to their needs for privacy and environmental conditions.

A series of galvanized metal, fixed horizontal louvres are attached to the exterior to protect the south and west façades, in particular, from solar gain. The bathroom is split into two components – a small WC with basin located against the rear wall next to the closet, and a self-contained glass pod at the other end of the space.

The bathing enclosure is contained by two curved solid walls which are joined by full-height panels of clear glazing. Inside, a bathtub and wet area shower benefit from views out into the sleeping floor, and beyond through the louvred exterior glazed walls.

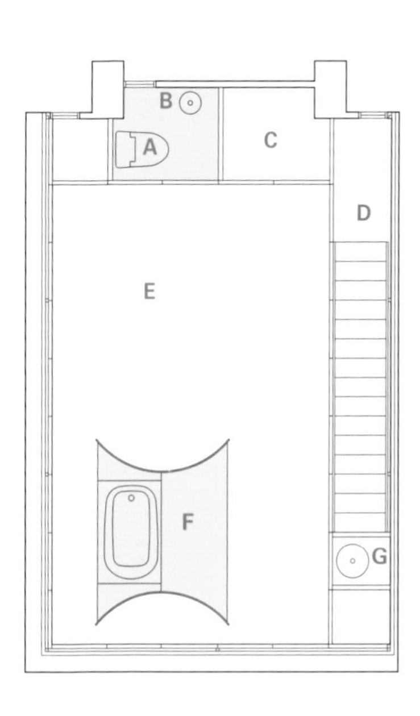

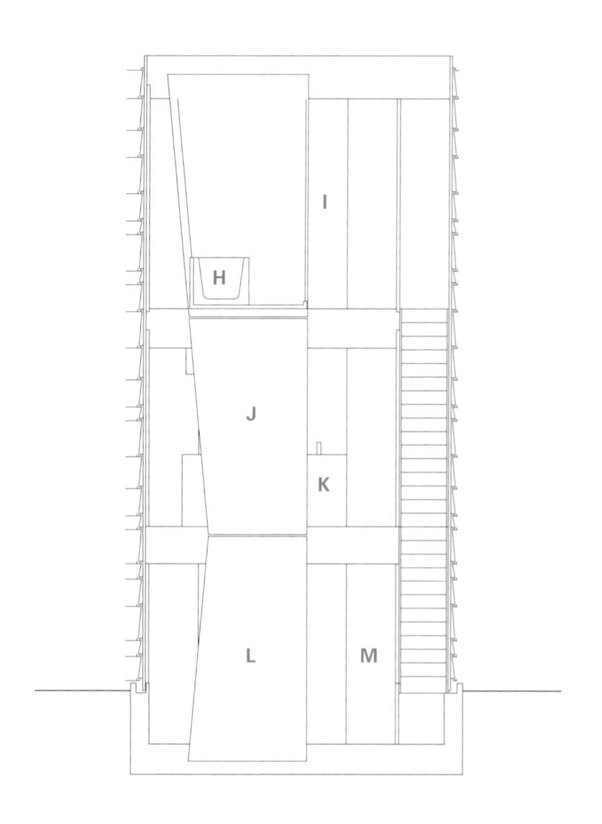

Opposite Left
The galvanized metal strips that cover the façade are interrupted only by white painted double steel doors – the one on the left for the shop and on the right for the residence upstairs.

Floor Plan
A WC
B Wash basin
C Closet
D Stair up from first floor
E Bedroom
F Bathroom
G Hot water cylinder
H Bathroom
I Bedroom
J Curved walls to living room
K Kitchen
L Dressing room
M Shop

Left
The compact floor plan still allows for plenty of bathing space. The bath and shower occupy the sculptural enclosure while a WC and closet are hidden behind folding acrylic doors at the rear of the space.

Bottom Left
Full-height glazing contains the bathing and showering enclosure while retaining views out through the external louvred façade.

Glass

EDH Endoh Design House
Natural Strips II
Tokyo, Japan

Bathroom Plan and Section A–A
1:20

1 Bent steel-plate curved structural walls to bath enclosure
2 Bath surround with white mosaic tiles
3 White ceramic bathtub
4 Stainless steel floor drain
5 Chrome-finish mixer tap and spout with separate shower head
6 White mosaic tiled ledge to shower area
7 Full-height fixed tempered glass wall with stainless steel patch fittings
8 Full-height glazed door with stainless steel patch fittings
9 White ceramic floor tiles
10 Angled glass screen to bath enclosure
11 Interior face of bent steel plate clad in white mosaic tiles
12 Stainless steel wall mountings for shower head
13 White mosaic tiled splashback
14 Painted waterproof plasterboard skirting

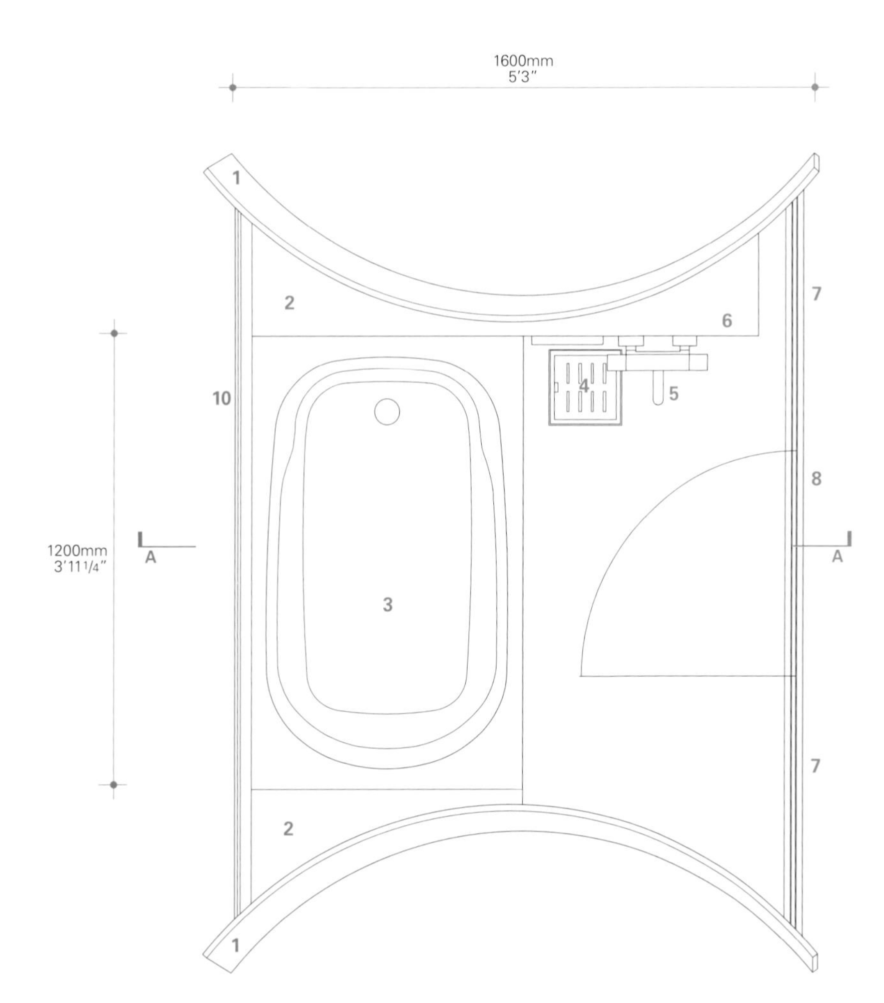

Materials
Benchtop White mosaic tiled with INAX IM-25P1/HN1
Joinery Tempered glass
Floor Tiled with INAX NPKC-200/PU1

Fixtures
Taps and Spout Thermostat system combination faucet, CERA HG13241S
Bath INAX ABR-1210/N92
Shower Head Hand shower head CERA HG28573R and shower hose CERA HG28276

Project Credits
Completion 2005
Client Ichiro Chino, Mituko Chino
Project Architects Masaki Endoh, Hiroaki Takada
Structural Engineers Masahiro Ikeda
Main Contractor Sobi Co.Ltd

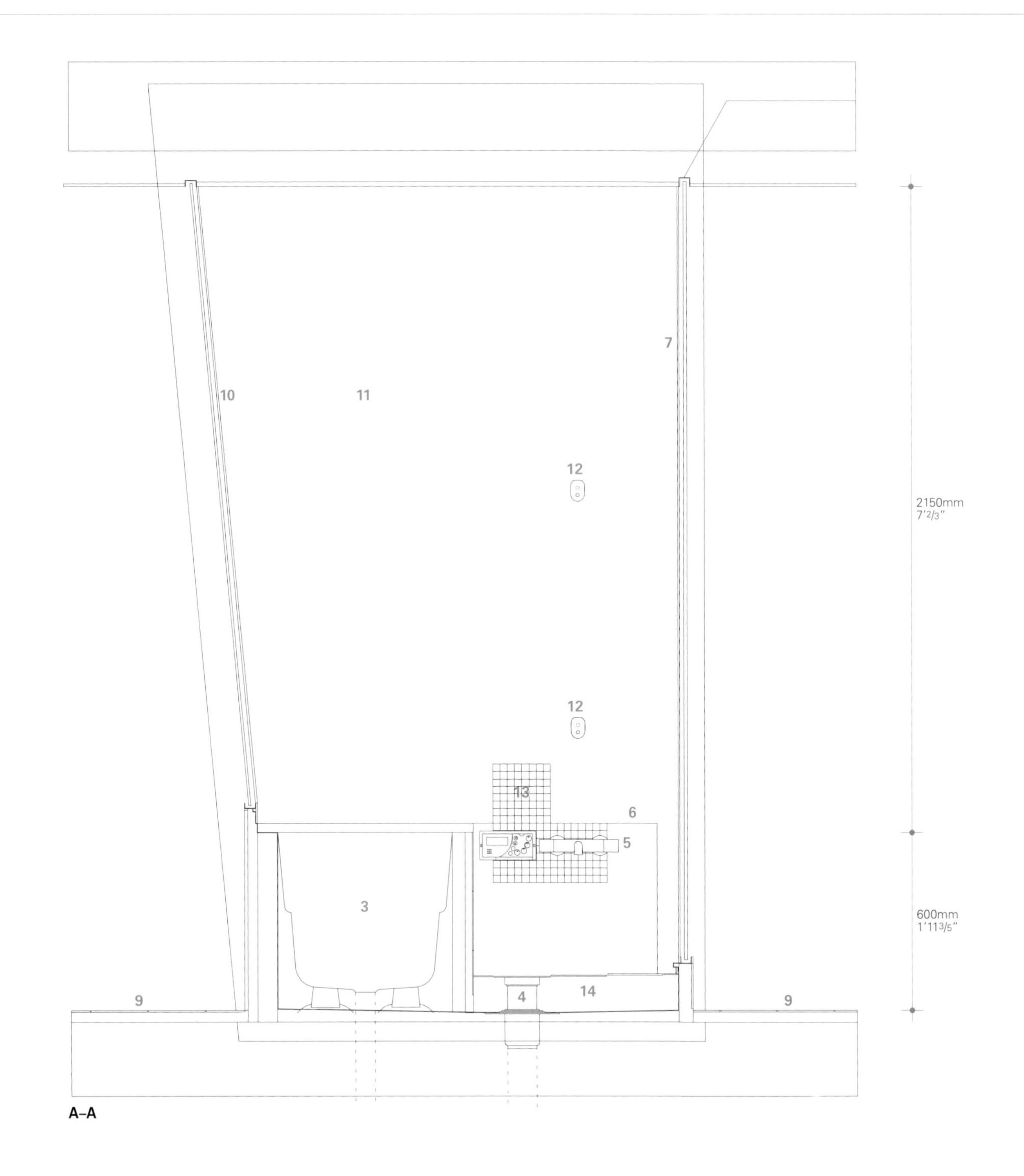

A–A

CCS Architecture

Lake Street Residence San Francisco, California, USA

The challenge in remodelling a poorly planned, five-bedroom Victorian house in San Francisco's Richmond District was to create a cohesive, well-lit, modern home for two. The solution lay in opening up the interior to make new spatial connections while bringing in light and views. The wide, shallow, two-level residence had two sets of rooms – one facing the street and receiving southern light, the other with views of Presidio Park to the north, but receiving less light. In general, most of the rooms were cellular, resulting in under-utilized spaces. With the help of skylights, windows, wall openings, and an open outlook between rooms, the new interior flows from front to back, as well as from left to right.

The central stair, which previously divided the house, was opened up to become a dramatic, light-filled, two-storey focal point. New rooms with new uses are orientated around the openings to create better clarity and flow. Art, sculpture and light liberate the space. On the first floor, a large, well-appointed kitchen makes a transition into the dining and living areas – essentially one 15 metre (50 foot) long space that looks out to the Presidio.

Along the street, a new media room, piano room / library have replaced two of the previous bedrooms. Both new rooms have few walls and are open to the other spaces. Upstairs, skylights and large windows illuminate the new master suite and home office. The serene and luxurious master bathroom has a large walk-in shower with walls of limestone and glass. Openable windows with high sills allow expansive views over the Presidio without compromising privacy.

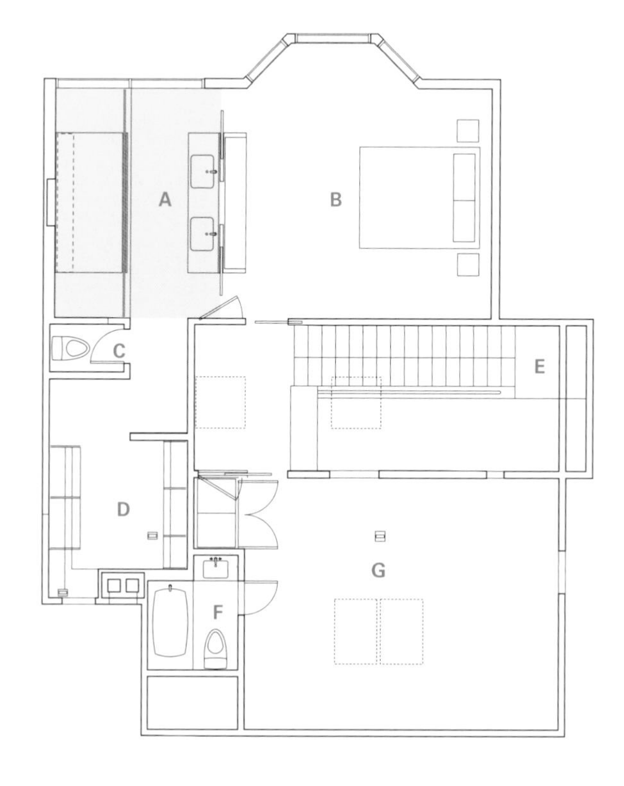

Opposite Left
The dignified exterior of this historic Victorian home belies an interior that has been completely transformed. The former dark, cellular layout is now a contemporary, light-filled, spacious home.

Floor Plan
- A Master bathroom
- B Master bedroom
- C WC
- D Dressing room
- E Stair up from ground floor
- F Bathroom
- G Home office / study

Above
A generously proportioned, stone-lined shower area is separated from the rest of the bathroom by a frameless and partially etched glass blade wall and lit from above with a large skylight.

Glass

CCS Architecture
Lake Street Residence
San Francisco, California, USA

Bathroom Plan and Elevations A, B and C
1:50

1 Stainless steel towel rail
2 Niche in stone-clad shower wall
3 Line of skylight over shower
4 Shower
5 Frameless, full-height glass screen
6 Doorway to WC and dressing room
7 Limestone tiles to floor
8 Sliding etched-glass door
9 White ceramic basin
10 Custom made terrazzo countertop
11 Mirror-clad wall behind basins
12 Storage to bedroom
13 Bedroom mirror
14 Shower head
15 Towel hook
16 Shower controls
17 Stainless steel, wall-mounted light fitting
18 Limestone wall tiles to shower area
19 Cylindrical glass pendant lights
20 Timber veneer drawer fronts
21 Timber veneer door fronts
22 Timber kickplate
23 Openable window with etched panel for privacy
24 Painted plasterboard wall

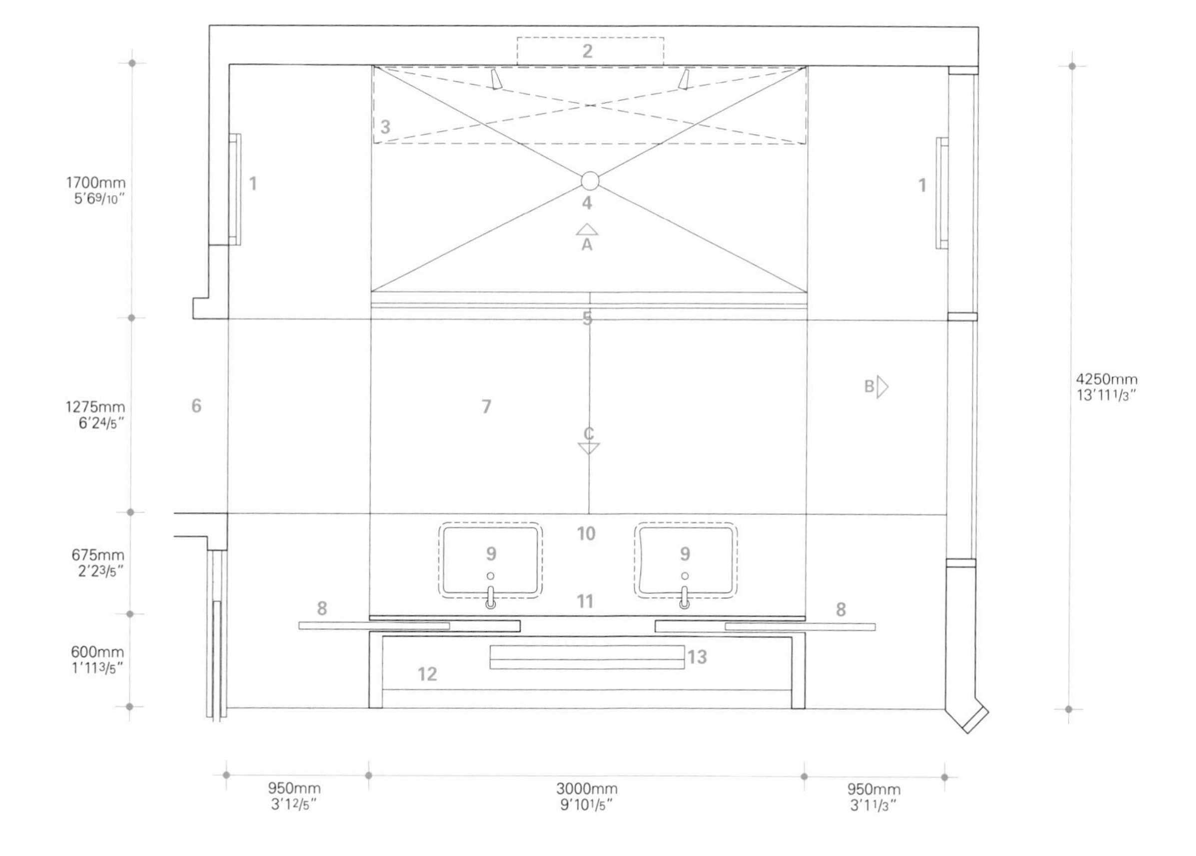

Materials
Benchtop Reconstituted stone top and side panels
Joinery Walnut drawer and door fronts
Floor Limestone tiles
Tiles Limestone

Fixtures
Basin Taps and Spout Dornbracht
Basin Kohler
WC Toto
Shower Head Dornbracht
Lighting BEGA recessed downlights and Resolute Pendants

Project Credits
Completion 2006
Project Architects Cass Calder Smith, Eduardo Perez
Interior Designer John Wheatman Associates
Structural Engineers John Yadegar Associates
Main Contractor Ben Davies Construction

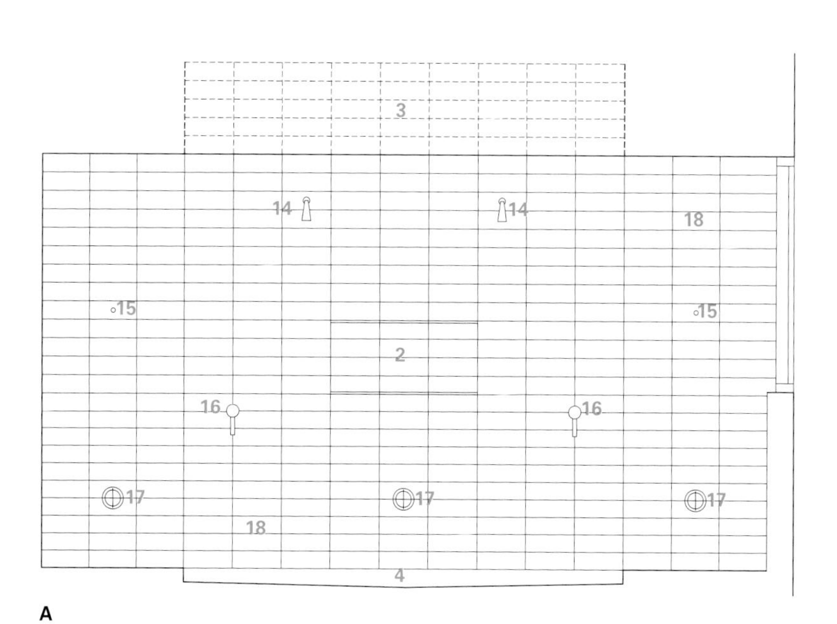

A

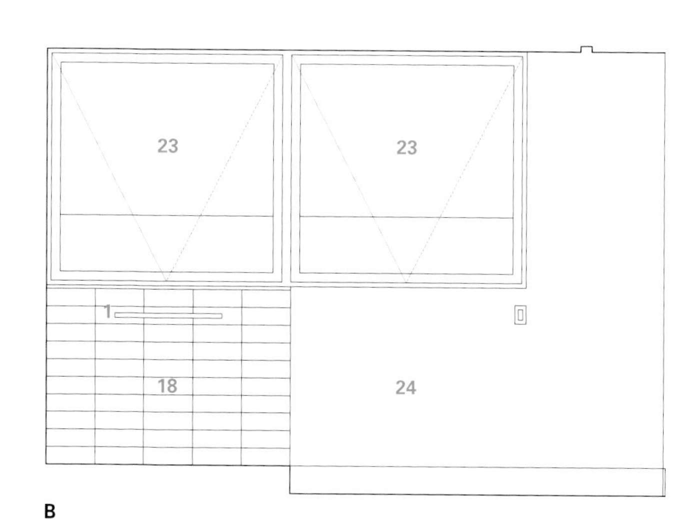

B

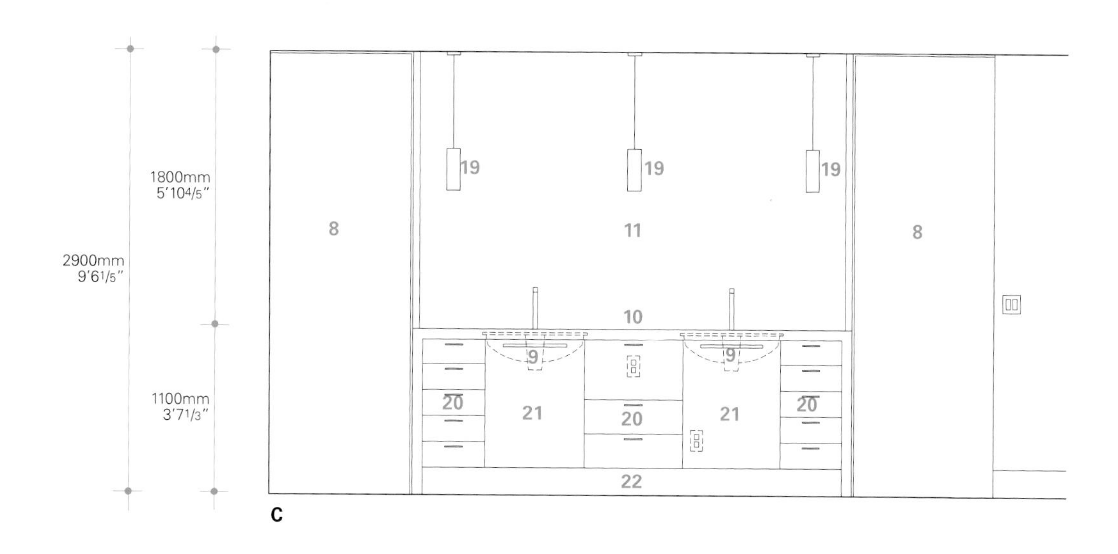

C

Glen Irani Architects

Hover House
Los Angeles, California, USA

This expansive family home includes a studio for the architect-owner, an artist's studio for his wife, a residence for four with guest quarters, ample outdoor living space and a swimming pool looking out over the canals of Venice. The success of the house is rooted in its programme, which advances the standards by which professionals work and live in the same structure by proposing stronger workspace connections to rejuvenating amenities such as the garden and swimming pool.

The ground-floor studios address the need for workspace accessibility and privacy by isolating the workspaces from the living areas above. However, the architecture studio readily converts to a living area by gliding the desks to one end on integrated rails. The living spaces hover above the ground level and are focused around a large southwest oriented sun-court. On the second floor a children's playroom and the living areas open onto the sun-court through large sliding glass panels.

The bathroom, located on the top floor, along with the master bedroom, is a luxuriously appointed bathing space that slots into a narrow space flanking the corridor to the master bedroom. It recalls naval architecture or, on a more extreme level, an airline bathroom, where amenities are seamlessly moulded into the space and every functional attribute is carefully calculated. Here, the tub, vanities and cabinetry are integrated into a single 'chassis' constructed from acrylic resin-coated MDO (exterior grade plywood coated with a smooth waterproof veneer).

The thin plane of glass around the bath transmits ample light and offers privacy from the courtyard beyond. Another thin plane of glass subdivides the WC and shower spaces while transmitting yet more light from the opposite wall of the bathroom.

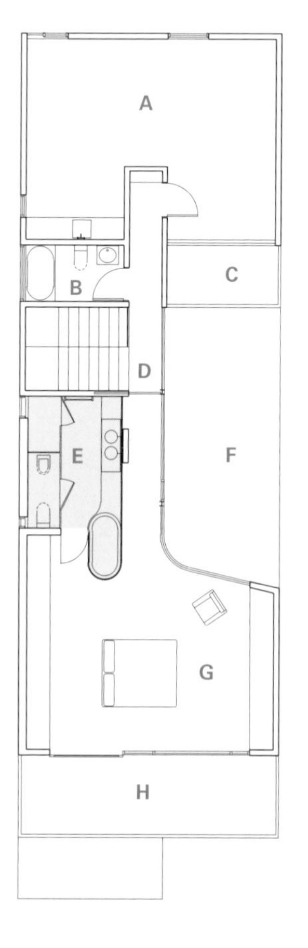

Opposite Left
View of the house from the canal. The three-storey strikingly contemporary home features over 40 colours, most visible from every area in the house. The colour design arose from a fledgling colour theory devised by the architect and artist owners.

Floor Plan
A Painting studio
B Bathroom
C Terrace
D Stair up from ground floor
E Master bathroom
F Void to courtyard below
G Master bedroom
H Terrace

Above Left
View of the bathroom from the bedroom. The curved glass wall around the bath and vanity screens the bathroom from the upper-level sun court (right).

Above Right
The entrance to the bathroom is located between a run of full-height dark timber cupboards and the curved glass screen.

Left
The bath surround and vanity joinery are designed as a continuous sculptural element. Where the basins needed to be raised to a useable height, a raised glass shelf is introduced, allowing the cabinets to continue uninterrupted beneath.

Glen Irani Architects
Hover House
Los Angeles, California, USA

Bathroom Plan, Section A–A and Elevation A
1:50

1 Wardrobes with bleached and dyed Birdseye Maple fronts
2 WC
3 Bidet
4 Glass door to WC
5 Glass partition between WC and shower
6 Shower head
7 Floor waste
8 Tiled finish to shower floor
9 Glass partition wall to shower and WC
10 Towel rail
11 Glass door to bathroom
12 Acid-etched glass screen to bath
13 Stainless steel frame to glass screen over
14 White ceramic bathtub
15 Continuous stone bath surround and countertop
16 White ceramic basin
17 Raised acid-etched glass countertop
18 Mirror-faced cupboards
19 Coloured concrete floor with acrylic sealer
20 Suspended glass sphere light fitting
21 Wall-mounted basin spout and mixer tap
22 White spray finished cupboard door
23 White spray finished drawers
24 White spray finished low bath surround

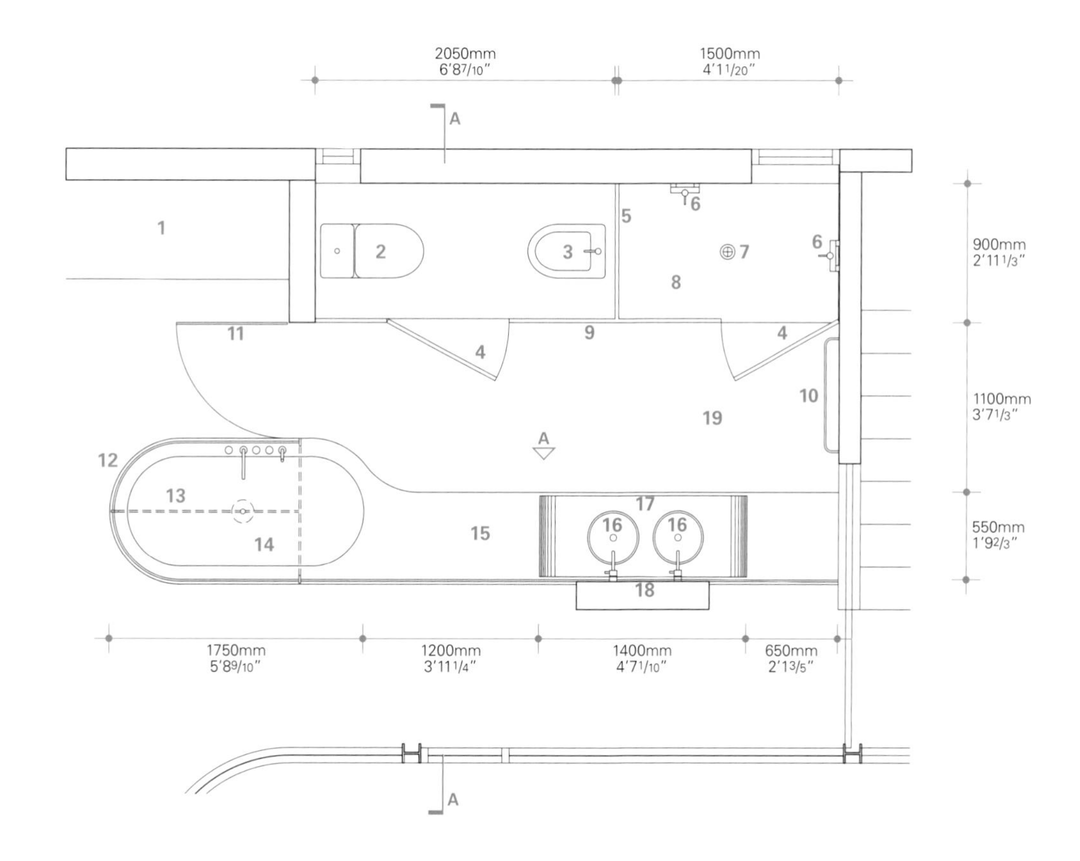

Materials
Countertop Frosted acrylic upper countertop
Joinery Acrylic resin coated MDF
Floor Coloured concrete with acrylic sealer
Tiles Orange Venetian glass mosaic tiles to shower
Lighting American De Rosa pendant globes

Appliances and Fixtures
Basin Taps Vola
Basin Lacava
Shower Taps Dornbracht
Shower Head Starck from Hansgrohe
Bath Taps and Spout Tara from Dornbracht
Towel Rails Detail, West Hollywood
WC Porcher Veneto
Bidet Duravit Metro

Project Credits
Completion 2005
Client Glen Irani
Project Architects Glen Irani, James Renny Caleca
Structural Engineers Parker Resnick Structural Engineers

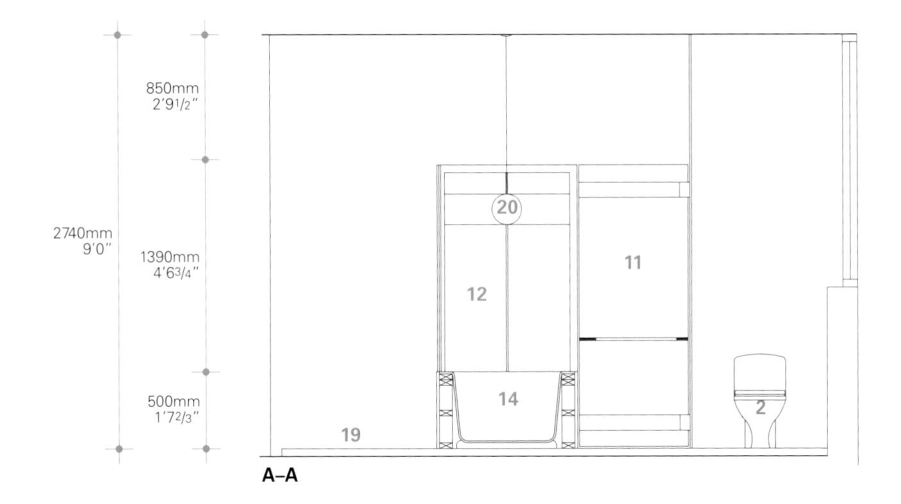

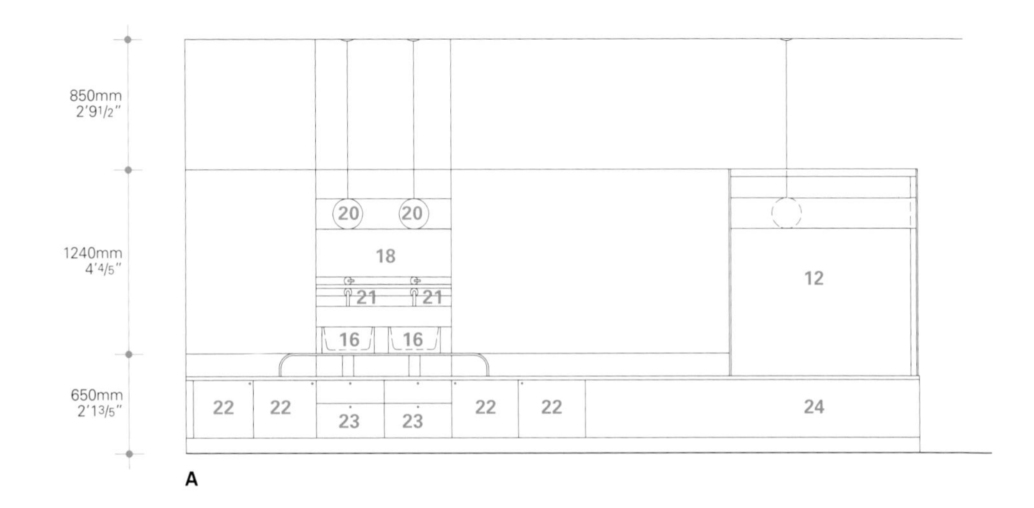

Crepain Binst Architecture

Loft
Antwerp, Belgium

This project for an office for up to 70 people as well as a private residence started life as a semi-derelict five-storey warehouse dating from c.1910. The building features beautiful cast-iron columns and vaulted brick arches in a handsome classical façade, all of which have been restored to their former glory.

The building was rearranged to create an inner courtyard with parking spaces and central access to both the office and the apartment. In place of the former industrial lift, a single central black-lacquered concrete shaft was built to house a new lift, staircase and all of the electrical and hydraulic services.

Levels three and four accommodate the private residence with sleeping quarters, a multipurpose room and a workshop on the third floor and living spaces including kitchen and dining room above, all arranged around the west-facing roof terrace which offers panoramic views of the city from both the front and the back of the building.

The master bedroom and bathroom occupy one structural bay at one end of the floor. A run of wardrobes has been added to the existing solid end wall to create a dressing area. The bathroom is separated from the bedroom by a three-quarter-height partition wall, allowing the existing structure to be seen above.

A change in floor level and finish (from timber to Corian) indicates the bathing area. Here, against mirror-clad wall panels on either side, are a custom made bathtub with Corian surround, and a wall-hung Corian countertop with two integrated basins and a cantilevered shelf below. Beyond these are an etched-glass wall with a sliding panel screen, the shower area and the WC. Located in the same services core, but opening onto the multi-functional area, are a second bathroom and laundry.

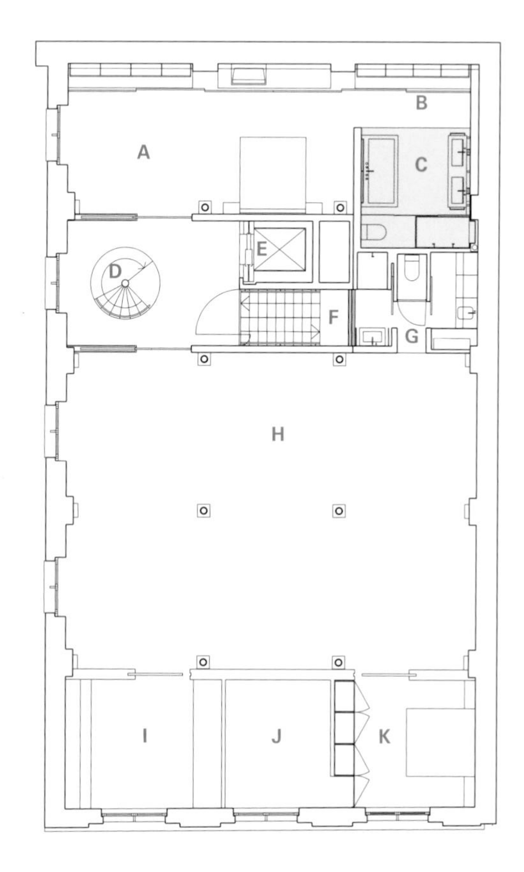

Opposite Left
View of the building from Antwerp Harbour. The renovated original brick façade (left centre) contrasts with new grey aluminium cladding to the apartment at the top of the building and the dark grey plaster to the office levels.

Floor Plan
A Master bedroom
B Dressing area and wardrobes
C Master bathroom
D Stair to upper level
E Lift
F Fire stair
G Guest bathroom
H Multi-functional space
I Studio
J Storage
K Guest bedroom

Left
View of the living room, study and library which features a band of high-level glazing. The apartment enjoys spectacular views of the city, including the spire of Antwerp Cathedral.

Below
The master bathroom is divided into two areas – the bathing area with white Corian double sink and shelf, and a shower and WC behind a wall of translucent glass.

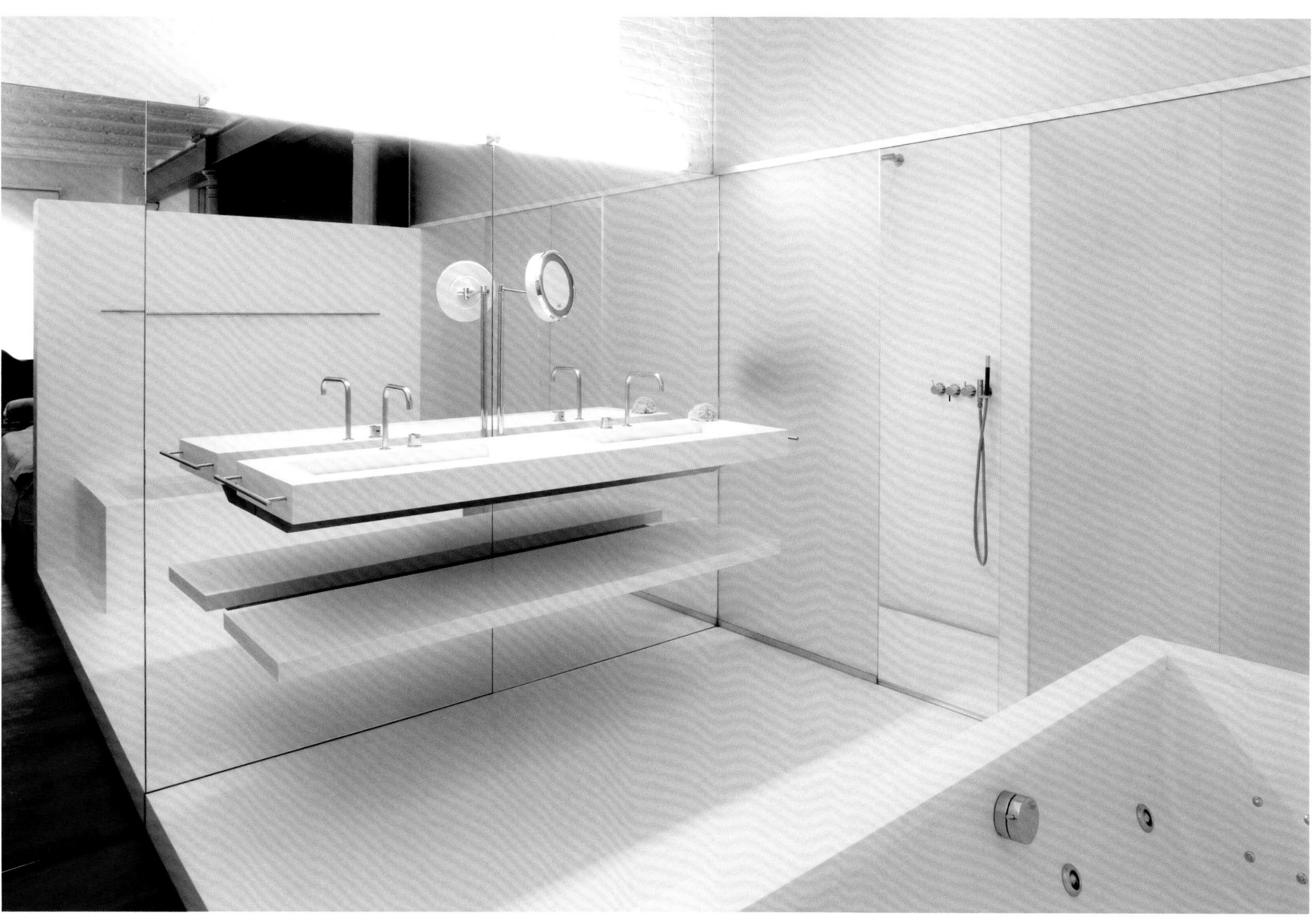

Glass

Crepain Binst Architecture
Loft
Antwerp, Belgium

Bathroom Plan and Sections A–A and B–B 1:50

1 Stainless steel towel rail above bath
2 Bath spout and mixer tap
3 Custom made bath with Corian surround
4 Stainless steel towel rail to basins
5 Custom made Corian basin
6 Basin spout and mixer tap
7 Corian basin surround and countertop
8 Raised Corian floor platform
9 WC
10 Glass screen to WC
11 Glass screen to shower
12 Custom made Corian shower tray
13 Shampoo niche to shower
14 Shower head
15 Shower to bathroom 2
16 Basin to bathroom 2
17 WC to bathroom 2
18 Laundry
19 Custom made cantilevered Corian shelf
20 Existing warehouse wall behind
21 WC flush button
22 Wardrobes to dressing room

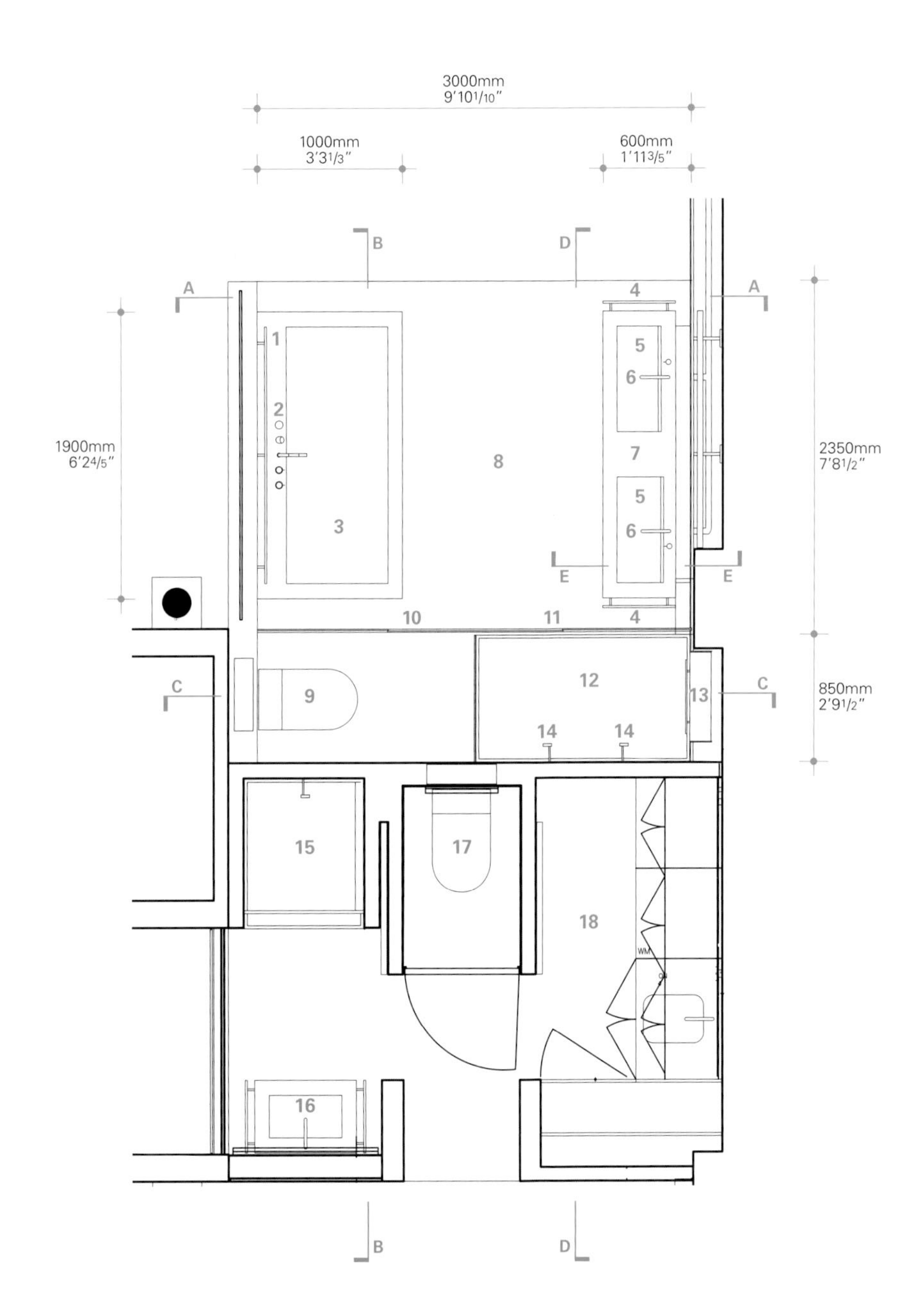

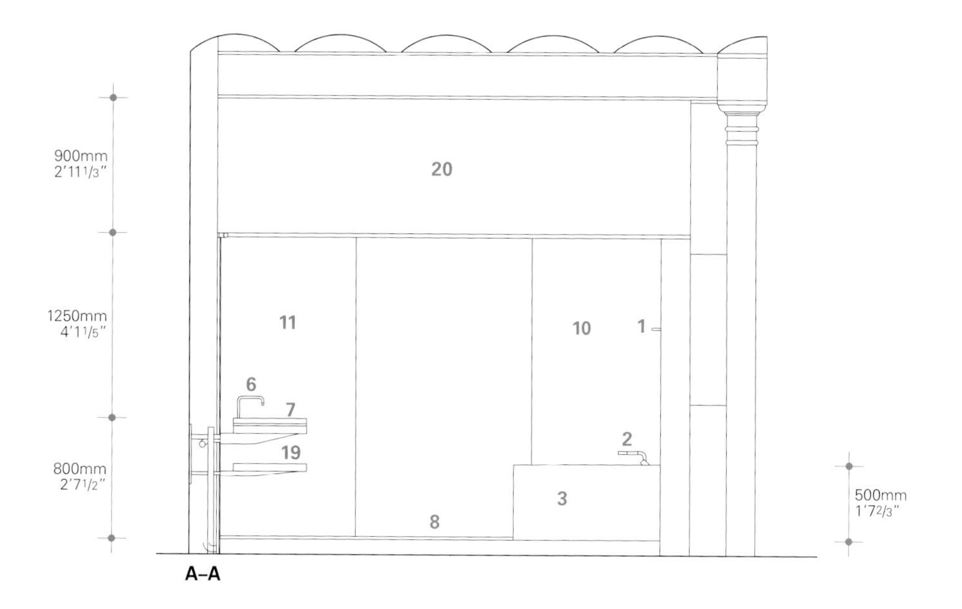
900mm
2'11 1/3"
1250mm
4'1 1/5"
800mm
2'7 1/2"
500mm
1'7 2/3"
20
11
10
1
6
7
19
2
3
8
A–A

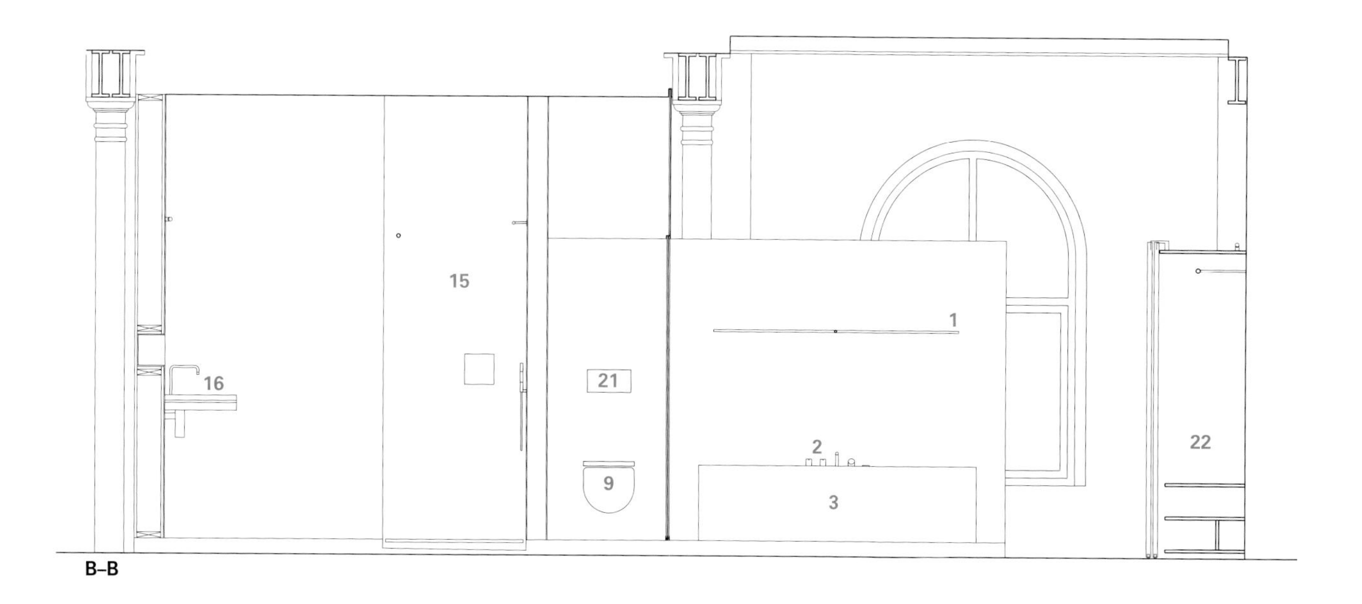
15
16
21
9
1
2
3
22
B–B

Glass

Crepain Binst Architecture
Loft
Antwerp, Belgium

Bathroom Sections C–C and D–D
1:50
1 Shower head
2 Shampoo niche
3 Hand held shower and mixer taps
4 Custom made Corian wall panels to shower
5 WC
6 WC flush button
7 Recessed down lights
8 Wardrobes to dressing area
9 Dressing area
10 Basin spout and mixer tap
11 Custom made Corian basin
12 Corian basin surround and countertop
13 Custom made cantilevered Corian shelf
14 Mirror-faced wall panel
15 Raised Corian floor
16 Glass screen to shower
17 Cupboards to laundry
18 Washing machines
19 Corian worktop to laundry
20 Laundry sink and spout
21 Cupboards below laundry sink
22 Full-height cupboards

Detail Section E–E
1:5
1 Corian edge panel
2 Corian basin surround
3 Corian bottom panel to basin
4 Basin spout
5 Mixer tap
6 Corian panel to take water spill
7 Stainless steel strut
8 Water outlet pipe
9 Corian back panel
10 Stainless steel ledge
11 Mirror-faced wall panel
12 Steel plate fixed to wall
13 Steel circular section fixed to steel plate
14 Corian shelf
15 Stainless steel structure

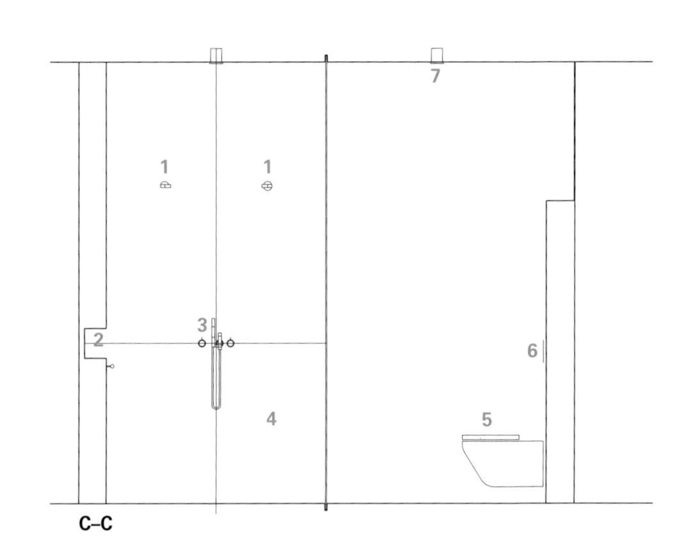

C–C

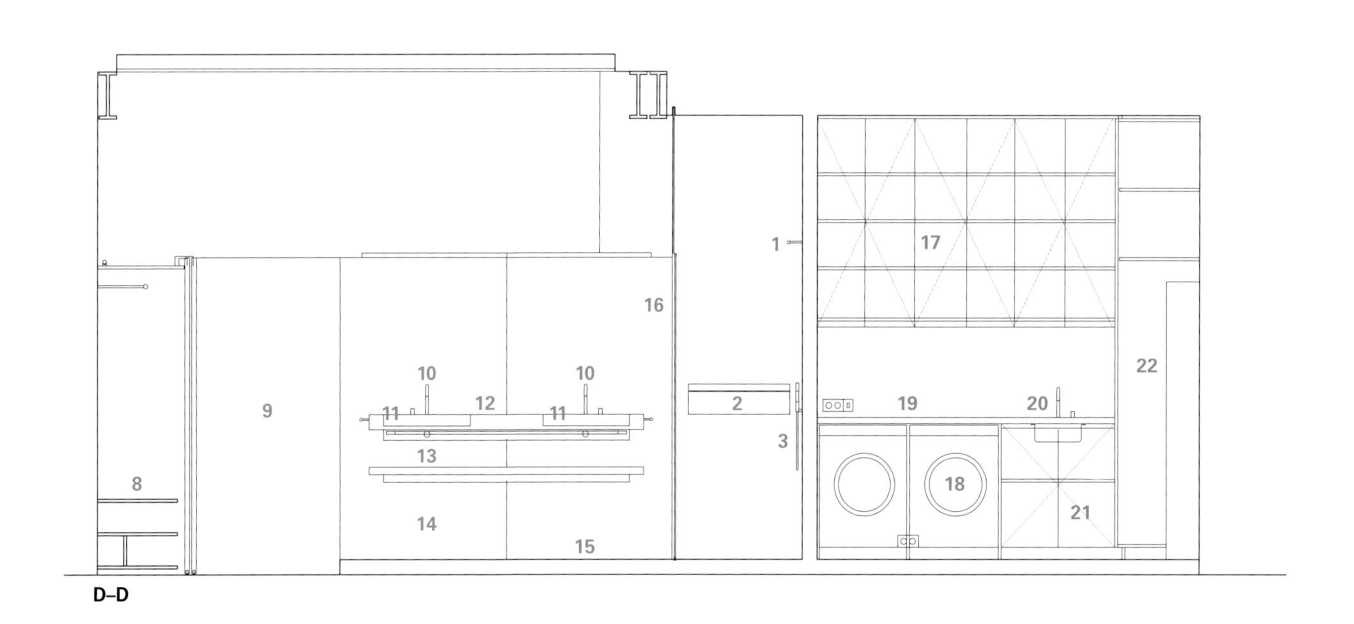

D–D

Materials
Countertop Corian
Floor Corian
Lighting Myriad, Sylvania, Philinea and Neon

Appliances and Fixtures
Basin Taps Vola 590
Basin Spout Vola 590
Basin Custom made Corian
Shower Taps Vola
Shower Head Vola
Bath Taps and Spout Vola
Bath Custom made Corian
Towel Rails Stainless steel
Toilet Duravit and Geberit

Project Credits
Completion 1997
Client Crepain Family
Structural Engineer Archidee
Quantity Surveyor Steven de Paepe and Jo Crepain
Main Contractor Van Rymenant nv
Interior Designer Nadia Pelckmans and Jo Crepain

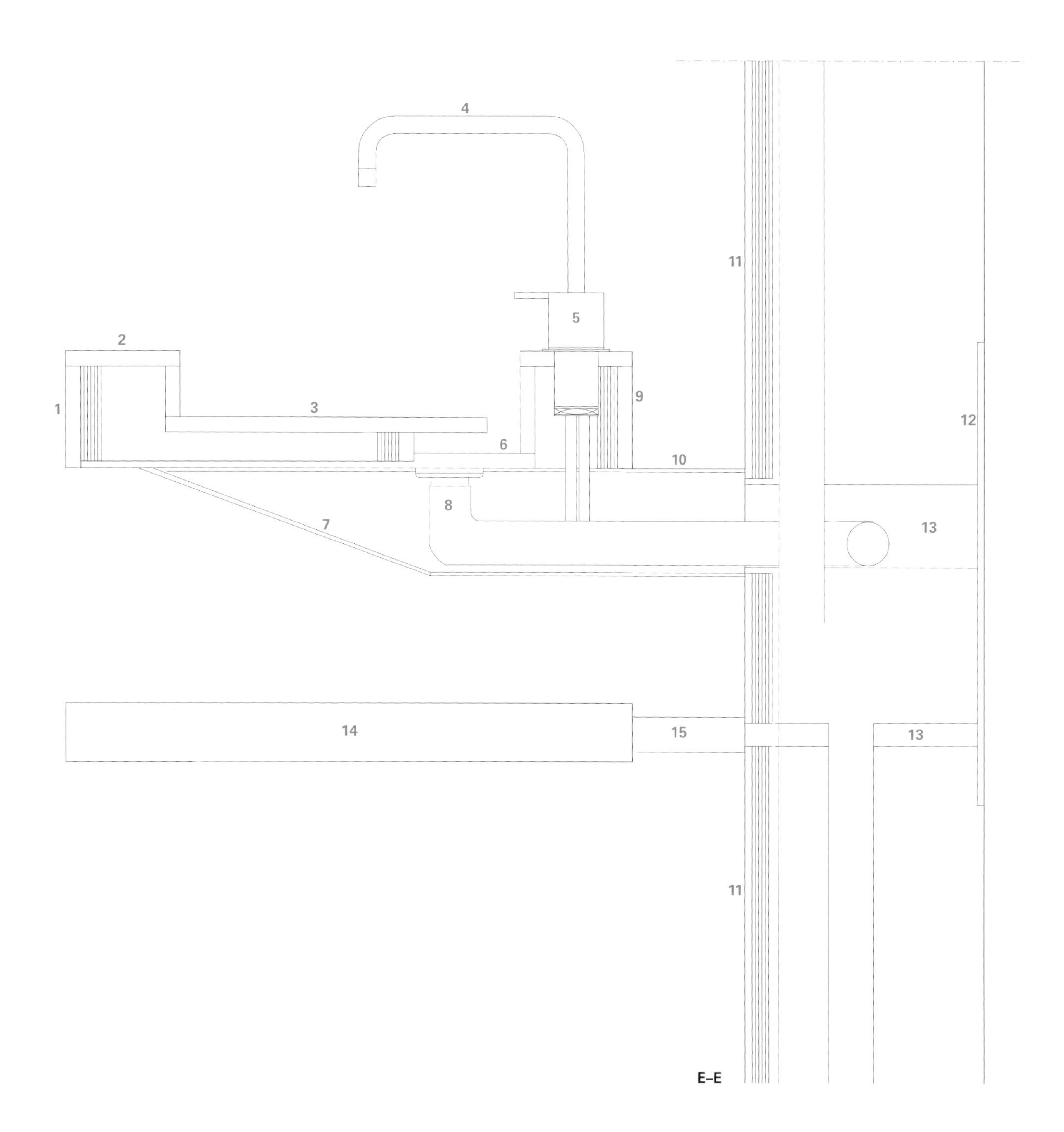

Steven Holl Architects, Ruessli Architekten

The Swiss Residence Washington, D.C., USA

The Swiss Residence is the official residence of the Swiss Ambassador to the United States in Washington, D.C. In addition to the Ambassador's domestic quarters, the building is an extension of the Swiss Embassy's work space and is used for official functions. The project was commissioned after an anonymous international competition in which ten other architects participated.

Sited on a hill with a direct view to the Washington Monument in the distance, the building's design is based on overlapping spaces drawn through a cruciform courtyard plan. From the entrance hall, one can see diagonally through the building to the terrace and on to the Monument. The residence is positioned on a plateau with an arrival square, a reflecting pool, a reception courtyard and a herb garden.

Among the public areas are two formal dining rooms, three salons, one reception hall and a stone terrace that offers spectacular views of the city. Each of these connects directly to an outdoor space that can accommodate groups of up to 200 people. The private areas are located on the second floor and include the Ambassador's living quarters, two guest rooms and staff rooms.

The materiality of the residence is an important feature of the design. The building's charcoal coloured concrete and sand-blasted translucent structural glass planks were inspired by the black rocks and white snow of the Swiss Alps. The residence is constructed according to Swiss 'Minergie Standards' to keep overall energy consumption low.

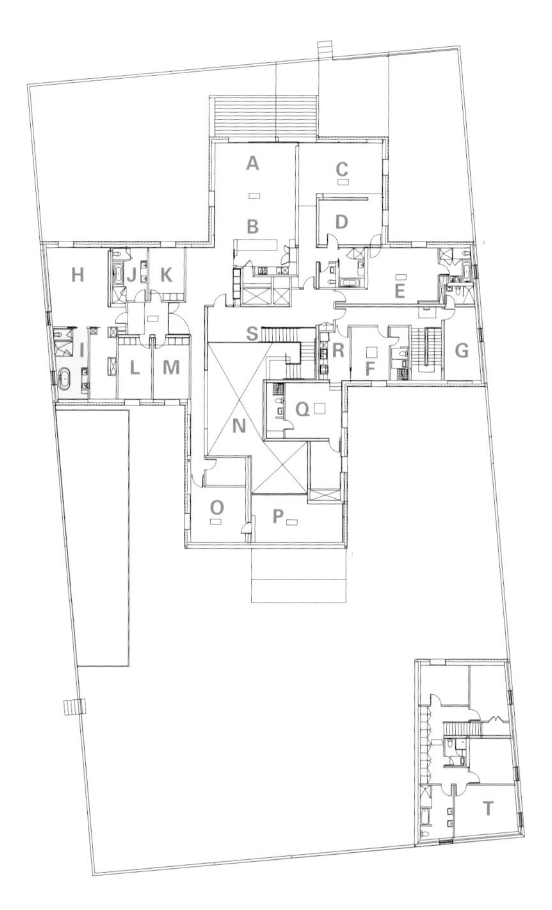

Opposite Left
From the entrance court, the minimal palette of materials and colours makes a dramatic impact. The black concrete entry façade is countered by a glazed porte cochere. Elsewhere, translucent glass planks allow diffused light in, and out, of the building.

Floor Plan
A Living room
B Kitchen
C Guest living room
D Guest dining room
E Guest bedroom
F Staff bedroom
G Staff bedroom
H Master bedroom
I Master bathroom
J Bathroom
K Bedroom
L Bedroom
M Bedroom
N Void overlooking ground floor below
O Reception room
P Private balcony
Q Staff bedroom
R Laundry
S Stair from ground floor
T Caretaker's house

Left
The master bathroom in the Ambassador's private quarters features simple white fixtures and white-painted plasterboard walls and ceiling which contrast with the dark timber floor. The Corian basins are integrated into a wall-hung vanity bench which sits opposite a free-standing white ceramic bathtub.

Glass

Steven Holl Architects, Ruessli Architekten
The Swiss Residence
Washington, D.C., USA

Bathroom Plan and Sections A–A and B–B 1:50
1 Sliding timber door to master bathroom
2 Toilet-roll holder
3 Spare toilet roll-holder
4 WC
5 Tiled shower enclosure
6 Wall-mounted shower set with hand held shower
7 Window
8 Bath spout and taps
9 Free-standing white ceramic bathtub
10 White roller blind to external window
11 Mirror-faced cabinet
12 Towel rail
13 Basin taps and spout
14 White Corian integrated basin in Corian countertop
15 Corian countertop
16 Wall-mounted mirror
17 Wall-mounted hook
18 Timber floor
19 Storage cupboards below countertop
20 Concealed recess for lighting and roller blind assembly
21 WC flush button

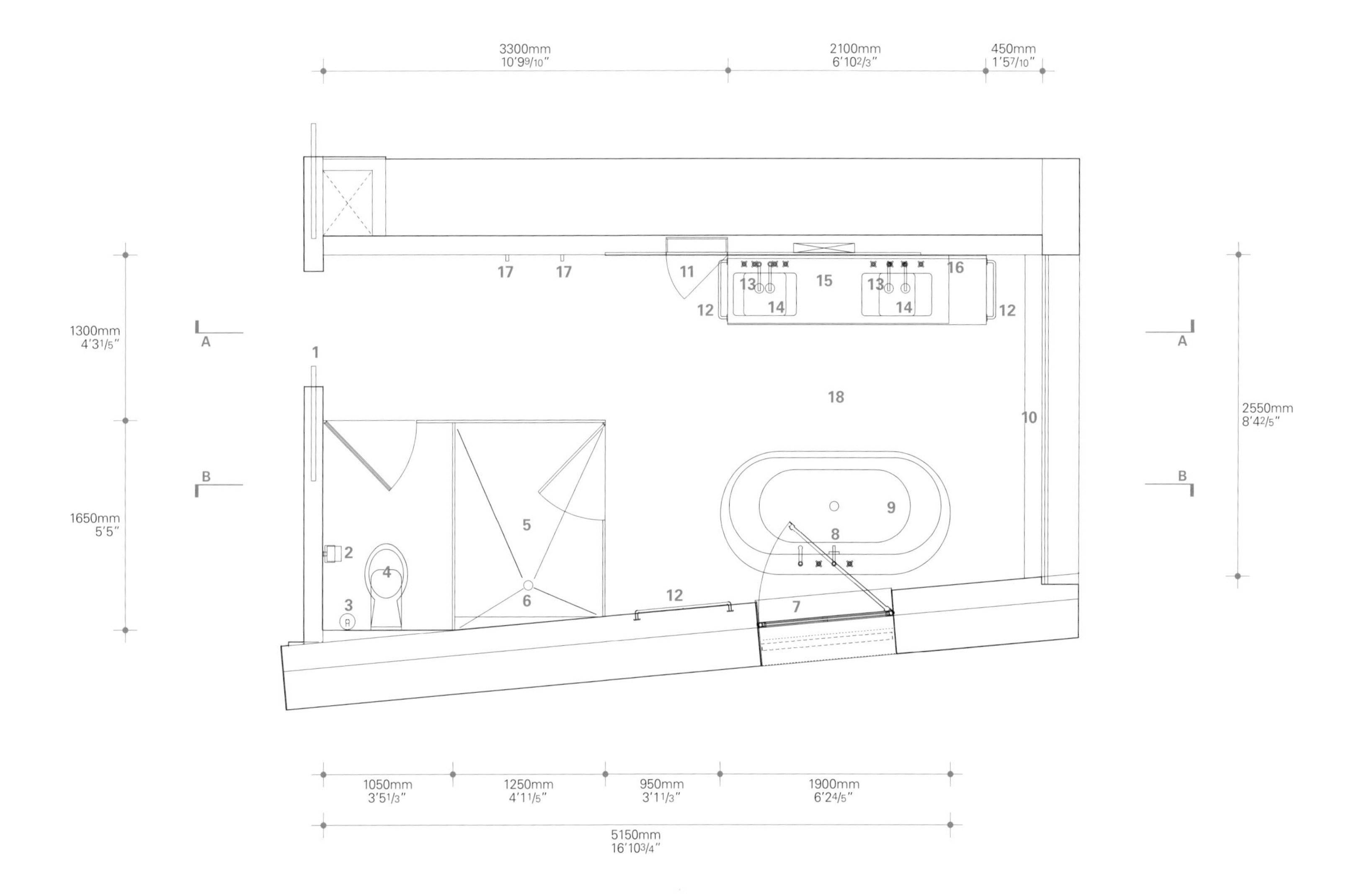

Materials
Countertop Custom made Corian countertop
Joinery Timber with white lacquered finish
Floor Dark stained bamboo
Splashback Custom made Corian panel
Wall Tiles White ceramic tiles
Lighting Fluorescent fixtures in light cove and Louis Poulsen Ballerup and Flos Train

Appliances and Fixtures
Basin Taps Dornbracht Tara
Basin Spout Dornbracht Tara
Basins Custom made Corian basins
Shower Taps Dornbracht Tara
Shower Head Dornbracht Tara
Bath Taps and Spout Dornbracht Tara
Bath Duravit Foster
WC Duravit Happy D

Project Credits
Completion 2006
Client Swiss Federal Office for Building and Logistics
Project Architects Steven Holl, Justin Ruessli, Olaf Schmidt, Stephen O'Dell, Arnault Biou, Peter Englaender, Annette Goderbauer, Li Hu, Irene Vogt, Mimi Kueh, Andreas Gervasi, Phillip Röösli, Rafael Schnyder, Urs Zuercher
Structural Engineers A.F. Steffen Engineers, Robert Silman Associates
Mechanical Engineers B+B Energietechnik AG, B2E Consulting Engineers

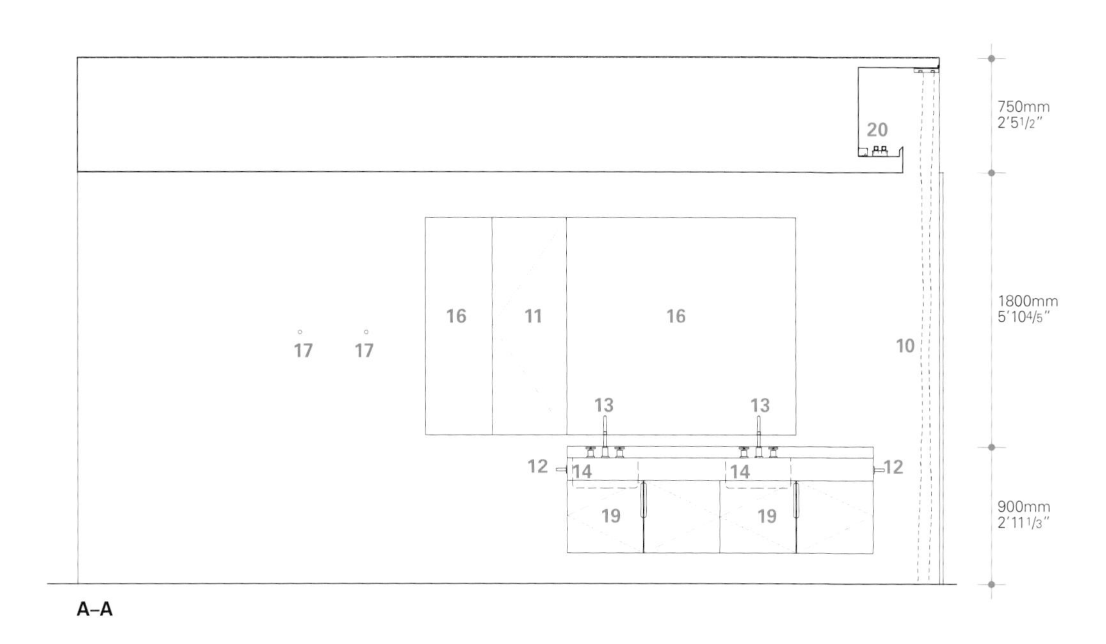

A–A

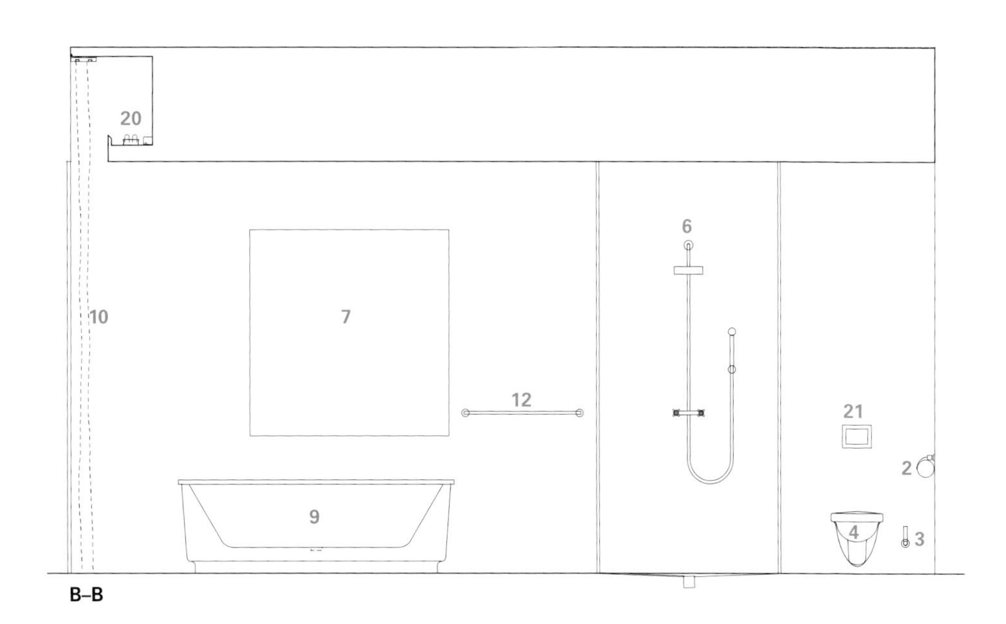

B–B

Kubota Architect Atelier

Hiroshima Residence Hiroshima City, Hiroshima Prefecture, Japan

This four-storey residence and clinic is situated on the banks of the Ota River in a suburb of Hiroshima. In a reversal of recent trends towards the separation of domestic and commercial buildings, this house refers back to ancient Japanese traditions of grouping sometimes disparate uses under one roof.

Here, a basement accommodates technical and plant rooms as well as staff lockers. The ground floor houses a reception space for the clinic, a discreet entrance to the residential quarters, and a garage. The first floor is divided in two, split between the operation suites for the clinic, and the master bedroom and bathroom for the residence.

The top floor, with expansive glazed walls overlooking the river, accommodates the main living spaces including the kitchen, dining and living areas, as well as the family bathroom and children's bedroom and play room. In one corner of this floor, separated from the living room by an open terrace, is a traditional Japanese tatami room used for tea ceremonies.

The main bathroom is located opposite the tatami room, separated from it by the lift core, storage room and a separate WC. The space is divided into three zones – the first with storage cupboards, vanity area and WC, the second housing a large bathtub and wet area shower which terminates in a large sliding glass door.

The third space opens directly from the bath room and is a private terrace surrounded by full-height walls for privacy but completely open to the elements. Here, a wall mounted shower provides the options for year-round outdoor bathing.

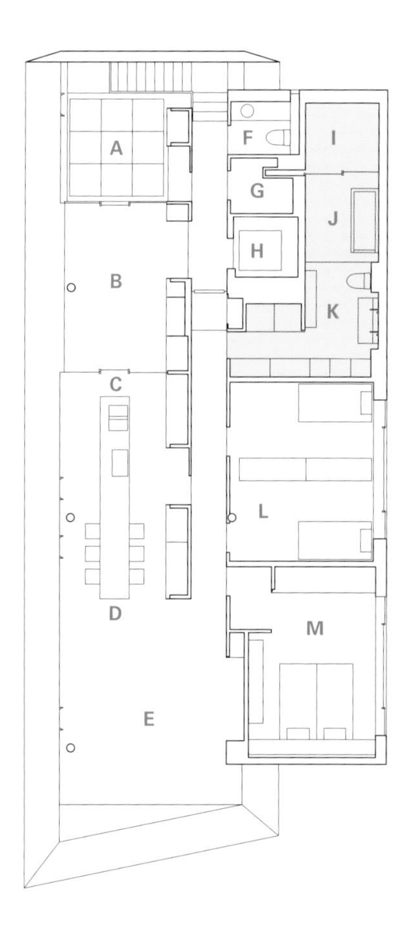

Opposite Left
View of the living and dining rooms on the top floor of the house. Expanses of full-height clear glazing provide views out over the river, while panels of glass louvres provide ventilation. The dining table is a continuous built-in bench that transforms into the kitchen island countertop.

Floor Plan
A Tea ceremony room
B Terrace
C Kitchen
D Dining room
E Living room
F WC
G Store room
H Lift
I Shower terrace
J Bath and shower
K Bathroom
L Playroom
M Bedroom

Left
In the bathroom, the bath and shower area open onto a walled terrace which is open to the sky.

Below Left
The bath and shower are arranged as a wet area, separated from the rest of the bathroom by a frameless glazed door.

Glass

Kubota Architect Atelier
Hiroshima Residence, Hiroshima City, Hiroshima Prefecture, Japan

Bathroom Plan and Sections A–A and B–B
1:50

1 White gloss mosaic tiled floor to walled shower terrace
2 Wall-mounted shower head
3 Sliding glass door to shower terrace
4 Polished chrome bath spout and taps
5 Acrylic resin bathtub
6 Wall-mounted shower set
7 Glazed screen and door to wet room
8 WC
9 Basin spout and taps
10 Double acrylic resin basin
11 Shelving
12 White gloss mosaic tiled floor
13 Storage shelves
14 Laundry cupboard
15 Wall-mounted mirror above basin
16 Towel rail

Detail Section Through Bathtub, C–C
1:10

1 Ceramic tiled floor on mortar bed over under-floor heating and insulation
2 Corian panel bath surround
3 White acrylic resin bath top
4 White acrylic resin bath
5 Bath support structure over rubber asphalt paint waterproofing
6 Wall-mounted bath spout
7 Stainless steel cover panel to concealed services
8 Wall-mounted bath taps
9 White mosaic tiled wall
10 Covered services

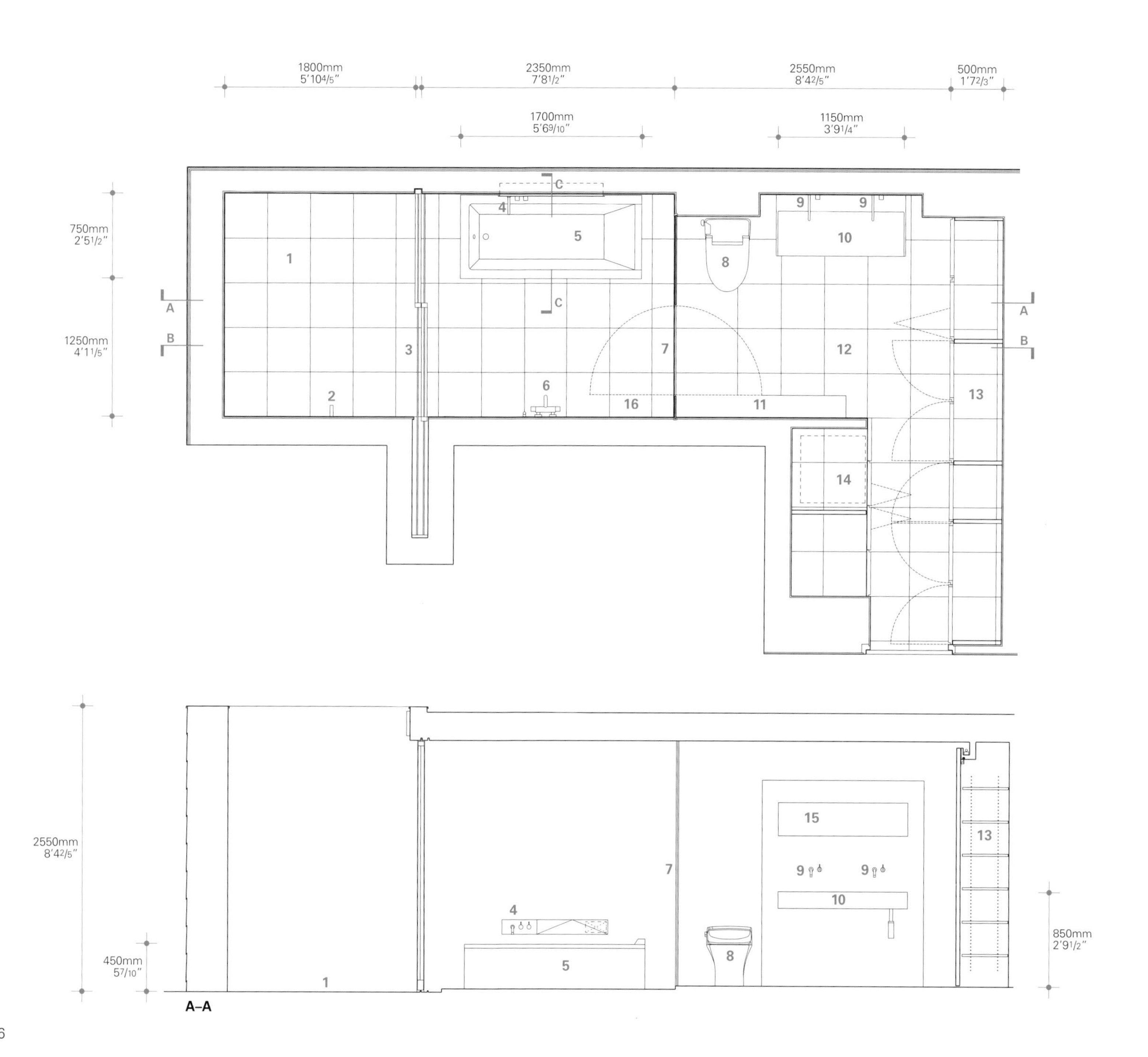

Materials
Floor Limestone-like ceramic tiles to floor of bathroom and terrace
Wall Tiles White glass mosaic tiles
Lighting Nippo fluorescent light concealed in ceiling

Appliances and Fixtures
Basin Taps Vola 110
Basin Spout Vola 110
Basin Bespoke brass design 'nude' acrylic resin basin
Shower Axor Hansgrohe hand shower and Axor Starck bar
Shower Head Axor Starck
Bath Taps and Spout Vola 620
Bath Bespoke acrylic resin
WC INAX 'Satis' with sheet warmer and electro-bidet

Project Credits
Completion 2005
Project Architects Katsufumi Kubota, Kazuya Toizaki, Yuko Mishima
Structural Engineer SAK – Takeo Sakuka
Main Contractor Nomura Architecture Construction

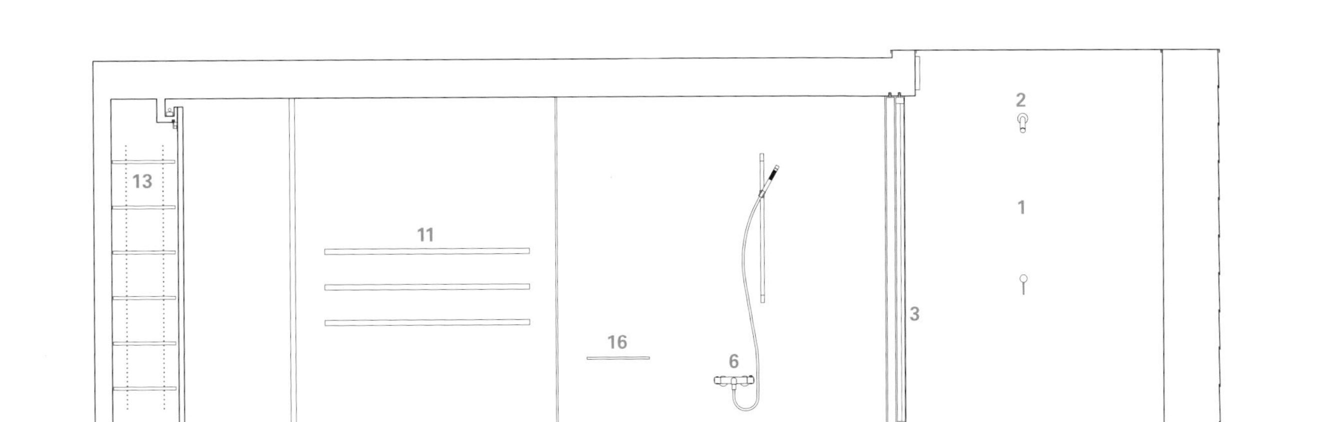

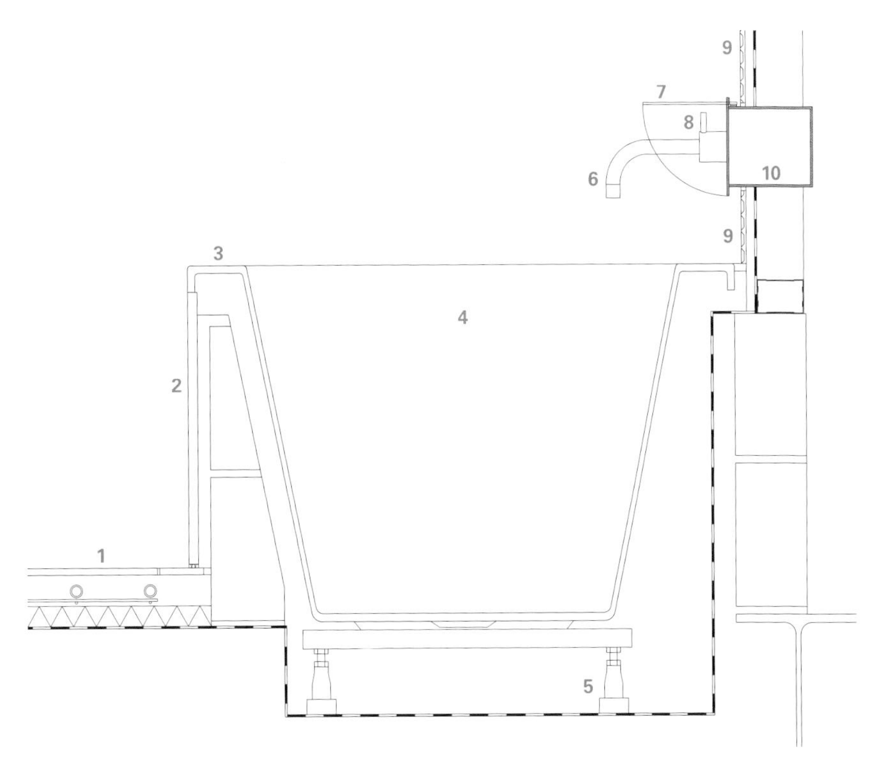

Architects' Contact Details

Australia

Coy + Yiontis Architects
387 Clarendon Street, South Melbourne
VIC 3205
T: +61 3 9645 7600
F: +61 3 9645 7622
cy@cyarchitects.com.au
www.cyarchitects.com.au

Craig Steere Architects
PO Box 7096, Shenton Park, Western
Australia 6008
T: +61 8 9380 4662
F: +61 8 9380 4663
craig@craigsteerearchitects.com.au
www.craigsteerearchitects.com.au

Marsh Cashman Koolloos Architects
Studio 401, 104 Commonwealth Street
Surry Hills, NSW 2010
T: +61 2 92114146
F: +61 2 92114148
architects@mckarchitects.com
www.mckarchitects.com

Stanic Harding
123 Commonwealth Street, Surry Hills
NSW 2010
T: +61 2 9211 6710
F: +61 2 9211 0366
architects@stanicharding.com.au
www.stanicharding.com.au

Tzannes Associates
63 Myrtle Street
Chippendale
NSW 2008
T: +61 2 9319 3744
F: +61 2 9698 1170
tzannes@tzannes.com.au
www.tzannes.com.au

Austria

Serda Architects
Palais Schönborn
Renngasse 4
1010 Vienna
T: +43 1 512 36 99/0
F: +43 1 512 36 99/11
architects@serda.at
www.serda.at

Belgium

Crepain Binst Architecture
Vlaanderenstraat 6
B 2000 Antwerpen
T: +32 3 213 61 61
F: +32 3 213 61 62
mail@crepainbinst.be
www.crepainbinst.be

Vincent Van Duysen Architects
Lombardenvest 34
B 2000 Antwerpen
T: +32 3 205 91 90
vincent@vincentvanduysen.com
www.vincentvanduysen.com

Germany

Schneider + Schmumacher
Niddastraße 91
D-60329 Frankfurt am Main
T: +49 69 25 62 62 62
F: +49 69 25 62 62 99
office@schneider-schumacher.de
www.schneider-schumacher.de

Japan

EDH Endoh Design House
#101, 2-13-8, Honmachi
Shibuya-ku
Tokyo 151 0071
T: +81 3 3377 6293
endoh@edh-web.com
www.edh-web.com

Kei'ichi Irie / Power Unit Studio
#2107, 12-1, Sarugaku-cho, Shibuya-ku
Tokyo 150 0033
T: +81 3 3461 9827
F: +81 3 3461 9829
info@pus.jp
www.pus.jp

Kengo Kuma and Associates
2-24-8 Minami Aoyama, Minato-ku
Tokyo 1070062
T: +81 3 3401 7721
F: +81 3 3401 7673
kuma@ba2.so-net.ne.jp
www.kkaa.co.jp

Kubota Architect Atelier
1–8–24 Imazu-cho, Iwakuni City,
Yamaguchi 740 0017
T: +81 827 22 0092
F: +81 827 22 0079
info@katsufumikubota.jp
www.katsufumikubota.jp

Waro Kishi + K. Associates Architects
4F Yutaka Bldg. 366 Karigane-cho
Nakagyo-ku, Kyoto 604 8115
T: +81 75 213 0258
F: +81 75 213 0259
kishi@k-associates.com
www.k-associates.com

Portugal

Ezzo
R. Gonçalves Zarco 1129 E. S. 126/127
4450–685 Leça Da Palmeira
T: +351 22 9969263
F: +351 22 9969265
cmmoreira@ezzo.pt
www.ezzo.pt

Atelier D'Arquitectura J. A. Lopes da Costa
Rua de Cabanões, 64
S. João de Ovar
3880-742 Ovar
T: +351 256 575 195
F: +351 256 587 875
geral@jalopesdacosta.com
www.jalopesdacosta.com

Spain

BAAS Jordi Badia / Mercé Sangenís Architects
Frederic Rahola 63
Baixos Local 1
08032 Barcelona
T: +34 93 35 80 111
F: +34 93 35 80 194
baas@jordibadia.com
www.jordibadia.com

Ramón Esteve
Plaza Pere Borrego i Galindo. 7
(Antigua Centenar de la Ploma)
46003 Valencia
T: +34 963 510 434
F: +34 963 155 534
info@ramonesteve.com
www.ramonesteve.com

Sweden

Wingårdhs Architects
Katarinavägen 17, SE 116 45 Stockholm
T: +46 8 447 40 80
F: +46 8 744 40 05
wingardhs@wingardhs.se
www.wingardhs.se

UK

David Nossiter Architects
70 Peckham Road
London SE5 8PX
T: +44 20 7708 5186
F: +44 20 7708 5186
mail@davidnossiter.com
www.davidnossiter.com

Hudson Architects
49-59 Old Street
London
ECIV 9HX
T: +44 20 7490 3411
F: +44 20 7490 3412
info@hudsonarchitects.co.uk
www.hudsonarchitects.co.uk

Paul Archer Design
13-27 Brunswick Place, Hackney
London N1 6DX
T: +44 20 7251 6162
F: +44 20 7253 9697
paularcher@paularcherdesign.co.uk
www.paularcherdesign.co.uk

Scape Architects
Unit 2, Providence Yard
London E2 7RJ
T: +44 20 7012 1244
F: +44 20 7012 1255
mail@scape-architects.com
www.scape-architects.com

Seth Stein Architects
Unit 15 Grand Union Centre, West Row,
London W10 5AS
T: +44 208 968 8581
F: +44 208 968 8591
admin@sethstein.com
www.sethstein.com

Turner Castle Architects
22 Iliffe Yard, Crampton Street
London
SE17 3QA
T: +44 20 7431 2507
office@turnercastle.co.uk
www.turnercastle.co.uk

Ullmayer Sylvester Architects
2 Whatcotts Yard, Palatine Road
London N16 8ST
T: +44 20 7503 0032
silvia@ullmayersylvester.com
www.ullmayersylvester.com

USA

Barton Myers Associates
1025 Westwood Boulevard
Los Angeles
CA 90024
T: +1 310 208 2227
F: +1 310 208 2207
p_robertson@bartonmyers.com
www.bartonmyers.com

CCS Architecture
44 McLea Court
San Francisco
CA 94103
T: +1 415 864 2800
F: +1 415 864 2850
info@ccs-architecture.com
www.ccs-architecture.com
180 Varick Street, No.902
New York,
NY 10014
T: +1 212 274 1121
F: +1 212 274 1122

Glen Irani Architects
410 Sherman Canal, Venice CA 90291
T: +1 310 305 8840
F: +1 310 822 1801
glen@glenirani.com
www.glenirani.com

Kaehler Architects
80 Greenwich Avenue
Greenwich
CT 06830
T: +1 203 629 2212
F: +1 203 629 0717
lek@kaehler-moore.com
www.kaehler-moore.com

Mark English Architects
250 Columbus Avenue, Suite 200
San Francisco
CA 94133
T: +1 415 391 0186
F: +1 415 362 9104
info@markenglisharchitects.com
www.markenglisharchitects.com

Steven Holl Architects
450 West 31st Street, 11th Floor
New York, NY 10001
T: +1 212 629 7262
F: +1 212 629 7312
nyc@stevenholl.com
www.stevenholl.com

Resources

The following are internet addresses for sourcing the fittings and appliances featured throughout the book. Unless otherwise indicated, these are international manufacturers and suppliers.

Abbey Kitchens
www.abbeykitchens.co.uk (Europe)

American De Rosa
www.americanderosa.com (US)

American Standard
www.americanstandard.com (US / CAN)

Aquaplus Solutions
www.aquaplussolutions.com (UK)

Aston Matthews
www.astonmatthews.co.uk (UK supplier)

Axor
www.axor-design.com

BEGA
www.bega.com

Bette
www.bette.co.uk (Europe)

Bisazza
www.bisazza.com

Caroma
www.caroma.com.au

Catalano
www.catalano.it

Cera
www.cera-india.com

Corian
www.corian.com

Cosmic
www.icosmic.com

Dornbracht
www.dornbracht.com

Duravit
www.duravit.com

Duscholux
www.duscholux.com

Erco
www.erco.com

Euroluce
www.euroluce.com.au (AUS)

Fagerhult
www.fagerhult.com

Fantini
www.fantini.it

Flos
www.flos.com

Franke
www.franke.com

Galassia
www.galassiacer.it (Europe)

Geberit
www.geberit.com

Grohe
www.grohe.com

Hansgrohe
www.hansgrohe.com

Ideal Standard
www.ideal-standard.co.uk (Europe)

Ifö Sanitär
www.ifosanitar.com

INAX
www.global.inax.co.jp

INR inredningsglas
www.inredningsglas.com

Kaldewei
www.kaldewei.com

Keramag
www.keramag.de

Kohler
www.kohler.com

Kreon
www.kreon.com

La Cava
www.lacava.com (US)

Louis Poulsen
www.louispoulsen.com

Madinoz
www.madinoz.com.au (ANZ, US)

Mora Armatur
www.moraarmatur.com

Nippo Lighting
www.nippo-web.com (US)

Omvivo
www.omvivo.com

Pazotti
www.pazotti.com.au (AUS)

Permesso
www.permesso.com (Europe)

Philippe Starck
www.philippe-starck.com

Plumb Warehouse
www.plumb-warehouse.co.uk (UK supplier)

Poliform USA
www.poliformusa.com (US)

Porcher
www.porcher.com (Europe)

Progetti
www.mgsprogetti.com

RAK Ceramics
www.rakceramics.co.uk (UK)

Roca
www.roca.com

Rogerseller
www.rogerseller.com.au (ANZ)

Royal Mosa
www.royalmosa.com

Toto
www.totousa.com

Vibia
www.vibialight.com (US / CAN)

Villeroy & Boch
www.villeroy-boch.com

Vola
www.vola.com

Waterside
watersidebathrooms.co.uk (UK)

Picture Credits

All architectural drawings are supplied courtesy of the architects

Photographic credits:

7 © Murray Fredericks
11 Richard Basic
13 Richard Basic
15 Norma Lopez
17 Norma Lopez
19 © Will Pryce
21 © Will Pryce
24 Shannon McGrath / shannon@shannonmcgrath.com
25 Shannon McGrath / shannon@shannonmcgrath.com
29 Shannon McGrath / shannon@shannonmcgrath.com
30 © Murray Fredericks
31 © Murray Fredericks
33 © Murray Fredericks
34 Steve Townsend / www.stownsend.com
35 Steve Townsend / www.stownsend.com
38 © Giorgio Possenti / VEGA MG
39 © Koen Van Damme / www.koenvandamme.be
44 Peter Clarke
45 Peter Clarke
47 Peter Clarke
48 © Edmund Sumner / VIEW
49 © Edmund Sumner / VIEW
52 © Eugeni Pons
53 © Eugeni Pons
57 © Eugeni Pons
58 © Jörg Hempel
59 © Jörg Hempel
62 © Keith Collie
63 © Keith Collie
67 © Keith Collie
68 Maite Piera / RBA
69 Maite Piera / RBA
72 © Koen Van Damme / www.koenvandamme.be
73 Karel Moortgat
76 Photography by Lyndon Douglas / info@lyndondouglas.com
77 Photography by Lyndon Douglas / info@lyndondouglas.com
79 Photography by Lyndon Douglas / info@lyndondouglas.com
80 © Kilian O'Sullivan / VIEW
81 © Kilian O'Sullivan / VIEW
84 James Silverman / james@jamessilverman.co.uk
85 James Silverman / james@jamessilverman.co.uk
88 Courtesy of the architects Kei'ichi Irie / Power Unit Studio
89 Courtesy of the architects Kei'ichi Irie / Power Unit Studio
92 © Yvonne Qumi / Yvonne@yqphotography.com.au
93 © Yvonne Qumi / Yvonne@yqphotography.com.au
97 © Yvonne Qumi / Yvonne@yqphotography.com.au
98 © John Gollings
99 © John Gollings
103 © John Gollings
106 Haiden & Baumann / Fotostudio Haiden and Baumann OEG
107 Haiden & Baumann / Fotostudio Haiden and Baumann OEG
111 Haiden & Baumann / Fotostudio Haiden and Baumann OEG
112 © Kilian O'Sullivan
113 © Kilian O'Sullivan
115 © Kilian O'Sullivan
116 Claudio Santini
117 Claudio Santini
120 Paul Gosney / paul@paulgosney.com
121 Paul Gosney / paul@paulgosney.com
125 Paul Gosney / paul@paulgosney.com
126 © Ciro Coelho / www.cirocoelho.com
127 © Ciro Coelho / www.cirocoelho.com
130 Hiroshi Ueda
131 Hiroshi Ueda
133 © Edmund Sumner / VIEW
134 © Richard Davies
135 © Richard Davies
138 João Ferrand
139 João Ferrand
142 Juan Rodriguez / RBA
143 Juan Rodriguez / RBA
148 Koichi Torimura
149 Koichi Torimura
152 Toon Grobet / www.toongrobet.be
153 Mich Verbelen
157 Mich Verbelen
158 Robert Frith / Acorn Photo Agency
159 Robert Frith / Acorn Photo Agency
161 Robert Frith / Acorn Photo Agency
162 Hiroyasu Sakaguchi
163 Hiroyasu Sakaguchi
166 Joe Fletcher Photography
167 Joe Fletcher Photography
170 © Undine Pröhl
171 © Undine Pröhl
174 Ludo Noël
175 © Toon Grobet / www.toongrobet.be
180 Andy Ryan
181 Andy Ryan
184 Hiroshi Ueda
185 Hiroshi Ueda

Acknowledgments

Thanks above all to the architects who submitted material for this book. Their time, effort and patience is very much appreciated. Special thanks to Hamish Muir and Sophia Gibb for the design and picture research respectively. Thanks also to Philip Cooper and Gaynor Sermon at Laurence King and to Justin Fletcher for editing the drawings. And finally a special thanks to my husband Vishwa Kaushal.